EDITED BY WILLIAM BORDEN

RESHAPING THEORY IN CONTEMPORARY SOCIAL WORK

Toward a Critical Pluralism
in Clinical Practice

Columbia University Press   *New York*

Columbia University Press
Publishers Since 1893
New York   Chichester, West Sussex
Copyright © 2010 Columbia University Press
All rights reserved

Library of Congress Cataloging-in-Publication Data
Reshaping theory in contemporary social work : toward a critical pluralism
in clinical practice / edited by William Borden.
p. cm.
Includes bibliographical references and index.
ISBN 978-0-231-14700-2 (cloth : alk. paper) —
ISBN 978-0-231-14701-9 (pbk. : alk. paper)—ISBN 978-0-231-51933-5 (e-book)
1. Social service. 2. Social work administration. I. Borden, William, 1954–
HV40.R387   2010
361.301—dc22   2009029433

∞

Columbia University Press books are printed on permanent
and durable acid-free paper.

This book is printed on paper with recycled content.
Printed in the United States of America
c 10 9 8 7 6 5 4 3 2 1
p 10 9 8 7 6 5 4 3 2 1

References to Internet Web sites (URLs) were accurate at the time of writing.
Neither the author nor Columbia University Press is responsible for URLs that
may have expired or changed since the manuscript was prepared.

For Sharon Berlin
scholar, teacher, and practitioner

CONTENTS

ACKNOWLEDGMENTS

THIS VOLUME ORIGINATES in a conference on the role of theory in contemporary social work practice, sponsored by the School of Social Service Administration at the University of Chicago in May 2007. The participants, leading scholars and practitioners in the field, were asked to address emerging developments in clinical theory from the vantage point of their own scholarship, research, or practice. The ideas and concerns explored over the course of the conference have shaped the chapters in this volume.

I thank the contributors for their thought, care, and generosity of spirit in preparing their accounts, and I thank my colleagues who joined the contributors as participants in the conference, especially Marie Connolly, Sarah Gehlert, Bernece Simon, Sara Taber, and Edwina Uehara. Jeanne Marsh, dean of the School of Social Service Administration, remains steadfast in her support of intellectual life, and I thank her and my colleagues for their ongoing conversation and support of scholarship in all its varied forms. I would like to express my gratitude to James Clark, collaborator on many projects, whose passion for ideas and conversation through the years have deepened my understanding of crucial concerns explored in this volume. It has been a special pleasure to work with

Lauren Dockett, our editor at Columbia University Press, who has provided encouragement and support over the course of the project. The volume is dedicated to Sharon Berlin, scholar, teacher, and practitioner, whose contributions to clinical theory over the last quarter-century continue to enrich the field.

INTRODUCTION

WILLIAM BORDEN

WE MUST FIND A THEORY THAT WILL WORK; AND THAT MEANS
SOMETHING EXTREMELY DIFFICULT; FOR OUR THEORY MUST MEDIATE
BETWEEN ALL PREVIOUS TRUTHS AND CERTAIN NEW EXPERIENCES.

—WILLIAM JAMES, LECTURE 6, *PRAGMATISM'S CONCEPTION OF TRUTH*
(1907, 76-91)

PLURALISM HAS BEEN an irrepressible feature of social work from
the start of the profession. A divergent range of thinkers, intellectual traditions, and theoretical perspectives have shaped the course of practice, over
the last century, and clinicians continue to make pragmatic use of ideas from
a variety of sources. Even so, theoretical concerns receive surprisingly little
consideration in the broader literature of the field as practitioners seek to
strengthen the empirical foundations of the discipline and negotiate the
demands of an applied profession. Theory is often marginalized in social
work education as a result of perceived conflicts with the practical concerns
of the profession; the emergence of generalist, skills-based courses of study,
and the growing emphasis on evidence-based practice.

This volume reaffirms the place of theory in social work practice and
shows how emerging perspectives enlarge ways of seeing, understanding,
and acting over the course of psychosocial intervention. At root, as William
James reminds us, theories are instruments, providing us with tools for
critical thinking, methods for carrying out our work, and justifications for
our actions. The following chapters, written by distinguished scholars and
practitioners especially for this volume, engage a range of essential concerns
in contemporary social work, reflecting the vitality, richness, and creativity of theorizing in our time. Social workers have centered on the concrete

particularities of persons and lives in their theory making from the beginnings of the profession, remaining close to the richness of lived experience and the human contexts of vulnerability, need, and possibility. As we will see, the contributors are careful to connect ideas and experience through case reports and clinical illustrations, showing how we bring ideas to bear in the give-and-take of day-to-day practice, reflecting the play and place of theory in our ongoing efforts to provide care, foster personal growth, and work toward social change.

Although most social workers endorse eclecticism as their orientation to practice, there is little consideration of the ways in which clinicians integrate ideas and methods from differing perspectives over the course of intervention. In the opening chapter I introduce critical pluralism and pragmatism as orienting perspectives in comparative approaches to clinical theory, drawing on the philosophical thought of William James, and show how mastery of differing theoretical models, therapeutic languages, and modes of intervention strengthens eclectic and integrative approaches to psychosocial intervention. By way of illustration, I examine a case from four theoretical perspectives, encompassing psychodynamic, behavioral, cognitive, and humanistic lines of understanding, and consider the ways in which a pluralist approach enlarges explanatory systems and facilitates efforts to integrate concepts, empirical findings, and technical procedures from divergent points of view. I emphasize the crucial role of ongoing dialogue across the foundational schools of thought, grounded in the concrete particulars of the clinical situation, in attempts to strengthen critical perspectives and enrich theoretically informed, pragmatic approaches to practice.

Chapters 2 and 3 explore recent developments in cognitive theory and psychoanalytic thought, and identify basic tasks in development of integrative approaches in psychosocial intervention. Although practitioners have employed cognitive approaches in a range of settings over the last quarter century, traditional versions of this mode of intervention have proven problematic in the field of social work because they fail to take sufficient account of actual experience in the outer world. Sharon Berlin, in chapter 2, reviews the basic assumptions and therapeutic methods encompassed in classical models of cognitive psychotherapy, considering their strengths and limits, and outlines the integrative perspective she has developed for social work practice.

As Berlin explains, classical thinkers have tended to locate the origins of dysfunction *within* the person, emphasizing cognitive distortions and failing to consider the realities of social, cultural, and environmental conditions that perpetuate problems in functioning. Moving beyond the traditional focus on the inner life of the individual, Berlin provides a crucial reorientation of the cognitive perspective for social work practice, situating the person in the larger social surround of demands and opportunities, helping practitioners take more account of oppressive or depriving conditions in the outer world that shape personal meaning and behavior.

Drawing on recent developments in neuroscience, personality theory, social psychology, relational psychoanalysis, narrative studies, experiential psychotherapy, and framing perspectives in the social work tradition, Berlin has developed an integrative model of practice that enlarges conceptions of person-environment interaction and core elements in psychosocial intervention. While her reformulations emphasize social and environmental domains of concern, she preserves a focus on the person as an individual, strengthening connections among personality theory, social-psychological perspectives, and clinical practice.

In chapter 3, Jerome Wakefield and Judith Baer trace the growing convergence of contemporary cognitive psychology and psychoanalytic thought and identify overlapping domains of concern that they view as fundamental in efforts to fashion an integrative theoretical perspective. By way of introduction, they present scientific and moral arguments for the development of integrative perspectives in social work practice and explore the strengths and limits of differing approaches to integration in the broader field of contemporary psychotherapy. Their conceptions of theoretical integration frame their account of the crucial points of contact between Sigmund Freud's classical psychoanalytic theory, contemporary cognitive science, and cognitive-behavioral perspectives. They consider notions of motivation, unconscious mental states, and mental representation in their analysis of the conceptual overlap between psychoanalytic understanding and cognitive perspectives.

Wakefield and Baer review models of intervention developed within each tradition, providing representative case illustrations, and describe shared concepts, themes, and facilitating processes in the clinical situation. They outline the ways in which psychodynamic perspectives promise to strengthen development of cognitive theory, showing how modular models of mind, conceptions of defense, and notions of conflict enlarge current understanding. They view Freud as a thinker from whom clinical scholars and practitioners can continue to learn in efforts to establish a hybrid cognitive-psychodynamic theory.

James Clark, in chapter 4, argues that theorizing should centralize the dignity of the human person; he explores the ways in which biography, the study of lives, and historical perspectives deepen our understanding of what it means to be a unique individual and the particular circumstances that shape one's experience of vulnerability, need, and problems in living. He examines contemporary issues in the study of persons and lives, exploring a range of philosophical and methodological concerns, and reviews recent work in the field of psychobiography, providing a trenchant analysis of the strengths and limits of work to date.

In the domain of practice, Clark shows how biographical and historical frameworks inform critical thinking and decision making in the clinical situation and facilitate development of protocols for assessment of clients and management of cases. He presents three case studies that document the crucial importance of biographical and historical data in psychosocial intervention. As he demonstrates, biographical and historical perspectives introduce complexity and longitudinal views, carrying critical implications for inclusion and exclusion of data that potentially lead to dramatically different interpretations of experience in case formulations and differing modes of intervention over the course of the helping process. His chapter shows how the promise of theory, as practiced in the pursuit of psychobiography, the study of lives, and the study of history, enriches psychological, social, cultural, and clinical understanding in social work practice.

In spite of claims to a professional jurisdiction framed by a person-environment perspective, models of social work practice continue to emphasize psychological theories and person-oriented approaches in psychosocial intervention. In chapter 5, Susan Kemp centers on conceptions of place in her efforts to rejuvenate environmental theory in direct practice. The centrality of place in human experience is the starting point for converging lines of inquiry in cultural anthropology, cultural geography, and environmental psychology, much of it shaped by phenomenological perspectives. Kemp explores what it means to speak of place in social work practice, emphasizing the ways in which everyday environments enrich or limit conceptions of self and relational life; health, well-being, and spirituality; and access to resources and opportunities. People make places, but places also make people, she explains, reminding workers that the dynamics of power and privilege operate in the concrete particularities of ordinary, everyday surrounds. The burdens of current environmental challenges fall inequitably on communities "for whom social workers are particularly accountable," she observes.

In the realm of direct practice, Kemp emphasizes the need for deeper appreciation of the experiential and material aspects of place in clients' lives and the crucial role of "place making" that transforms people and surrounds. Drawing on empowerment perspectives, she emphasizes the importance of a critically reflective focus on personal agency and structural factors, on local knowledge, and on participatory and dialogic approaches to place-based knowledge and change. She outlines basic tasks in efforts to facilitate "place-sensitive" practice, encompassing strategies to engage and validate local knowledge; narrative perspectives; a range of visual activities, including photography, video, and other art forms; and geographic information systems that provide ways of mapping person-place relationships. Kemp urges practitioners to follow the example of the early social workers in the settlement house movement and the charity organization societies, who remained close to the everyday worlds of their clients, "observing and absorbing the texture of daily life in place."

The field of mental health, shaped by the medical model and classical psychoanalytic thought, emphasized conceptions of individual psychopathology and family deficits well into the late twentieth century, failing to recognize sources of strength that sponsor efforts to negotiate adversity and misfortune. Over the course of her work, Froma Walsh has challenged this paradigm, working to enlarge understandings of resilience, coping, and growth in her studies of family functioning and the social surround. In chapter 6, she reviews theoretical and empirical lines of inquiry that have informed conceptions of resilience over the last three decades and introduces a multisystemic perspective that integrates developmental theory and ecological domains of concern.

Walsh describes the core elements of a family resilience model, focusing on belief systems, organization patterns, and communication processes, that provides a pragmatic framework for clinical and community-based intervention and prevention. As she shows in her account of intervention with Bosnian and Kosovar refugee families, the concept of family resilience centers on strengths in the context of adversity and lends itself to a wide range of applications in our efforts to help families and communities negotiate crises and ongoing life challenges.

The last three chapters of this book explore the relationship among theory, practice, core values, and essential concerns in the broader social work tradition.

Janet Finn centers on the meaning and power of love and the search for social justice in social work practice, considering the ways in which the value base of the profession influences theorizing and practice. She wonders whether the forces of professionalization and the postmodern practice of social work have silenced a more intimate discourse of human connection and undermined motives for social action, denigrating a connection to our fundamental humanness as a core value base in the profession. Drawing on Sharon Berlin's seminal essay on the value of acceptance and the politics of knowledge that have shaped the profession over the last century, she reviews emerging conceptions of relationship, love, and justice, and examines the implications of the turns toward more reflexive and dialogical approaches in psychosocial intervention. In doing so, she describes the development of her own political and theoretical work over the last decade, integrating the contributions of structuralist and poststructuralist thought, feminist theorists, strengths perspectives, and empowerment-based approaches to practice.

With her colleague, Maxine Jacobson, Finn has introduced a social justice framework that emphasizes themes of personal meaning, context, power, history, and possibility. She reviews the defining features of this orienting perspective, providing clinical illustrations, and shows how core concepts are translated into action through facilitating processes that link theory and practice, including engagement, teaching and learning, activity, accompaniment, evaluation, critical reflection, and celebration. The perspective emphasizes conceptions of relationship, mutuality, and participation, translating the theory, politics, and ethics of social justice into praxis for personal and social transformation.

Theoretical understanding promises to strengthen emerging models of evidence-based practice, informing assessment, case formulation, and treatment planning in psychosocial intervention. In chapter 8, Stanley McCracken and Tina Rzepnicki examine the crucial functions of theory in evidence-based practice. They define theory broadly, encompassing a range of explanatory or predictive propositions set forth in formal knowledge structures subject to evaluation by researchers, as well as personal knowledge structures that help practitioners organize and understand clinical phenomena.

McCracken and Rzepnicki outline basic steps in the implementation of evidence-based practice, offering clinical illustrations, and explore the ways in which theoretical understanding strengthens efforts to carry out empirically supported intervention. In doing so, they show how conceptions of "mindful practice" and "logic modeling" help workers clarify the ways in which they engage differing perspectives in the clinical situation. As they emphasize, theoretically informed conceptions of evidence-based practice show how practitioners can make flexible use of technical procedures and the experiential dimensions of the helping process in light of the nature of specific problems in functioning and the individual, social, and cultural characteristics and contexts of the client.

A growing number of thinkers are exploring the development of practice wisdom in contemporary social work, seeking to better understand the ways in which clinicians generate knowledge through experiential learning and bring understanding to bear in the course of their day-to-day activities. In doing so, scholars emphasize the limits of the predominant theories that currently guide conceptions of intervention and urge practitioners to reformulate ideas and establish perspectives that better reflect the pragmatic character and diverse contexts of contemporary social work. In the closing chapter, Malcolm Payne provides a critique of clinical theory and describes core elements of practice wisdom that promise to deepen understanding of basic tasks and facilitating processes in psychosocial intervention.

In his analysis, formal practice theory is problematic in two respects. First, it is "universalist," in the sense that theorists assume that social workers can carry out their practice on the basis of research-based behavioral prescriptions. Such perspectives fail to take account of the complexities, ambiguities, and demands of particular situations and settings that shape actual practice in the real world. Payne argues that we must deepen our understanding of the ways in which context, contingency, and experiential learning influence intervention in continued development of practice knowledge. A second limitation of current practice theory lies in its emphasis on behavioral and social change. Payne reminds us that a good deal of clinical social work involves provision of ongoing care and support rather than efforts to facilitate change as such. He reviews conceptions of caring, support, resilience, emotional intelligence, and basic elements of the helping process, providing representative clinical illustrations, and identifies crucial domains of concern in continued development of theoretical understanding and models of practice.

Although the writers explore divergent concerns in contemporary theory and practice, their accounts reaffirm the framing perspectives and core values that have shaped the profession from the start, including (1) the crucial focus on person and environment; (2) humanistic conceptions of the self, emphasizing the inherent worth and dignity of the individual, the influence of life history on personal meaning, resilience, and inherent capacities for change and growth; (3) the role of relationship and social life in health and well-being; and (4) fundamental commitments to caring, notions of social justice, and the common good.

At the same time, the writers identify challenges and tasks in the continuing development of theory and practice in our time, emphasizing the need to elaborate integrative models of treatment; to take greater account of place, social surround, context, and history in conceptions of intervention; to link theoretical understanding with empirical findings, technical procedures, and clinical experience in more complex formulations of evidence-based practice; and to address fundamental tensions and contradictions among the core values, ethical foundations, and moral claims of the profession and the politics of theory and practice. The contributors are hopeful that their accounts and reflections will help establish a basis for greater dialogue across the divergent perspectives that shape the field and foster continued development of theory, research, and practice.

RESHAPING THEORY IN CONTEMPORARY SOCIAL WORK

PART ONE

THEORY AND PRACTICE

Orienting Perspectives

1   TAKING MULTIPLICITY SERIOUSLY

Pluralism, Pragmatism, and Integrative Perspectives
in Clinical Social Work

WILLIAM BORDEN

YOU MUST BRING OUT OF EACH WORD ITS PRACTICAL CASH-VALUE,
SET IT AT WORK WITHIN THE STREAM OF YOUR EXPERIENCE.... THEO-
RIES THUS BECOME INSTRUMENTS.... PRAGMATISM UNSTIFFENS OUR
THEORIES, LIMBERS THEM UP.

—WILLIAM JAMES, *PRAGMATISM*

A RANGE OF intellectual traditions have shaped the collective wisdom of social work practice over the decades, and clinicians continue to
make pragmatic and creative use of ideas and methods from a variety of
theoretical perspectives. Although most clinicians endorse eclecticism as
their fundamental orientation to practice, there is surprisingly little discussion of the ways in which workers integrate differing concepts, empirical data, and technical procedures over the course of intervention. In this
chapter I introduce critical pluralism and pragmatism as orienting perspectives in comparative approaches to clinical theory and show how mastery
of the foundational schools of thought strengthens eclectic, integrative
approaches to psychosocial intervention.

In the first section I review the growing emphasis on integrative perspectives in contemporary practice and examine the role of theory in eclectic, individualized approaches to treatment. In the second part I introduce
conceptions of pluralism and pragmatism, drawing on the work of William
James, and show how they provide critical perspectives in comparative
approaches to clinical theory. I examine a case from four theoretical perspectives and illustrate the ways in which a pluralist orientation strengthens formulations of psychosocial intervention. In the third section I review
lines of inquiry that have shaped integrative models of intervention, broadly

characterized as technical eclecticism, common factors approaches, and theoretical integration, and identify exemplars of each perspective. Further discussion of the case report presented in the preceding section illustrates core elements of the differing approaches to integration. Finally, I consider the relative merits of pluralist points of view and integrative models of psychosocial intervention and emphasize the importance of ongoing dialogue across divergent schools of thought in continued development of critical perspectives and theoretically informed practice.

INTEGRATIVE PERSPECTIVES IN CONTEMPORARY PRACTICE

Representatives of the foundational schools of thought in contemporary psychotherapy have increasingly come to appreciate the strengths and limits of differing perspectives, over the last decade, and there is growing dialogue across the therapeutic traditions in efforts to identify common elements and clarify differences. Practitioners have integrated core concepts and methods of intervention from divergent points of view in their attempts to engage a wider range of clients, broaden the scope of intervention, strengthen the empirical base of treatment, and improve therapeutic outcomes.

Thinkers have drawn on psychodynamic, cognitive, behavioral, humanistic, family, and ecological perspectives in building integrative models of practice. For example, Paul Wachtel has developed a psychodynamic approach that links core concepts in relational psychoanalysis with cognitive, behavioral, experiential, and systemic perspectives, extending earlier integrations of psychoanalytic constructs and behavioral theory (1977, 1997, 2008). Marsha Linehan has integrated behavioral and cognitive approaches with relational concepts and Eastern mindfulness practices in developing her model of dialectical behavior therapy (1993). Sharon Berlin has introduced an integrative cognitive perspective that encompasses core concepts in neuroscience, the foundational schools of thought in contemporary psychotherapy, ecological points of view, and framing perspectives in the social work tradition (2002). James Prochaska and Carlo DiClemente conceptualize differing stages and levels of change in their transtheoretical framework, integrating psychodynamic, behavioral, cognitive, humanistic, and family systems perspectives (2002).

I strongly support efforts to deepen our understanding of common elements that operate across the major schools of thought and to integrate core concepts and technical procedures in pragmatic approaches to psychosocial intervention. In doing so, however, I believe it is crucial to preserve the distinct identities of the foundational therapeutic traditions for two reasons.

First, if clinicians fail to develop an understanding of the major theories of the field, they do not have conceptual frames of reference to understand the constructs, empirical findings, and methods they are trying to integrate in practice. Technical procedures are deprived of context, in the absence of theoretical understanding, and clinicians run the risk of carrying out reductive, mechanized approaches to treatment by protocol (see Borden, 2008b). Second, as clinical scholars have emphasized, integrative approaches themselves cannot evolve unless thinkers preserve the integrity of the core theoretical systems in their own right (see Gurman & Messer, 2003; Liddle, 1982). There is a generative tension between the purity of approach that defines the foundational schools of thought and the pragmatism of integrative perspectives that sponsors dialogue and development in both domains of activity.

In light of these concerns, I believe it is critical to introduce the major theoretical perspectives as distinct systems of thought in social work education and clinical training. The foundational theories of contemporary psychotherapy set forth compelling accounts of the human situation, offering divergent conceptions of self, relational life, the social surround, and therapeutic action. As such, they provide orienting perspectives for differing renderings of persons and lives. Although each line of understanding inevitably fails to capture the variety and complexity of human experience, they are crucial because they set forth distinct visions of reality and world views (Messer & Winokur, 1984) and help practitioners appreciate the implications of certain ideas by pressing them to their limits (Strenger, 1997).

In introducing the theoretical systems, it is important to consider the historical circumstances and intellectual traditions that have shaped the development of understanding and practice. In exploring the history of ideas within the differing traditions, students and clinicians develop an appreciation of the social, cultural, political, and economic conditions that have influenced conceptions of personality, relationship, and social life; renderings of health, well-being, and the common good; and recognitions of vulnerability, need, and problems in living.

Practitioners come to realize the ways in which persons and lives, problems in living, practice settings, and the social surround have influenced particular ways of working—how, for example, the contributions of Jane Addams and the culture of the settlement house influenced the development of group methods and ecological approaches, or the ways in which the values of the social democratic movement of central Europe and the free psychoanalytic clinics of Vienna, Berlin, and Budapest enlarged conceptions of vulnerability and social justice in the broader psychodynamic tradition. Without an appreciation of the intellectual traditions, world views, and essential concerns that have shaped understanding and practice in the therapeutic traditions, as Alan Gurman and Stanley Messer (2003) remind us, clinicians are likely to find theories "rather disembodied abstractions that seem to evolve from nowhere, and for no known reason" (p. 5).

In the domain of psychosocial intervention, comparative analysis of the theoretical systems clarifies differing conceptions of the helping process; the structure of intervention; the range of application; the functions of the therapeutic relationship and the role of interactive experience; strategies and technical procedures; curative factors, facilitating conditions, and change processes; and methods of monitoring progress and evaluating outcomes.

A growing number of graduate social work programs have established generalist, atheoretical, skills-based courses of study. Such approaches are problematic in that they fail to introduce the foundational theories of the field and fail to provide opportunities to develop the critical analytic capacities needed to negotiate the concrete particularities, complexities, and ambiguities of clinical practice. As Jeffrey Applegate (2003) observes in his critique of social work education, the knowledge base of direct practice has increasingly neglected the dynamics of inner life, personal meaning, and facilitating processes believed to sponsor change and growth.

The orienting perspectives and ethos of the social work tradition urge practitioners to approach the person as an individual—not as an object but as a subject—"as a human being first and last," in the phrase of Oliver Sacks, engaging "the experiencing, acting, living 'I'" (1984, p. 164). While students learn how to implement technical procedures in skills-based courses of study, they do not develop knowledge of the conceptual foundations needed to carry out what Donald Winnicott would call "experiments in adapting to need" that serve as the basis for individual approaches to intervention (Borden, 2009).

In the domain of social work practice, the psychodynamic, behavioral, cognitive, humanistic, and ecological perspectives focus our attention on overlapping realms of experience from differing points of view and enlarge ways of seeing, understanding, and acting in the clinical situation. What counts as theory, as Carlo Strenger reminds us, is always "an attempt of other therapists to make sense of their attempts to do the best they could" (1997, p. 144), and the cumulative experience that they have tried to represent and characterize in their formulations enlarges our understandings of what carries the potential to help in the clinical situation. Practitioners realize, however, that theory itself cannot replace the power of critical thinking and judgment.

CRITICAL PLURALISM AND PRAGMATISM

In this section I show how conceptions of pluralism and pragmatism provide orienting perspectives in efforts to engage differing theoretical perspectives and integrate core concepts with empirical findings and technical procedures over the course of intervention. In doing so, I draw on the work of William James, who increasingly elaborated notions of pluralism and pragmatism in his later writings on psychology, religion, and morality (James, 1907/1946; 1909/1977; 1911). I examine a case from four theoretical perspectives in order to illustrate the ways in which pluralist points of view enlarge concepts of change and therapeutic action in the clinical situation. Finally, I review exemplars of pluralist points of view in contemporary clinical practice.

James argues that human understanding is inherently limited, and he urges thinkers and practitioners to approach concerns from multiple, independent perspectives. He assumes that no single theory can in itself fully grasp the variety and complexity of human experience. There are equally valid points of view that inevitably challenge or contradict one another, he argues, and divergent perspectives potentially lead to insight, understanding, and action. For James, theories are tools for thinking. He writes: "Theories . . . become instruments, not answers to enigmas, in which we can rest. We don't lie back on them, we move forward. . . . Pragmatism unstiffens all our theories, limbers them up and sets each one at work" (1907/1946, p. 53). Each theoretical system has its own history, root metaphors, domains of concern, purposes, rules, methods, strengths, and limits.

Pluralist thinkers thereby challenge notions of grand theory, which presume to set forth universal truths, and assume that theoretical formulations provide only fragmentary renderings of experience. Practitioners do not try to find a synthesis between differing theories or fashions encompassing systems of understanding. To the grand theorist, James would say: "Ever not quite," reasoning that the concrete particulars of ordinary everyday experience, of life as we live it, are messy.

James met Sigmund Freud in September 1909 at a special convocation to celebrate the twentieth anniversary of Clark University. By his accounts he was uncomfortable with Freud, uneasy with his efforts to develop a grand theory of personality, psychopathology, and therapeutic treatment, calling him "a man obsessed by fixed ideas" (see Simon, 1998, p. 363).

The world we live in, James reminds us, is unfenced and untidy, presenting us with multiplicities and complexities, confusions and contradictions, ironies and ambiguities. Accordingly, the pluralist does not base decisions on abstractions, preferring to engage the concrete particularity of the individual case, seeking to understand the complexities, ambiguities, and uncertainties that grand theoretical schemes inevitably fail to represent (see Viney, King & King, 1992, p. 94). The pluralist turns away from "abstraction," "absolutes," "fixed principles," and "closed systems," searching for fact, concreteness, action, and adequacy (James, 1907/1946, pp. 43–81).

From a Jamesian perspective, then, pluralism encourages free exploration of alternative ways of seeing and understanding without the constraints of pure theoretical systems. Areas of agreement may emerge from independent lines of inquiry, which provide a basis for belief, for our best guess as to the truth of the matter, but the pluralist is willing to let many things stand alone, ever attuned to the dangers of presuming to know too much. There is an appreciation of gaps in understanding.

As biographers have emphasized, James's approach to knowledge and understanding was fundamentally developmental, emphasizing process, growth, ever shifting frames of reference. He saw the world itself much as he thought of the field of vision: "There is always a fringe, there is an ever shifting horizon, and no static vantage point from which we can make the big claim" (Viney, King & King, 1992, p. 94). In working from comparative perspectives, scholars, researchers, teachers, and practitioners can better realize the possibilities and limits of varying points of view and enlarge notions of truth.

For James, *what matters is what works*, and his conceptions of pluralism are closely linked to notions of pragmatism set forth by C.S. Pierce and John Dewey. Briefly, pragmatism emphasizes the practical implications of our beliefs and the ways in which they contribute to effectiveness in the conduct of life. Louis Menand captures the essence of the pragmatic outlook in his seminal study of James, Oliver Wendell Holmes, and Charles Pierce, *The Metaphysical Club*: "An idea has no greater metaphysical stature than, say, a fork. When your fork proves inadequate to the task of eating soup, it makes little sense to argue about whether there is something inherent in the nature of forks or something inherent in the nature of soup that accounts for the failure. You just reach for a spoon" (2001, p. 361).

In his pragmatic conception of truth, James proposes: "The true is the name of whatever proves itself to be good in the way of belief and good, too, for definite, assignable reasons" (James, 1907/1946, p. 76). If we take an idea to be true, he wants to know, "what concrete difference will its being true make in any one's actual life? . . . What, in short, is the truth's cash value in experiential terms?" (James, 1907/1946, p. 200). The crucial question is not "Is it true?" but rather "How would our work or our lives be better if we were to believe it?" *What is the use of a truth?*

For James, truth _happens_ to an idea; it becomes true—is made true—through experience. In following the pragmatic method, he writes, "You must bring out of each word its practical cash-value, set it at work within the stream of your experience. It appears less as a solution, then, than as a program for more work, and more particularly as an indication of the ways in which existing realities may be changed" (1907/1946, p. 53).

CRITICAL PLURALISM AND CLINICAL PRACTICE

In the conception of critical pluralism I describe here, practitioners engage multiple theoretical models, therapeutic languages, and modes of intervention, drawing on ideas and methods from a variety of perspectives in light of the particular circumstances of the clinical situation. Differing perspectives allow clinicians to approach human problems from a range of positions and to shift points of entry in light of particular needs, tasks, and conditions.

Practitioners engage a range of models and methods as they carry out their work, without committing themselves to any single school of thought, tacking back and forth between higher level theoretical concepts and application of ideas and methods in the concrete particularity of the helping process. Following pragmatic conceptions of utility, practitioners judge the validity of concepts and methods on the basis of their effectiveness—their "cash value"—in the particular clinical situation.

The foundational schools of thought provide _contexts of understanding_ for engagement of differing ideas, empirical findings, and technical procedures over the course of intervention. I consider the following case from four theoretical perspectives in order to illustrate the ways in which a pluralist approach strengthens understanding of essential concerns, change processes, and potential approaches to intervention over the course of psychotherapy.

CASE ILLUSTRATION

The client, age twenty-six, was referred for psychotherapy by his physician following onset of insomnia, diffuse anxiety, signs of depression, and dissociative states seven months after his return from military service in Iraq. What he had experienced there, he related, was beyond his ability to render into words. He described fluctuating periods of numbing detachment and intrusive recollections of traumatic events from his tour of duty, where he had witnessed the deaths of civilians and soldiers, and he reported recurring dreams of running through endless fields of bodies. He had been injured when an explosive device detonated while he was driving patrol in Bagdad. He had completed a course of rehabilitation following recovery from injuries, and was living with an aunt who had raised him following his mother's death in childhood. He related a growing sense of hopelessness, helplessness, and dread—"I feel like my life is over"—and described a series of symptoms that met diagnostic criteria for posttraumatic stress disorder (PTSD).

Beyond the impact of his experience in Iraq, further sources of vulnerability emerged in exploration of the client's developmental history and accounts of earlier life events. His mother had died when he was six, and he and his brother had been adopted by their aunt. He described ongoing conflict in family life through childhood and adolescence. He had struggled as a student, describing himself as an "underachiever," and had been unable to find meaningful employment following graduation from high school. He explained that he had joined the military in an effort to "get a new start in life" following the death of his brother in a gang shooting.

His experience of dependency and withdrawal following his injuries had intensified longings for closeness and connection with others, but he found himself avoiding contact with friends and extended family, fearful that they would want him to talk about what he had witnessed in Iraq. Although the client's primary goal was to address the immediate problems in functioning associated with the posttraumatic stress disorder, he explained that he also wanted to restore contact with family members, strengthen relationships with friends, and proceed with life tasks: "I want my life back."

COMPARATIVE PERSPECTIVES

The explanatory systems of the four major schools of thought in contemporary psychotherapy, set forth in the psychodynamic, behavioral, cognitive, and humanistic traditions, provide divergent accounts of the core activities and change processes in psychosocial intervention. I briefly consider the ways in which thinkers from each tradition focus our attention on overlapping concerns and potential courses of action in the therapeutic situation.

PSYCHODYNAMIC PERSPECTIVES

Contemporary psychodynamic theories focus on conceptions of self and relational life, emphasizing the ways in which earlier patterns of care, social environments, and critical events have shaped personality development, unconscious conflicts, defenses, patterns of coping and adaptation, and particular ways of being, relating, and living. In approaching the case from a psychodynamic perspective, the clinician explores the meaning of traumatic events in light of earlier developmental experience, relationships, life events, and losses.

The relational schools of thought focus the practitioner's attention on subjective experience, patterns of interpersonal functioning, and social life. From the perspective of self psychology, the clinician centers on the client's loss of cohesion in sense of self and disruptions in relational life that have perpetuated his experience of vulnerability, demoralization, and fragmentation. Object relations perspectives emphasize the ways in which the client's internal models of self, others, and interactive experience have influenced his perceptions of traumatic experience, current relationships, and patterns of interpersonal behavior in the therapeutic situation. The core concepts of the interpersonal school focus the clinician's attention on feared domains of internal and external experience, defensive operations, and vicious circles of thought, feeling, and action that perpetuate problems in functioning.

In a psychodynamic framing of the therapeutic process, the clinician seeks to help the client integrate traumatic experience, restore cohesion in sense of self, enlarge the range of coping strategies, and strengthen capacities to engage relationships and participate in social life. Conceptions of intervention emphasize the sustaining functions of the therapeutic relationship and the constancy of care in the holding environment. The clinician considers the client's modes of attachment and patterns of interpersonal functioning in light of the early loss of his mother, assessing his capacities to establish a therapeutic alliance and engage in the interactive experience of the therapeutic process. The practitioner uses interpretive procedures to deepen understanding of reactions to traumatic events in light of earlier losses and defensive behaviors, and actively engages sources of experiential learning and task-centered approaches in efforts to strengthen problem-solving skills, coping strategies, and interpersonal functioning.

Relational schools of thought stress the importance of processing transference reactions that emerge in the therapeutic relationship as the client works through unconscious elements of traumatic experience. The clinician's awareness of countertransference experience is also crucial, as reactions to the client's accounts of traumatic events potentially strengthen or undermine the therapeutic alliance and course of treatment (for extended accounts of psychodynamic strategies and techniques, see Borden, 2009; Curtis & Hirsch, 2003; Ford & Urban, 1998).

BEHAVIORAL PERSPECTIVES

The broader behavioral tradition encompasses conceptions of classical conditioning, operant conditioning, and social learning, emphasizing the ways in which patterns of learning and environmental conditions or situational factors shape behavior. In approaching the case from a behavioral perspective, the clinician focuses on the content, dynamic organization, and contexts of specific patterns of behavior that perpetuate problems in functioning. The practitioner specifies the particular types of responses and environmental factors involved in patterns of behavior and describes their functional antecedent and consequent relationships, clarifying the conditions that activate, reinforce, and maintain the problematic patterns. Contemporary thinkers increasingly encompass the phenomenology of subjective experience in their conceptions of behavior, and the clinician regards physiological processes, emotion, cognition, and imagery related to traumatic events as focal concerns in assessment of functioning and treatment planning.

In behavioral conceptions of the therapeutic process, the practitioner and client specify problem behaviors and identify criteria for monitoring progress and evaluating outcomes. The clinician develops an individualized treatment plan, using evidence-based guidelines, engaging a range of methods and technical procedures in view of symptoms and focal concerns.

The core activities of intervention potentially include incremental exposure to feared domains of inner and outer experience through verbal processing of traumatic memories and guided imagery to desensitize stimuli; modification of environmental conditions or situational factors that reinforce avoidance behaviors; task assignments, behavioral rehearsal and role playing; communication and social skills training; problem-solving training; and modeling of alternative behaviors. Acceptance- and mindfulness-based treatment approaches could be used in efforts to help the client regulate inner states of self (for extended accounts of behavioral strategies and techniques, see Antony & Roemer, 2003).

COGNITIVE PERSPECTIVES

Contemporary cognitive perspectives are based on conceptions of psychological constructivism, emphasizing the active nature of perception, learning, and knowing. Thinkers assume that individuals develop mental structures or schemata that mediate emotion and behavior, encompassing assumptive worlds, belief systems, automatic thoughts, and personal narratives. In approaching the case from a cognitive perspective, the clinician explores the ways in which traumatic experience has disrupted core schemata, activating dysfunctional cognitive processes that predispose the client to dysfunctional memory structures, distorted interpretations of experience, patterns of arousal and numbing, and avoidance of activity.

The clinician centers on the ways in which the client misinterprets experience as dangerous, reinforcing maladaptive, inflexible views self, others, and the world (see Hembree & Foa, 2003). In framing the therapeutic process, the clinician seeks to help the client identify, disrupt, and change maladaptive beliefs and cognitive distortions associated with the traumatic experience that perpetuate his experience of fear, demoralization, and disengagement from activities. The clinician employs a range of methods and strategies in efforts to help the client identify and challenge maladaptive schemata ("the world is a dangerous place"), working assumptions ("my family really doesn't want to spend time with me"), and automatic thoughts ("my life is over"), and develop more adaptive ways of processing experience and generating meaning that take account of earlier events and actual circumstances (for extended accounts of cognitive strategies and techniques, see Berlin, 2002, and chapter 2, this volume; Leahy, 2004; Reineke & Freeman, 2003; Wakefield & Baer, chapter 3, this volume).

HUMANISTIC PERSPECTIVES

Humanistic perspectives emphasize inherent capacities for change, growth, and realization of potential in the development of the self. Embracing a phenomenological perspective, thinkers view the self as process and center on the experiential character of personal functioning, emphasizing the crucial role of awareness and attention in ongoing assimilation of information. Humanistic conceptions of psychotherapy encompass a range of approaches developed in the person-centered, experiential, and existential traditions.

According to person-centered theory, the fully functioning individual is distinguished by "openness to experience"; "existential living," reflected in spontaneous, flexible, and adaptable ways of being in light of moment-to-moment experience; and "organismic trusting" that shapes decision making and action in light of differing needs, core values, and essential concerns (Rogers, 1961). Problems in living originate in incongruities between the person's immediate experience and constructed versions of the self. In maladaptive functioning, the individual has failed to revise conceptions of self in light of inner needs and outer realities, and is constricted by defensive patterns of behavior.

In framing intervention from this perspective, the clinician focuses on the development of the therapeutic relationship, emphasizing the core conditions of unconditional positive regard, warmth, empathy, and authenticity, and facilitates the client's integration of traumatic experience and enlarged conceptions of self through exploration, reflection, and processing of perceptions, thoughts, and feelings. Practitioners assume that the therapeutic process itself activates inherent self-righting, self-healing tendencies, sponsoring change and growth (see Bohart, 2003).

In an experiential approach, the clinician departs from the nondirective stance of the Rogerian, person-centered perspective and focuses on exploration of emotion in efforts to help the client assimilate and reorganize traumatic memories, change problematic patterns of behavior, and proceed with life tasks (see Greenberg, 2002, for a review of an emotion-focused approach to trauma). Technical procedures outlined in focusing-oriented psychotherapy strengthen exploration, processing, and integration of subjective experience related to traumatic events (Gendlin, 1996). Existential perspectives center on the meaning and implications of the traumatic experience, potentially helping the client clarify essential concerns as he attempts to establish a sense of direction and purpose (Yalom, 1980; for an extended review of humanistic strategies and techniques, see Bohart, 2003).

THE PROCESS OF INTERVENTION

In the context of the pluralist perspective described here, the clinician's understanding of the psychodynamic, behavioral, cognitive, and humanistic perspectives provides conceptual foundations for use of differing constructs, empirical findings, and technical procedures from each tradition over the course of intervention. The practitioner engages elements from a range of sources in light of the specific circumstances of the clinical situation and emerging tasks over the course of intervention. Transition from one perspective to another is guided by the nature of the client's presenting problems; conceptual schemes that guide explanations of difficulties and understandings of the helping process; the focal concerns of intervention; capacities to engage and use differing elements in the therapeutic process; and the relative effectiveness of particular strategies. The clinician seeks to maintain an appreciation of higher level theoretical formulations *and* a focus on the practical implementation of concepts and procedures in the concrete particularity of the helping process, moving back and forth between ideas and experience.

As the review of the case shows, the explanatory systems of the psychodynamic, behavioral, cognitive, and humanistic traditions bring differing elements of traumatic experience into sharper focus, clarifying core domains of concern in approaching the therapeutic process. The comparative perspective broadens the range of phenomena that provide potential points of entry over the course of intervention, encompassing symptoms and circumscribed problems in functioning; conceptions of self, subjective experience, and meaning; interpersonal conflicts and relational life; dysfunctional behaviors; and maladaptive cognitions. In proceeding with the therapeutic process, the clinician and client would clarify the goals of intervention through dialogue and consider the core activities of treatment in light of immediate concerns, understanding of problems in functioning, and expectations of the helping process.

EXEMPLARS OF THE PLURALIST OUTLOOK

As we engage the seminal thinkers of our theoretical traditions, we discover certain figures who introduce distinctive points of view that encompass a range of perspectives, making pluralism a defining feature of their work. In doing so they demonstrate what Strenger characterizes as one of the "prime virtues" of pluralism: "the ability to maintain one's voice while containing within oneself a multiplicity of voices" (1997, p. 141). I briefly consider exemplars of theoretical pluralism in psychoanalysis and contemporary psychotherapy.

DONALD WINNICOTT AND THE INDEPENDENT TRADITION

In the domain of psychoanalytic understanding, Donald Winnicott and the other clinicians who formed the Independent Tradition in Great Britain exemplify Jamesian conceptions of pluralism and pragmatism in their approach to theory and practice. This group emerged as an alternative to the theoretical orthodoxy of Melanie Klein and Anna Freud in the British Psychoanalytic Society in the 1940s, and it remains a forceful voice in contemporary psychotherapy and social work practice.

The Independent thinkers draw on a divergent range of thinkers and ideas, but they are uneasy with grand statements or encompassing conceptions of personality, psychopathology, or therapeutic practice. They reject objective or rational concepts of knowledge and truth, arguing that we can never know the "truth" of the "whole," and they challenge ideas that seem removed from the experience of everyday life; as Adam Phillips shows in his account of Winnicott, there is seldom radical intent in their theorizing (1988).

Winnicott refuses to codify his ideas in a cohesive theoretical system, and he chooses ordinary words over the technical language of the social and behavioral sciences. He is a natural observer, ever searching for the unnoticed obvious, and his ideas emerge from the concrete particulars of clinical practice, following his empirical disposition. His work is marked by an ongoing concern with observation and empathy, as Phillips observes, and he demonstrates a steadfast belief in our ability to make ourselves known and understood through our words and actions (1988, p. 11).

The attitudes and sensibilities of the Independent Tradition predispose practitioners to remain open, measured, and modest in their approach to theory itself. While some critics find them tentative in their use of it, they see their uncertainty as a condition of critical thinking, seeking to acknowledge the limits of their understanding and to avoid the risks of presuming to know too much

As a group, their commitment to individuality, creativity, pluralism, and pragmatism allows them to approach their work from multiple points of view, without privileging one position over another, without recourse to dogma or notions of absolute truth (see Borden, 1998). Winnicott emphasizes that he does not conduct "standard psychotherapy" but rather tries to carry out "experiments in adapting to need," using whatever ideas and methods carry the potential to help in light of the possibilities and constraints of the particular clinical situation (Borden, 2009; Winnicott, 1971).

CONTEMPORARY EXEMPLARS

A growing number of contemporary thinkers have engaged conceptions of pluralism in their writings on clinical theory and therapeutic practice. Drawing on the philosophical contributions of Isaiah Berlin, Strenger has explored the tensions between "purism" and "pragmatism" in his writings on the development of therapeutic voice and style in the clinical situation (1997, 2002). In the field of relational psychoanalysis, Stephen Mitchell has engaged divergent thinkers in his formulations of the relational paradigm (1988, 1997, 2000). In introducing the editorial philosophy of the journal *Psychoanalytic Dialogues*, he wrote: "We need to learn to regard differences in theoretical perspectives not as unfortunate deviations from accurate understanding but as fortunate expressions of the complex ways in which human experience can be organized." (1991, p. 6). Over the course of his writings, he urges clinicians to recontextualize and integrate differing ideas in ongoing efforts to fashion a personal synthesis. Other practitioners have elaborated Winnicott's developmental and clinical formulations, drawing on a range of psychoanalytic thinkers in exploring the functions of theory and personal idiom in therapeutic practice (Bollas, 1989; Borden, 1998, 2009; Wright, 1991).

In the field of cognitive psychology, Michael Mahoney has emphasized the importance of cross-theoretical dialogue, exemplifying the pluralist point of view in the development of his constructivist perspective (1995). Donald Meichenbaum has engaged a range of thinkers in fashioning his cognitive-behavioral models of intervention, emphasizing the role of subjective experience, narrative process, and personal meaning (1995). In the humanistic tradition, Leslie Greenberg has brought a depth of understanding and practical flexibility to the development of his experiential psychotherapy, drawing on psychodynamic, cognitive, and behavioral perspectives (2002). Although the foregoing thinkers have introduced distinctive points of view, they demonstrate the importance of dialogue across the therapeutic traditions in pragmatic consideration of ideas and methods, making pluralism a central feature of their work.

INTEGRATIVE PERSPECTIVES

Growing appreciation of the strengths and limits of the differing schools of thought has deepened interest in integrative conceptions of psychosocial intervention, and thinkers have drawn on psychodynamic, behavioral, cognitive, humanistic, and ecological theories in their attempts to apply a wider range of technical procedures, identify common elements that sponsor change, and develop unified conceptions of personality, psychopathology, and therapeutic action. In this section I expand earlier accounts of integrative perspectives (Borden, 2008b) and briefly consider the preceding case example in light of differing concerns explored in each line of inquiry.

Three perspectives have shaped attempts to integrate theory, empirical findings, and technical procedures in the field of psychotherapy. These are broadly categorized as technical eclecticism, common factors approaches, and theoretical integration (Arkowitz, 1992; Goldfried & Norcross, 1995). In each approach thinkers attempt to strengthen practice by looking beyond the bounds of single schools of thought, but they emphasize differing domains of phenomena and levels of analysis in attempts to facilitate change and improve outcomes. I describe the defining features of each perspective and identify exemplars associated with the approaches.

TECHNICAL ECLECTICISM

In this form of integration clinicians apply technical procedures pragmatically on the basis of presumed efficacy (Arkowitz, 1992; Safran & Messer, 1997). Practitioners match specific methods with circumscribed problems in functioning on the basis of empirical evidence and clinical knowledge; in a prescriptive version of this approach, clinicians employ standardized treatment protocols linking particular diagnostic categories and specific procedures that have been validated in controlled clinical trials. For example, empirical findings and clinical experience provide evidence for the effectiveness of behavioral and cognitive procedures in treatment of problems in functioning associated with posttraumatic stress disorders and borderline personality organization. Clinical researchers frequently outline procedures in manuals that guide application of specific techniques over the course of intervention.

The foundation is empirical rather than theoretical, and it is the most technically oriented approach to integration. Thinkers assume that methods can be applied independently of the theories from which they are derived, and practitioners draw procedures from differing sources without necessarily endorsing—or even understanding—the supporting conceptual foundations (Goldfried & Norcross, 1995). Representative examples of technical strategies include graded exposure to feared domains of experience, systematic desensitization, interpretive procedures, cognitive restructuring, and stress inoculation training.

This form of integration is exemplified in Arnold Lazarus's (2002) multimodal therapy, encompassing behavioral, cognitive, and experiential methods, and Larry Beutler's (2004) prescriptive model of treatment, specifying strategies and procedures for circumscribed problems in functioning.

In approaching the foregoing case from the perspective of technical eclecticism, the practitioner focuses on circumscribed symptoms or problems in functioning and combines methods from a range of sources on the basis of outcome studies and clinical experience. Potential strategies of intervention include exposure-based behavioral procedures to desensitize trauma-related stimuli; cognitive techniques to facilitate processing of traumatic memories and revise dysfunctional beliefs; stress inoculation training, coping skills training, and eye-movement desensitization and reprocessing (EMDR).

COMMON FACTORS PERSPECTIVES

This approach to integration assumes that the major therapeutic systems exert their effects through core factors that operate independently of technical procedures associated with particular schools of thought. In a seminal paper published more than seventy years ago, Saul Rosenzweig argued that all forms of psychotherapy share basic elements that account for their effectiveness, emphasizing the crucial functions of the therapeutic relationship and the role of conceptual schemes that provide explanations of problems in functioning and curative factors in therapeutic intervention (1936). Drawing on Rosenzweig's formulations, Jerome Frank argued that all modes of psychological healing share core elements that sponsor change and growth (Frank & Frank, 1991). He centered on the sustaining functions of the therapeutic relationship, the healing setting, conceptual schemes that provide explanations of what is the matter and what carries the potential to help, and the rituals or core activities of psychosocial intervention. Bruce Wampold has extended Frank's work, emphasizing the central importance of the therapeutic relationship and explanatory schemes in therapeutic outcomes (2007).

Half a century of psychotherapy research has documented the comparable effectiveness of diverse forms of intervention, and growing evidence points to the widespread operation of common factors in beneficial outcomes. Such findings challenge the power of the medical model of psychosocial intervention, which links specific treatment effects with specific diagnoses (Messer & Wampold, 2002; Wampold, 2007).

The common factors approach seeks to clarify "the profile of factors that are most strongly associated with positive therapeutic outcome" (Arkowitz, 1992, p. 275). Clinicians engage differing elements in fashioning individualized approaches to treatment on the basis of client characteristics, presenting problems, and experiential learning over the course of intervention. Sol Garfield's integrative perspective, emphasizing insight, hope, and experiential learning, serves as an example of the common factors perspective (2000).

In approaching the case from a common factors perspective, the clinician centers on basic elements believed to facilitate change and growth, including the development of the client-practitioner relationship and the therapeutic alliance; the constancy of care in the holding environment of the therapeutic setting; conceptual schemes that offer plausible explanations of problems in functioning and curative elements in psychosocial intervention; and the core activities, strategies, and procedures of the helping process. The clinician shifts ways of working in light of the client's concerns and responsiveness to differing elements. At the start of treatment, for example, the client may find cognitive-behavioral procedures most helpful in efforts to manage symptoms associated with PTSD. In time, as he restores a sense of mastery and strengthens coping skills, he may find process-oriented approaches most useful, exploring interactive experience in the therapeutic relationship to deepen understanding of issues and develop more adaptive ways of negotiating problems in living.

THEORETICAL INTEGRATION

In this approach, practitioners move beyond integrations of technical procedures or common elements and reformulate or translate ideas across theoretical traditions in their efforts to develop unified conceptions of personality, psychopathology, and practice methods (Safran & Messer, 1997; Stricker & Gold, 2003). Although the intervention strategies of the integrative system potentially incorporate procedures used in technical eclecticism, there are major differences in the assumptions and formulations that guide decision making and application of strategies and techniques (see Stricker & Gold, 2003). The conceptual frameworks broaden the range of phenomena that potentially serve as the focus of treatment and offer differing points of entry over the course of treatment.

The initial version of Wachtel's model, linking psychoanalytic perspectives with behavioral theory, is widely regarded as the first example of theoretical integration (Wachtel, 1977). In subsequent elaborations of the approach, Wachtel has integrated the core concepts of relational psychoanalysis with cognitive, behavioral, experiential, and systemic points of view (2008). Other examples of theoretical integration, mentioned earlier, include Berlin's cognitive-integrative perspective (2002; chapter 2, this volume) and the transtheoretical model of Prochaska and DiClemente (2002). Messer (2001) introduced a fourth perspective, assimilative integration, which incorporates developments in theoretical integration and technical eclecticism (see Gurman & Messer, 2003; Stricker & Gold, 2003). In assimilative approaches, practitioners integrate various techniques within a central thera-peutic framework that differs from the context in which the procedures were developed (see Wakefield & Baer, chapter 3, this volume, for further discussion of integrative strategies).

In approaching the case from the perspective of an integrative conceptual model, the clinician considers a range of phenomena in assessment of prob-lems in functioning, encompassing intrapsychic, experiential, cognitive, behavioral, interpersonal, and systemic domains of concern. In carrying out intervention, the clinician engages concepts and technical procedures from models that may have been considered incompatible in traditional forms of therapeutic practice. In Wachtel's integrative approach, for example, the cli-nician uses psychodynamic approaches and behavioral methods in efforts to deepen self-understanding and disrupt "vicious circles" of thought, feeling, and action that perpetuate problems in living.

Following conceptions of change encompassed in most integrative approaches, the practitioner seeks to help the client deepen awareness and understanding of conscious and unconscious domains of experience; restruc-ture cognitive processes and reorganize structures of meaning (conceptual-ized as schemata in cognitive theory or as working models of self, others, and interactive experience in object relations theory); learn new behavioral skills; engage stimuli that perpetuate fear and anxiety; enrich capacities to experience emotion; and revise maladaptive patterns of interpersonal func-tioning (see Stricker & Gold, 2003, for further discussion of change processes encompassed in integrative approaches).

Empirical studies have demonstrated the effectiveness of integrative approaches across a range of models, including dialectical behavior therapy (Linehan, 1987, 1993); prescriptive therapy (Beutler, Alomohamed, Moleiro & Romanelli, 2002); transtheoretical therapy (Prochaska & DiClemente, 2002); and process-experiential psychotherapy (Greenberg, 2002). For reviews of specific findings, see Glass, Arnkoff & Rodriguez, 1998; Messer & Warren, 1995; Roth & Fonagy, 2005; Stricker & Gold, 2003). Practitioners emphasize the need to better reflect the complexity of clinical phenomena and the contexts of intervention in continued development of process and outcome research on integrative approaches (see Safran & Messer, 1997, for discussion of methodological issues in continued development of research on integrative practice).

PLURALISM, INTEGRATIVE APPROACHES, AND CRITICAL PERSPECTIVES

Social workers must inevitably negotiate fundamental tensions between more pure conceptions of the therapeutic endeavor and more pragmatic renderings of the helping process over the course of their training and practice. As I have observed, most clinicians come to characterize their approach as eclectic, drawing on ideas and methods from a variety of sources. Even so, there has been little consideration of the ways in which practitioners engage differing theoretical perspectives, empirical findings, and technical procedures over the course of their work.

I have introduced critical pluralism and pragmatism as orienting perspectives in comparative approaches to clinical theory and argued that mastery of the foundational schools of thought strengthens eclectic, integrative approaches to psychosocial intervention. In this closing section I consider the relative merits of pluralist and integrative approaches, emphasizing the crucial functions of dialogue in continued development of critical perspectives.

As we have seen, pluralist points of view maintain the distinct identities of the core theoretical systems and make the multiplicity of differing approaches a defining feature of clinical practice. Presumably, all theories are necessarily limited, and thinkers emphasize the importance of ongoing dialogue across the therapeutic traditions in efforts to clarify differences and integrate concepts, empirical findings, and technical procedures in pragmatic approaches to intervention.

Although pluralist perspectives broaden the scope of understanding and strengthen critical thinking and decision making in psychosocial intervention, they place considerable demands on the worker in the clinical situation. The practitioner must engage multiple models, languages, and modes of intervention, negotiating tensions between a particular approach and alternative points of view, moving back and forth between higher level constructs and the specifics of the clinical situation. Following the pragmatic orientation of critical pluralism, the clinician searches for what works, judging the validity of differing ideas and methods on the basis of their effectiveness. The fundamental challenge in working from a pluralist orientation is to establish a point of view that encompasses a range of perspectives *and* preserves the distinctive therapeutic style and personal idiom of the clinician (see Borden, 2008b; Strenger, 1997; 2001).

Experienced practitioners of all orientations use methods that work, engaging methods from divergent perspectives, and a growing number of practitioners argue that integrative perspectives best reflect what most clinicians "actually *do* rather than what they were *trained to do*" (Stricker & Gold, 2003, p. 344; italics added). It is useful to reconsider briefly the three forms of integrative practice in light of the theoretical concerns explored here.

The approaches encompassed in technical eclecticism guide workers in pragmatic application of specific strategies in treatment of circumscribed problems in functioning on the basis of empirical findings and clinical knowledge. Although this approach to integration strengthens conceptions of evidence-based practice, most models consider technical procedures independent of their underlying theoretical systems. In the absence of conceptual frames of reference, practitioners run the risk of implementing reductive, mechanized approaches to treatment.

Further, such approaches generally fail to address the ways in which the context of the therapeutic process itself may influence differing perceptions and use of methods. As critiques of technical eclecticism have emphasized, the meaning and impact of procedures varies with differing therapeutic contexts (Messer & Warren, 1995; Safran & Messer, 1997). For example, a client engaged in a psychodynamically oriented treatment could experience the clinician's introduction of behavioral techniques as an attuned and responsive effort to help or as an impinging element that disrupts the therapeutic process. Differing theoretical perspectives deepen the practitioner's understanding of the dynamics of inner life, personal meaning, and the crucial functions of interactive experience in the therapeutic situation. Finally, prescriptive approaches are limited in that they fail to consider variations in functioning over the course of the therapeutic process. Safran and Messer recommend that practitioners to use a "process diagnosis" rather than a "fixed diagnosis" and apply procedures flexibly in view of changing needs and emerging capacities (1997).

Meta-analyses exploring the relative efficacy of differing therapeutic approaches continue to show that all treatments are approximately equally effective. Such findings challenge conceptions of intervention that posit specific treatment effects for particular disorders, emphasizing the importance of common factors rather than technical procedures (Messer & Wampold, 2002; Wampold, 2007). As we have seen, a second approach to integration emphasizes differing use of core elements in individualized, eclectic approaches to treatment. While this perspective clarifies common factors that would appear to be central in all forms of intervention, it fails to take account of the distinctive features of differing therapeutic systems and the ways in which clinicians carry out intervention in the context of differing frameworks of meaning (see Messer & Winokur, 1984; Safran & Messer, 1997).

The models developed in the third approach to integration offer unified conceptions of personality, problems in living, and the helping process. In doing so, they broaden the scope of intervention, and encompass ideas and methods that are potentially excluded from the core therapeutic systems, extending the range of options in clinical practice (Stricker & Gold, 2003). In the translation and reformulation of core concepts across perspectives, however, thinkers potentially diminish the nuance and richness of the distinctive theoretical systems (see Safran & Messer, 1997; Messer & Winokur, 1984).

Some scholars have argued that the epistemological differences underlying the foundational therapeutic systems are so fundamental as to limit coherent synthesis of core concepts and methods. In their critique of integrative trends in psychotherapy, Safran and Messer (1997) advocate a more "contextually-based, pluralistic approach" to clinical theory and an "atmosphere of confronting and discussing difference rather than shunning it" (p. 149). Drawing on contemporary philosophical perspectives, they show how dialogue across diverse perspectives helps practitioners move beyond preconceptions, consider different points of view, and deepen appreciation of phenomena (see, e.g., Gadamer, 1980; Habermas, 1979; Rorty, 1982). Richard Bernstein's philosophical position of "engaged fallibilistic pluralism" provides an alternative to relativistic points of view that perpetuate a facile acceptance of all theoretical orientations and practices (1993). He urges thinkers and practitioners to take their fallibility seriously; while they may be committed to particular styles of thinking, they are "willing to listen to others without denying or suppressing the otherness of the other" (1993, p. 336).

Given the diverse perspectives, models, and methods that we have come to encompass in contemporary practice, it is clear that we cannot reduce the complexity of the clinical situation to any single vision of the human situation or form of therapeutic practice. As James would remind practitioners, the world is full of "partial purposes" and "partial stories"—is "one" in some respects, and "many" in others (James, 1911, p. 134). As we have seen, pluralist approaches recognize the particularity and the irreducible ambiguity of the clinical situation, focusing on fact, concreteness, action, and adequacy. Pragmatic lines of understanding emphasize the effectiveness or "cash value" of differing ideas and the importance of flexibility and common sense in our efforts to help. Ongoing dialogue across the divergent schools of thought, grounded in the concrete particulars of everyday social work, promises to enrich critical perspectives and theoretically informed approaches to integrative, eclectic practice.

REFERENCES

Antony, M., & Roemer, L. (2003). Behavior therapy. In A. Gurman & S. Messer (Eds.), *Essential psychotherapies* (pp. 182–223). New York: Guilford.

Applegate, J. (2003). Full circle: Returning psychoanalytic theory to social work education. *Psychoanalytic Social Work*, 11 (1), 23–36.

Arkowitz, H. (1992). A common factors therapy for depression. In J.C. Norcross & M.R. Goldfried (Eds.), *Handbook of psychotherapy integration* (pp. 402–432). New York: Basic.

Berlin, S. (2002). *Social work practice: A cognitive-integrative perspective.* New York: Oxford University Press.

Bernstein, R. (1993). *The new constellation.* Cambridge, Mass.: MIT Press.

Beutler, L. (2004). *Prescriptive psychotherapy.* London: Oxford University Press.

Beutler, L., Alomohamed, S., Moleiro, C., & Romanelli, R. (2002). Systematic treatment selection and prescriptive therapy. In J. Lebow (Ed.), *Comprehensive handbook of psychotherapy, Vol. 4: Integrative-eclectic* (pp. 255–272). New York: Wiley.

Bohart, A.C. (2003). Person centered psychotherapy and related experiential approaches. In A. Gurman & S. Messer (Eds.), *Essential psychotherapies* (pp. 107–148). New York: Guilford.

Bollas, C. (1989). *Forces of destiny.* London: Free Association Books.

Borden, W. (1998). The place and play of theory in practice: A Winnicottian perspective. *Journal of Analytic Social Work*, 5 (1), 25–40.

Borden, W. (1999). Pluralism, pragmatism, and the therapeutic endeavor in brief dynamic treatment. In W. Borden (Ed.), *Comparative approaches in brief dynamic psychotherapy* (pp. 7–42). Binghamton, N.Y.: Haworth Press.

Borden, W. (2008a). Contemporary object relations psychology and psychosocial intervention. In A.R. Roberts (Ed.), *Social workers' desk reference* (pp. 259–264). New York: Oxford University Press.

Borden, W. (2008b). Comparative theory and integrative perspectives in psychosocial intervention. In A.R. Roberts (Ed.), *Social workers' desk reference* (pp. 305–310). New York: Oxford University Press.

Borden, W. (2009). *Contemporary psychodynamic thought and social work practice.* Chicago: Lyceum Press.

Curtis, R., & Hirsch, I. (2003). Relational approaches to psychoanalytic psychotherapy. In A. Gurman & S. Messer (Eds.), *Essential psychotherapies* (pp. 69–106). New York: Guilford.

Ford, D., & Urban, H. (1998). *Contemporary models of psychotherapy.* New York: Wiley.

Frank, J., & Frank, J. (1991). *Persuasion and healing.* Baltimore: Johns Hopkins University Press.

Gadamer, H. (1980). *Dialogue and dialectic.* New Haven, Conn.: Yale University Press.

Garfield, S. (2000). Eclecticism and integration: A personal retrospective view. *Journal of Psychotherapy Integration*, 10, 341–356.

Gendlin, E. (1996). Focusing-oriented psychotherapy: A manual of the experiential method. New York: Guilford.

Glass, C., Arnkoff, D., & Rodriguez, B. (1998). An overview of directions in psychotherapy integration research. *Journal of Psychotherapy Integration*, 8, 187–210.

Goldfried, M., & Norcross, J. (1995). Integrative and eclectic therapies in historical perspective. In B. Bongar and L. Beutler (Eds.), *Comprehensive textbook of psychotherapy* (pp. 254–273). New York: Oxford University Press.

Goldstein, H. (1990). The knowledge base of social work practice: Theory, wisdom, analogue, or art? *Families in Society* (January), 32–43.

Greenberg, L. (2002). *Emotion-focused therapy*. Washington, D.C.: American Psychological Association.

Gurman, A., & Messer, S. (2003). Contemporary issues in the theory and practice of psychotherapy. In A. Gurman and S. Messer (Eds.), *Essential psychotherapies* (pp. 1–24). New York: Guilford.

Habermas, J. (1979). *Communication and the evolution of society*. Boston: Beacon Press.

Hembree, E., & Foa, E. (2003). Promoting cognitive therapy in posttraumatic stress disorder. In M. Reinecke & D. Clark (Eds.), *Cognitive therapy across the lifespan* (pp. 231–257). Cambridge, U.K.: Cambridge University Press.

James, W. (1907/1946). *Pragmatism*. New York: Longmans, Green.

James, W. (1909/1977). *A pluralistic universe*. Cambridge, Mass.: Harvard University Press.

James, W. (1911). 'The one and the many.' In *Some problems in philosophy: A beginning of an introduction to philosophy* (pp. 113–146). New York: Longmans, Green.

Lazarus, A. (2002). The multimodal assessment treatment method. In J. Lebow (Ed.), *Comprehensive handbook of psychotherapy, Vol. 4: Integrative-eclectic* (pp. 241-254). New York: Wiley.

Leahy, R. L. (Ed.). (2004). *Contemporary cognitive therapy: Theory, research, and practice*. New York: Guilford.

Liddle, H. A. (1982). On the problems of eclecticism: A call for epistemologic clarification and human scale theories. *Family Process*, 21, 81–97.

Linehan, M. (1987). Dialectical behavior therapy for borderline personality disorder. *Bulletin of the Menninger Clinic*, 51, 261–276.

Linehan, M. (1993). *Cognitive-behavioral treatment of borderline personality disorder*. New York: Guilford.

Mahoney, M. (Ed.) (1995). *Cognitive and constructivist psychotherapies: Theory, research, and practice*. New York: Springer.

Meichenbaum, D. (1995). *Cognitive and constructive therapies: Theory, research, and practice*. New York: Springer.

Menand, L. (2001). *The metaphysical club*. New York: Farrar, Straus & Giroux.

Messer, S. (2001). Applying the visions of reality to a case of brief therapy. *Journal of Psychotherapy Integration*, 10, 55–70.

Messer, S., & Wampold, B. (2002). Let's face it: Common factors are more potent than specific therapy ingredients. *Clinical Psychology: Science and Practice*, 9, 21–25.

Messer, S. & Warren, S. (1995). *Models of brief psychodynamic psychotherapy*. New York: Guilford.

Messer, S., & Winokur, M. (1984). Ways of knowing and visions of reality in psychoanalytic psychotherapy and behavior therapy. In H. Arkowitz & S. B. Messer (Eds.), *Psychoanalytic therapy and behavior therapy: Is integration possible?* (pp. 63–100). New York: Plenum.

Mitchell, S. (1988). *Relational concepts in psychoanalysis*. Cambridge, Mass.: Harvard University Press.

Mitchell, S. (1991). Editorial philosophy. *Psychoanalytic Dialogues*, 1, 1–7.

Mitchell, S. (1997). *Influence and autonomy in psychoanalysis*. Hillsdale, N.J.: Analytic Press.

Mitchell, S. (2000). *Relationality: From attachment to intersubjectivity*. Hillsdale, N.J.: Analytic Press.

Norcross, J., & Goldfried, M. R. (Eds.) (1992). *Handbook of psychotherapy integration*. New York: Basic Books.

Phillips, A. (1988). *Winnicott*. Cambridge, Mass.: Harvard University Press.

Prochaska, J., & DiClemente, C. C. (2002). Transtheoretical psychotherapy. In J. Lebow (Ed.), *Comprehensive handbook of psychotherapy, Vol. 4: Integrative-eclectic* (pp. 165–184). New York: Wiley.

Reineck, M., & Freeman, A. (2003). Cognitive therapy. In A. Gurman & S. Messer (Eds.), *Essential psychotherapies* (pp. 224–271). New York: Guilford.

Rogers, C. (1961). *On becoming a person*. Boston: Houghton Mifflin.

Roth, A. & Fonagy, P. (2005). *What works for whom? A critical review of psychotherapy research*. New York: Guilford.

Rorty, R. (1982). *Consequences of pragmatism*. Minneapolis: University of Minnesota Press.

Rosenzweig, S. (1936). Some implicit common factors in diverse methods of psychotherapy. *American Journal of Orthopsychiatry*, 6, 412–415.

Sacks, O. (1984). *A leg to stand on*. New York: Touchstone Books.

Safran, J., & Messer, S. (1997). Psychotherapy integration: A postmodern critique. *Clinical Psychology: Science and Practice*, 4, 140–152.

Simon, L. (1998). *Genuine reality: A life of William James*. New York: Harcourt Brace.

Strenger, C. (1997). Hedgehogs, foxes, and critical pluralism: The clinician's yearning for unified conceptions. *Psychoanalysis and Contemporary Thought*, 20 (1), 111–145.

Strenger, C. (2002). *The quest for voice in contemporary psychoanalysis*. Madison, Conn.: International Universities Press.

Stricker, G., & Gold, J. (2003). Integrative approaches to psychotherapy. In A. Gurman & S. Messer (Eds.), *Essential Psychotherapies* (pp. 317–350). New York: Guilford.

Stricker, G., & Trierweiler, S. J. (1995). The local clinical scientist: A bridge between science and practice. *American Psychologist*, 50, 995–1002.

Ursano, R., et al. (2004). Practice guideline for the treatment of patients with acute stress disorder and posttraumatic stress disorder. Washington, D.C.: American Psychiatric Association.

Viney, W., King, C., & King, B. D. (1992). William James on the advantages of a pluralistic psychology. In M. Donnelly (Ed.), *Reinterpreting the legacy of William James* (pp. 91–100). Washington, D.C.: American Psychological Association.

Wachtel, P. (1977). *Psychoanalysis and behavior therapy*. New York: Basic Books.

Wachtel, P. (1989). *The poverty of affluence: A psychological portrait of the American way of life*. Philadelphia: New Society Publishers.

Wachtel, P. (1993). *Therapeutic communication*. New York: Guilford.

Wachtel, P. (1997). Psychoanalysis, behavior therapy, and the relational world. Washington, D.C.: American Psychological Association.

Wachtel, P. (2008). *Relational theory and the practice of psychotherapy*. New York: Guilford.

Wampold, B. (2007). Psychotherapy: The humanistic (and effective) treatment. *American Psychologist*, 2 (8), 857–873.

Winnicott, D. W. (1945/1965). *The maturational process and the facilitating environment*. New York: International Universities Press.

Winnicott, D. W. (1971). *Therapeutic consultations in child psychiatry*. New York: Basic.

Wright, K. (1991). *Vision and separation*. Hillsdale, N.J.: Jason Aronson.

Yalom, I. (1980). *Existential psychotherapy*. New York: Basic.

PART TWO

INNER EXPERIENCE AND OUTER REALITIES

2 WHY COGNITIVE THERAPY NEEDS SOCIAL WORK

SHARON BERLIN

OVER THE LAST quarter-century cognitive therapy has emerged as a popular and effective form of treatment for a range of mental health problems. Since Aaron Beck published his original cognitive conceptualization of depression almost forty years ago, cognitive approaches have steadily been elaborated, tested, applied, and revised (Leahy, 2004). This evolution of cognitive therapy has followed a more general trend in the psychotherapy field, in which theorists extend existing theories of therapy by reaching beyond the traditional conceptual boundaries of a given approach to integrate ideas from multiple schools of thought. Recent developments in cognitive therapy draw on work from neuroscience, relational psychology, social psychology, social work, decision theory, and cognitive psychology to provide more comprehensive, complex, and precise explanations of how mental health problems develop and can be treated (Berlin, 2006).

Despite the growing emphasis on integration, there are still multiple versions of cognitive therapy specified in the psychotherapy literature. These differ from one another to varying degrees with respect to theoretical assumptions, types of problems addressed, and kinds of intervention methods employed. The most basic version of cognitive therapy is Beck's model of cognitive therapy for depression (Beck, Rush, Shaw & Emery, 1979). It constitutes the base from which other models have been elaborated and is probably the most widely used and most thoroughly investigated.[1] Beck's cognitive therapy has been translated into a treatment manual that specifies clear-cut steps to be accomplished within a relatively short course of treatment (e.g., Barlow, 2001). These features of brevity and specificity make cognitive therapy an appealing candidate for research investigations. Indeed, cognitive therapy has been subjected to numerous empirical tests and has emerged as a premier evidence-based practice, especially for problems of depression and anxiety (e.g., Chambless & Peterman, 2004; DeRubeis et al., 1999; Evans et al., 1992; Hollon & DeRubeis, 2004; Teasdale et al., 2001). Because of its specificity, short-term applications, and empirical support, health insurance companies and mental health agencies often promote cognitive therapy as the treatment of choice for a number of mental health disorders.

Since social workers constitute the majority of mental health providers and are in a position to draw on cognitive therapy approaches to inform work with clients, it is important that practitioners understand both the richness and limits of cognitive conceptions of problems and of change. Over the years I have worked to extend the explanations and change strategies that constitute cognitive therapy to make them more useful for clinical social work practice. In this chapter I share my latest thinking about the give-and-take relationship that I believe would strengthen both cognitive therapy and social work. First, I offer my reading—my own translation and in some instances, elaboration—of the underlying assumptions and therapeutic methods that characterize most forms cognitive therapy. Second, I raise concerns about the ways that prevailing cognitive and constructive perspectives tend to disregard the influence of environmental forces (sociocultural, economic, and political forces). By arguing that reality is the product of subjective constructive processes, these perspectives minimize the independent role of the environment in shaping experience (Kemp, Whittaker, & Tracy, 2002). Finally, I describe a cognitive-integrative model of cognitive therapy that I have designed to specifically take account of the environmental dimensions of personal problems (Berlin, 2002). This model is especially appropriate for social work practice.

FUNDAMENTALS OF COGNITIVE THERAPY

In general, cognitive therapy works to help people operate outside of their restrictive memory representations of difficult past experiences as they respond to current life circumstances. The theoretical basis for this approach is a set of ideas that explain how organized memories of the past guide current responses. The fundamental notion is that as we engage in interactions in the world, our memory systems represent and store these experiences—not just our thoughts about them, but also the motivations, emotions, images, and actions that are part of our overall response. Over the course of similar experiences, memory representations of situations and our reactions to them form relatively stable memory patterns or networks (sometimes called *schemas*) that we then automatically use to process and respond to new occurrences. Among other things, these memory patterns or schemas give us a view of the current circumstances, a sense of ourselves within them (for example, as confident, frightened, victimized, or relieved), and a set of actions to take (for example, leave, attack, placate, listen, soothe) to respond to them. From our insider's perspective, however, it seems as if the content of our moment-to-moment thoughts, emotions, motivations, and actions are fresh constructions, totally elicited by and appropriate to what is happening now. For the most part, we feel quite certain that we are living in and responding to the present.

The more we apply a particular schema to events, the more elaborate and accessible the schema becomes, to the point that a small subset of situational features will be enough to automatically activate the whole network of memories. Thus, for example, when someone undermines our efforts to achieve an immediate goal, that impediment, perhaps in combination with a certain tone of voice or facial expression on their part, or our own preexisting mood, or even the state of the weather (for example, overcast and chilly) is likely to activate predesigned, unintentional explanations, predictions, and body responses, which combine to give us that old familiar feeling—say, of hopeless, self-demeaning passivity (Teasdale, 1997).[2]

Presumably, our capacity to draw on memory representations of past experiences to make sense of the present and anticipate the future proved to be an advantage in the course of human evolution. And as we think about it, the benefits seem obvious. Why go through all the trouble of analyzing or "overthinking" every event or object that we encounter, when we can rely on our history of past choices and past outcomes to generate responses that usually serve us well? (Bargh & Barndollar, 1996). By the same token, evolutionary processes have also given humans the ability to notice discrepancies, including things that stand out from context, things that pique our curiosity, things that have changed, and emerging opportunities that bear on our goals. Under ordinary circumstances we register and accommodate such differences. In other words, we change our minds. And yet, for a variety of reasons, sometimes we don't. Sometimes we tenaciously hang on to patterns of understanding, acting as if nothing had changed or could change even more if we played our part a little differently. Following the familiar pathways requires less effort from all of us, and yet we have also evolved to notice and adjust to differences. So the question is: what gets in the way of this adaptive capacity?

First, we are less likely to revise our fundamental memories about who we are, what we can do, and what the world has to offer, if we have an implicit sense that our current way of apprehending and responding is protecting us in some way (for example, protecting us from trusting too much and getting let down again, or from being assertive and bringing on rejection). In response to feelings of vulnerability, and in the service of the defensive inclination that such feelings evoke, our attentional focus automatically narrows to keep us vigilant for additional threats and by extension, impervious to anything that might distract us from our attempts to stay safe. Ordinarily, this protective system works very well, but on the downside, it can keep us from noticing and making the most of "positive discrepancies"—in other words, discrepancies that could signal to us that we are safer than we had thought or that opportunities (to grow, explore, resolve, restore) seem to be available and are worth checking out (Berlin, 2003; Greenberg, 2002; Teasdale, 1997; Wachtel, 2005). And even if we become weary of the strictures of our defensive reactions and make a conscious effort to scan for opportunities to operate outside them, efforts to move beyond our "safety zone" can trigger anxiety that in turn causes us to retreat to our more circumscribed routines. Back in "familiar territory," the anxiety abates, and we are left with the sense that we were right the first time—that our best course is to play it safe, to stay with what we know and with what makes us feel most secure (Wachtel, 1993, 2005).

Second, we are less likely to notice opportunities to adjust our responses if we don't have some sense of how things could be different. We need at least a fragment of an idea, or feeling, or image that suggests there might be another, more useful and more freeing way of responding. Coupled with this sense that things could be better, we also need to be able to access the skills that would allow us to fill out this nascent "vision" and turn it into action. In other words, we need to be able to develop a growing sense of "what else?": If avoiding humiliation is not going to be my main motivating principle and life goal, then what else? Maybe risking and trusting? Maybe giving and receiving comfort and appreciation? Maybe disarming rather than extending the sting of criticism or embarrassment? Have I ever responded in these ways? What existing memories can I build on? How can I turn down the high emotional amplitude that occurs when I even consider risking a difference? And how, specifically, can I add to the motivating, attention-getting power of my new goal (say, of paying more attention to the needs of others and reaching out to them) in my life, today? What can I do to act according to it—what are the steps and where are the choice points?

In line with Markus and Nurius's (1986) classic work on positive self-memories, as people consciously inch their way toward a new way of thinking/feeling/acting, these shifts are retained in memory to contribute to a progressively more elaborate and accessible memory pattern of what they hope to accomplish and are accomplishing. In turn, this developing memory pattern supplies a more detailed, complex experiential base for guiding subsequent, goal-oriented efforts. Memory representations of goals that actually work to compel new responses are specific, detailed, and laced with compelling emotion. It is the longing, pride, curiosity, or love that is a part of this new goal or possibility that directs our attention to goal-related opportunities and generates the energy to persist, despite continuing obstacles, in making use of them (Bargh, 1982; Klinger, 1996).

Third, in order for these new visions and actions to sustain, develop, and come to fruition, they need to be recognized and reinforced by others within the relevant life-domain. The point is that at least *someone*—some significant family member, friend, employer, teacher, or other authority—needs to respond to our emerging new perspectives, feelings, and actions in a positive way. Of course, the best-case scenario is that we will encounter early and consistent signals from a variety of sources that this new approach we are taking actually works (Bandura, 1986; Markus & Cross, 1990).

Finally, (and this is the part that traditional cognitive therapy theorists hardly ever emphasize) we don't make significant memory revisions and adjustments if our ongoing circumstances continue to supply us with the kinds of cues that fit well enough with the old memory patterns to add to them and keep them active. The main issue here is not so much that individuals fail to detect positive discrepancies in the flow of incoming information (although some of that may be going on), but rather that the environment fails to provide enough positive discrepancies to notice. When the events of daily life continue to generate fairly consistent messages—say, of deprivation and powerlessness—there is little basis on which to revise one's memory-based patterns about what one's life is, could be, and will be like (Berlin, 2002). Although practitioners who specialize in work with trauma survivors fully understand the impossibility of lessening the effects of trauma while individuals remain in dangerous circumstances (Briere & Scott, 2006), for some reason this insight has not been applied more broadly.

Under one, or more usually some combination, of these circumstances—compelling inclinations to preserve a sense of familiarity and security; absence of vision, skills, or reinforcing feedback; absence of discrepant information in the environment—we are likely to get stuck within fairly narrow memory frameworks for understanding, feeling, and acting. Moreover, our subjective sense is that the perceptions, conceptions, inclinations, and feeling these frameworks give us are fresh, real, and appropriate to the immediate situation. In the moment, we are not likely to have any inkling that we are remembering past experiences of mistrust and applying those experiences to Mr. X. Because of something that he just did or said, we know that we don't trust him, and as far as we can tell, this feeling is all because of him.

This is the kind of impasse in which a good cognitive therapist has the potential to help—by prompting us to examine the constrained and constraining nature of the thoughts, feelings, and actions we are generating, and to understand these responses as *habits of mind*. Through various means, the therapist would try to help us catch on to how our automatic reliance on familiar memory patterns is creating a constricting and sometimes an almost unbearable reality.

In typical accounts of cognitive therapy (for example, A. T. Beck et al., 1979; A. T. Beck, 2005; J. Beck, 1995), the therapist leads the client through a process of breaking out of these old mental habits by first imagining and then trying out other, more freeing ways of understanding and responding. The protocol usually calls for self-monitoring in order to observe one's own mind tendencies and essentially catch oneself in the act of applying these overused memory constructions (for example, "Here it is again . . . that old feeling that I *have* to *fix things* . . . I *have* to make it work . . . I have to make sure *everyone* is happy . . . Okay . . . so I'll just note this on my 'daily record of dysfunctional thoughts'"). The next steps involve carefully considering the ways in which these reactions are no longer useful, generating some sense of what kind of response (primarily thoughts and behaviors) might better serve one's more growth-oriented goals, and then strengthening and fine-tuning these alternative conceptualizations and action plans by trying them out in the course of daily life. Often there is an additional step that includes exploring one's basic beliefs about the kinds of compromises one has assumed were necessary in order to make it in the world, reflecting on their origins and the purpose they served in that original context, and then holding them up to the light of day to see if they are still necessary or adaptive.

Although the original cognitive therapy protocol gives primary emphasis to noting, examining, and changing thoughts—the word-based, interpretive aspect of mental activity—subsequent revisions take account that our brains generate emotional responses before they organize the words and concepts that we use to describe what is happening and how we are feeling. In these later versions, additional attention is given to changing the emotional quality or overall feel of problematic responses (Greenberg, 2002; Klosko & Young, 2004; Segal, Williams, & Teasdale 2002; Teasdale, 1997).

These are the fundamentals of the basic cognitive therapy approach. To my mind, they provide a complex, compelling, and plausible explanation of how people get stuck in inflexible and constraining mental patterns and how they can move beyond them. They also include a set of therapy guidelines that, by most empirical accounts, have been quite successful. But, as attractive as this body of knowledge is, it sells itself short by minimizing or otherwise glossing over the ways in which current life circumstances can also play a powerful role in prompting personal change or in signaling that nothing has changed or will ever change—except perhaps, for the worse. This shortcoming limits the scope of work carried out by a full range of clinicians and clients, but it is particularly constraining for social workers and their clients. The kinds of difficulties that most of our social work clients face press us to find explanatory and practice frameworks that take account of the force of daily life circumstances on clients' states of mind and behavior.

LIMITED PERSPECTIVE ON ENVIRONMENTAL INFLUENCES

When cognitive therapy theorists do address the context in which the person lives and functions, the focus takes three main forms. First, explanations of the origins of psychological difficulties point to early interactions with caregivers as generating the information that forms the foundation of key memory patterns. Theorists acknowledge that ongoing events and conditions play a role in reactivating versions of these foundational memories. They also concede that the current flow of life events serves to extend and even revise preexisting patterns, but here, they fail to fully appreciate and make use of the fact that the information generated through the dynamics of daily life (in a particular time, place, culture, and power structure) can either give people more reasons to respond in the ways that they always have or suggest the possibility that something is or could be different. It is as if *all* the important environmental influences occurred in childhood and can *only* be tempered now by helping the person realize that their old, memory-based responses are neither necessary nor useful in the current circumstances. As a consequence, when clinicians apply these assumptions in practice, they focus their clients on altering maladaptive schematic patterns and give little if any emphasis to also understanding and changing the nature of present life circumstances that maintain and extend these patterns.

Second, attention is sometimes focused on how environmental factors operate as barriers to treatment. Here, a therapist may work to minimize the environmental impediments that make it hard for the client to attend sessions and engage in the therapeutic process. The practitioner might help a person access baby-sitting resources or resolve transportation difficulties so that she can actually get to the session and work on her *real* problems, which are usually framed as her dysfunctional ways of understanding herself and her options. Admittedly, attending to environmental barriers to treatment is a positive step. The mystery here is why cognitive therapists who are concerned about material and sociopolitical constraints as barriers to treatment don't go on to consider that these same conditions (inadequate economic resources, overburdened social networks, discrimination) are also likely to be heavily implicated in the problems the client is wanting to resolve.

It is not uncommon for therapists (cognitive therapists and others) to observe that a particular client's situation is horrible, but at the same time, to suggest that to get involved in trying to address it is beyond the therapeutic purview. "Helping my client get food stamps, or a warm winter coat, or a doctor's appointment or . . . isn't my job." Sometimes the strategy in this kind of situation is to "divvy up" the client problems, so that the psychotherapist works on the client's psychological issues, but refers the client to the social worker for help in managing concrete needs. Or in another variation, the social worker will focus on the psychotherapeutic tasks and refer the client to the case manager for assistance with issues of heat, food, shelter, work, and so on. In some situations these types of arrangements may seem to be the most practical and affordable way to ensure that *someone* is attending to the most basic sources of the client's distress. Yet when therapists find a way to directly or indirectly offer clients concrete help, these efforts are generally viewed as occurring *outside* of the therapeutic frame.

A final way in which context is considered within traditional cognitive therapy takes the form of analyzing how the individual actually pulls for or elicits the kind of environmental response that she has come to expect. The underlying idea, which comes from a partial reading of an interactionist or person-environment perspective, is not only that the person creates her own version of reality in memory, but that her reliance on this (or any) memory pattern implicitly shapes the responses of others to her. Thus, she also creates her current actual environment (Caspi, 1993, 2005). In many accounts of this process, the individual's assessments and actions also incorporate a paradoxical element (Wachtel, 1993).

By way of illustration, consider the case of an insecure person, Jane, who relates to others in a domineering way in order to command their attention, care, and admiration. The paradox is that the very behaviors that are meant to ensure that others will affirm and want to be close to her drive them away. As the paradox plays out, Jane is left with a confirmation of her own worst fears, but without insight into the role that her automatic expectations and responses play in keeping her isolated and lonely. This kind of analysis inevitably leads to a treatment emphasis on how Jane, in operating off memory-based schemas, is actually inadvertently prompting or provoking others to reject her. If family members continue to target her as the scapegoat, then explorations are likely to focus on the ways she continues to play the role of victim; if coworkers at the restaurant ridicule her and gossip about her, the primary consideration is how she is misinterpreting these communications or might find some more effective way of dealing with them; if she is overlooked for promotions, the focus is likely to gravitate to improving her skills and/or learning assertive communication. Of course, these strategies are not all wrong, but it is wrong to imagine that because of an unfortunate past, Jane is now the *sole* author of her difficulties. If others are now behaving badly toward Jane, rather than take a serious, clear-eyed look at how people and structures and circumstances may be playing a fairly independent role in making her life hard, cognitive therapists tend to focus primarily on how Jane—with her misperceptions, inadequate communications, or lack of workplace skills—is complicit in this turn of events.

The point here is not that the perspectives detailed above are completely off track or that they don't lead to constructive work. Nor is it fair to paint all cognitive theorists and therapists with the same brush, as if there are no variations or exceptions. Rather, the argument is that, in general, cognitive therapy conceptualizations of person-environment interaction are insufficient. They don't fully capture the more extensive and complicated ways that past *and* current environmental factors make their way into all our personal experiences, including experiences of being stuck in difficulties and of finding a way out.

How should we understand this limited perspective on environmental influences? There are probably multiple, interrelated reasons for it, but central among them is the person-centered tradition of mainstream, European-American psychology. This discipline was conceived and developed as a science of the inner workings of the self. Accordingly, internal self-qualities (states, dispositions, motives, and feeling) are understood as the primary sources of action and adaptation in the world. Although the self is described as interacting with its context, it still tends to be viewed as quite separate or independent from it (Kitayama, 2002; Markus & Kitayama, 1997). Mainstream psychology carved out this internal territory for study and has more or less stuck with it.[3]

Moreover, the psychological perspective has flourished within a culture in which conceptions of individualism run deep. While psychology favors individualistic accounts of personal distress, even more generally, American society has been steeped in notions regarding the promise of personal initiative, the importance of personal responsibility, and the exhilaration of personal independence—to the extent that it is hard to think outside them.

Despite all this, the interactionist perspective, which stems from propositions regarding the reciprocal and constitutive interactions of open systems (Bertalanffy, 1968; Magnusson, 1990; Meyer, 1983; Ungar, 2002) seems to offer an alternative to the psychocentric bias we find in cognitive therapy and, indeed, in practically all other forms of psychotherapy. The central assumption of the interactionist perspective is that the individual develops and functions through dynamic, continuous, and reciprocal processes of interaction with his or her environment. In this view, no single system contributing to personhood—mental, biological, or environmental—functions in isolation from the others. Each shapes and responds to the others in contributing to a dynamic, organized, whole person, but not necessarily in a clear-cut, linear way, nor in an equal way. By the same token the individual, by virtue of his or her interpretations and actions, contributes to the context in which he or she functions, but is certainly not the sole contributor to this environment and often not the most powerful one.

These notions seem sound enough, and yet they have not pulled us very far from the traditional, internal psychological emphasis. In the case of cognitive therapy, the continuing tendency to lean toward the psychological interior is helped along by the ascendancy of constructivist notions of the person as meaning-maker—as an active, constructive, *co-creator* of his own experiences (Mahoney, 1995). Even though theorists who champion this constructivist meaning-making perspective describe it as interactionist, unfortunately, as their explanations unfold, the *co-* in *co-creator* drifts to the periphery, and it is the meaning-maker who creates reality. The constructivist idea as applied here is that people bring different histories of experience and thus different memory criteria to bear in interpreting the nature and personal impact of the current situation: "What's happening now—is it something funny, trivial, horrible, humiliating, irrelevant?" It depends. Reality depends on what one makes of the ongoing experiential stream.

This constructivist perspective was shaped by the cognitive revolution within psychology and sister disciplines, and takes its place alongside other tenets of postmodern thought that question the existence of realities beyond our individual or collective constructions of them (Bruner, 1990; Gardner, 1987; Miller 2003). Notions regarding the person as a meaning-maker have gained widespread appeal in both popular culture and academic circles. And they have imbued interactionist perspectives with an unmistakable person-centered tone: persons create environments, persons cannot be separated from environments, persons are active agents, and so on. Even though environmental situations are still gauged as influential, this is by virtue of the psychological meaning that a person gives to them (e.g., Magnusson, 1990; Caspi, 1993; Mischel, 2004).

To further illustrate, depending on the personal meaning or "psychological demand" of a situation in which one person is teasing another person, one individual may not even notice that he or she is being teased, another might read the teasing as an insult, and a third might see it as a sign of inclusion and affection (Mischel, 2004). All of this seems quite unremarkable; most of us can readily report scenarios in which different people see similar situations quite differently. But as we follow and affirm this line of analysis, it brings us to the conclusion that the material, social, cultural, and political features of situations are inevitably trumped by individuals' interpretations of them. This line of thinking provides a rationale for searching for sources of problems in the meanings that people construct—and by extension in the meaning-makers themselves—and for deemphasizing the environmental sources of such meanings. Is this a negative event, a stressful event, a situation of injustice or oppression or deprivation? According to the framework we have been exploring, the answer largely depends on the meaning the individual gives it. Even though the reasoning that takes us out on this limb is hard to dispute, once there, it feels quite precarious. We find ourselves wondering how we got into this predicament and wanting to retreat to a more secure and defensible position.

According to David Smail (2001), community psychologist and critic of the psychocentric bias in psychology, whenever theories provide clinicians *any* avenue or *any* loophole through which we can gravitate back to individualistic, internal explanations and courses of action, our socialization within an individualistic culture and our education within mainstream psychological models automatically prompts us to take it. Smail is further convinced that it is not necessary to resort to references to "murky" internal processes in trying to understand how external processes and events affect human functioning, and that whenever we do so, we are at risk of abandoning attention to the external conditions themselves. In his words, "it is perfectly possible to subscribe to a *psychological theory* [concerned with individual experience and action] whose fundamental concepts are material, social, and environmental rather than moral, individual and interior" (2001, p. 164). "Our mistake," he says, "is to take our *experience* of the operations of power as the force that moves us rather than concentrating on the influences that give rise to the experience in the first place" (p. 165).

Smail's point—that we move too quickly, mindlessly, and automatically, from a focus on the external sources of experience to the experience itself and then make it the focus of change—deserves our careful and sober consideration. He is right in suggesting that it would be easier to avoid being pulled away from consideration of external sources of experience if we were to discount internal sources altogether. I believe this also would be a mistake. By necessity, each person relies on memory to understand situations and organize efforts to manage them. In this way, memory records of experience not only influence the way we construct the past, but also bear on what we think, feel, and do now, and how we anticipate our futures. At the same time, the situations that we encounter as a part of our daily lives are not simply neutral phenomena waiting to be given form and significance according to our individual constructive processes (Hobfoll, 1989, 2003). By virtue of their attributes and context, situations also afford particular meanings and are likely to exert influence even when these forces operate outside of awareness.

By way of illustration, in an economy where blue-collar jobs that pay a living wage and provide benefits are hard to come by, a job loss is likely to trigger a range of negative consequences no matter how the individual frames it. Whether Joe views the termination of his job at the plant as a crisis or as an opportunity, it still interferes with his ability to make mortgage payments, brings employer health insurance coverage to a halt, puts additional strain on family relationships, and so on. In other words, environmental conditions may exert influences that fall outside the individual's immediate sense of what they mean.

Of course, the meanings that Joe constructs still matter; for example, if he is able to maintain a sense of optimism and self-worth in the midst of his unemployment, he will be more likely to persist in looking for another job and more likely to land one, than otherwise. But even so, his cognitive-emotional perspective is not the whole story.

For one thing, situations vary according to the degree that they are amenable to the efforts of individuals to change them or to buffer their impact by ignoring them or somehow reframing them. Similarly, the broader contexts in which situations are embedded differ in the extent to which they give people access to resources (for example, social and economic supports) that can be used to counter or buffer situational demands (Hobfoll, 2003). Joe doesn't have the means to change the job market. He can't get his old job back. Working for the political candidate who promises to create jobs or give tax breaks to working-class families could be a useful step in giving Joe the feeling that he is doing something to remedy oppressive conditions, and joining with others to take collective action may lead to positive change in the long run. Even so, there is no guarantee that his candidate will win the election or be able to make these changes or be able to make them quickly enough to benefit Joe in his immediate circumstances.

But depending on other circumstances, Joe still might be able to give himself a competitive edge in getting a new job. In this regard, it will matter whether or not Joe has the economic means to enter an educational program that can prepare him for a different occupation, or whether a reasonably good program even exists, or whether Joe has access to financial support to help maintain his family in the meantime—or access to a social worker who will stick with him in helping him to understand both the structural and personal aspects of his difficulty and to find inroads that he might take to buffer their effects.

If these resources exist, whether or not Joe is able to notice, cultivate, and take advantage of them, depends on how he sees them. If, in the course of Joe's life, he has encountered one instance after another of just eking by—in a family that could barely make ends meet, in a school system that was underfunded and understaffed, in a neighborhood that was the last to receive services or improvements, in a city in which he (and others of his race and class) were alternately viewed as a danger or a victim—and if his parents, friends, teachers, neighbors, and Joe himself stored these experiences in memory to generate feelings of demoralization and distrust, then the odds of Joe noticing and exploiting potential opportunities are less than if he were able to draw on organized memories of making the most of positive (or potentially positive) circumstances.

Still, we know that people tend to be highly adaptive. The resilience literature tells us that individuals who have adequate cognitive capabilities and have experienced a solid foundation of early care are often able respond positively to opportunities that emerge within a stream of relatively negative life events (Masten & Coatsworth, 1998; Walsh, 2003; Walsh, chapter 6, this volume). Perhaps this will be the case with Joe. But even here, the positive opportunities need to present themselves. This is not to say that opportunities necessarily come to us fully formed, just waiting to be pounced upon, but rather to suggest that, at the least, circumstances need to be responsive to an individual's efforts to build a renewed sense of safety, connection, and competence.

Of course, here is the rub: What if environmental circumstances are not responsive? Of course, we have to keep on looking for inroads. In the meantime, we can also help our clients develop ways of responding that will decrease their suffering and at least not make the situation worse. If, for example, we are able to help Joe notice and let go of his tendency to load the job loss situation with negative judgments, he is likely to feel better and be more able to actually notice or create and take advantage of opportunities related to his goal of providing for his family. Keeping Smail's caution in mind, in so doing, it will be important and difficult not to let the concern with how Joe is construing his job loss completely shift our combined attention away from the social and economic sources of experience to the experience itself. It is not that Joe has a problem because he gets down on himself. He has a problem because the plant closed, and he and hundreds of others were laid off. Even if we can't change these kinds of environmental forces in the short term, it is critically important to understand them, frequently acknowledge them, and consider strategies for changing them in the long term.

If we agree that the environment is not neutral—that situations and their contexts afford particular meanings and often result in particular consequences; that situations and contexts vary in the extent to which they provide access to resources and supports that might be used to buffer difficulties or open opportunities for change; that it is difficult to change one's mind about dangers and deprivations in the environment as long as they actually persist; and that cognitive therapy conceptualizations tend to overlook these influences and lead us to an overly narrow focus—then what? What are the implications of this understanding for social work practice?

There could be any number of useful responses to this question, and certainly some that are more radical than my own. But given a belief in the importance of relationship-based work with people and recognition of the potential richness of cognitive therapy, my consideration of this question has led me to develop an approach to practice that broadens the person-centered focus of traditional cognitive therapy and provides guidelines for maintaining the elusive person-environment balance that seems called for in the example given here and in our direct practice of social work.

The Cognitive-Integrative (C-I) perspective (Berlin, 2002) not only offers a framework for considering how a person's patterns of thinking might be constricting his or her experience, but in addition, offers a strong rationale for examining how available information from the current environmental context is also at play. It provides a set of guidelines that spell out how to bring environmental conditions into the cognitive therapy frame so that they become central considerations and not simply barriers or afterthoughts or something that we attend to as extra-therapeutic work (Kemp, Whittaker, and Tracey, 2002; Kemp, chapter 5, this volume; Miller, 2002).

HOW THE COGNITIVE-INTEGRATIVE PERSPECTIVE TAKES THE ENVIRONMENT INTO ACCOUNT

The Cognitive-Integrative perspective is designed around two fundamental and linked ideas: First, people are meaning-makers; to some significant extent, we operate on the basis of what we think things mean. Second, the meanings that we construct are shaped by both the ongoing information generated by environmental sources and personal sources (feedback from our own immediate thoughts, behaviors, emotions, and other body feelings), and the memory patterns we use to organize and understand this information. This broader focus on cognitive schemas and on available information helps us out of an untenable position of suggesting to the person whose life situation is by any standard a cause for feeling deprived or scared or depressed that she is constructing her own problems.

Since people change their minds when they repeatedly encounter events or circumstances or personal capacities that *are discrepant* from what they already know, it follows that in our social work helping role, we need to make sure that there are actually discrepancies to be noticed. We need to find them, create them, and help the client focus on experiencing the difference. How this actually plays out depends on the case at hand. But creating discrepancies—or, to put it in more positive terms, *creating new options or opportunities*—often means doing the kinds of practical things for clients that social workers already know how to do. For example, this could mean helping a family with a disabled child gain access to good respite care, or helping a lonely and mentally ill person find a support group that fits with his sensibilities, or not only finding the right budget counselor to help an individual overwhelmed with credit debt to get back on her feet, but also finding a way to explore with her the ways that we are all programmed to believe that having more material possessions will resolve our loneliness, or anxiety, or sense of exclusion; or it could mean sticking with the client no matter how many times she forgets or doesn't show up or doesn't follow through, perhaps addressing these issues, but also showing her a kind of loyalty that she has never experienced before.

Concrete help creates concrete differences that are relatively easy to notice and that tend to mean a great deal. In some situations, it will be enough to create these differences. They will draw the client's attention, actually remove or diminish sources of threat and worry, and activate feelings of progress and improvement. Yet, when old habits of feeling and understanding are highly developed and automatically accessible, we are also called upon to help our clients learn to consciously minimize the influence of these old memory patterns so that they do not overpower emerging new ones. In this situation, we can help clients learn to notice, understand, and accept their habitual responses and also to experiment with allowing difference, in the sense of trying on alternative ways of conceptualizing a situation and one's relationship to it, searching for additional emotional reactions to it, and learning and employing alternative action responses to it. In short, we work both to generate new streams of information and to help the individual develop the attentional capacity to notice these differences, the cognitive and emotional capacity to conceptualize and feel their significance, and the skills to act on them—to make the most of them.

Changing environments is hardly ever easy, but even when we've located and created potential opportunities, circumventing well-established memory patterns in order to develop new ones can also be complicated. As discussed earlier, people can get stuck in a certain way of feeling, understanding, and acting because to do otherwise prompts anxiety. Traditional cognitive therapy offers us useful avenues to pursue in assisting clients over this barrier. In taking up this interactive work, it is critically important to stay alert to the possibility of automatically drifting toward an exclusively internal cognitive focus. Even though social work practitioners have staked out a relatively broad person-environment focus, for the reasons I have noted, we are still not immune to the pull of a psychology of internal processes.

And yet, more than any other therapeutic profession, because of our intimate knowledge of the ways in which poverty, danger, deprivation, and powerlessness force restrictive and defensive responses, we are in a position to take the lead in drawing attention to social causes and finding ways to alter at least some of their noxious features. We will still be in a position to help clients learn how to respond to these situations in a way that will deflect their worst damage, but this should not be our sole strategy or necessarily our major strategy. Of course, a careful assessment of the nature of the client's difficulties and the client's own perspective will influence how we focus and balance our work, but when we find ourselves completely taken up with concerns about dysfunctional thoughts, emotion regulation, and motivational impairments, we need to take a step back to acknowledge and then figure out how to ameliorate the situational factors that are currently fueling these mental states.

Although as clinical social workers we are undoubtedly influenced by what seems to be a pervasive, culturewide dispositional bias (Jones & Nisbett, 1971; Batson & Marz, 1979: Batson, O'Quin & Pych, 1982), we can still correct for this leaning. In the same way that we ask clients to notice, understand, and accept their well-rehearsed memory patterns and then to consider ways to bring in additional information in the service of adding breadth and flexibility to habitual responses, we need to ask ourselves to do the same. Even though we are prone to focus too narrowly on internal sources of difficulties, that does not mean we should not focus on them at all. If, for example, it is the case that one brief moment of wondering about a client's out-of-awareness motivations sets the stage for an exclusive focus on early unconscious conflicts and disregard of current constraining circumstances, then we will need to notice this "relapse" and readjust. In other words, the "abstinence model" is not a good solution here. For good reasons, clinical social workers have positioned themselves in this ambiguous person-environment territory. And if we stay vigilant, we are quite capable of dealing with the ambiguity in order to find the most useful balance of emphasis for each client. We understand that situations are not completely determinative nor are individuals autonomous agents. Instead of opting for the clarity of an either-or position, we operate with the view that life situations create personal psychology, and that even though massive power differentials often exist between individuals and larger social forces, people can and do create environmental change. In the end, we understand that meaningful life changes usually require shift all the way around.

NOTES

1. Unless otherwise noted, I use the term *cognitive therapy* to refer to versions of cognitive therapy that adhere closely to Aaron Beck's original description of cognitive therapy for depression (Beck, Rush Shaw & Emery, 1979).

2. Increasingly, neuropsychologists are able to pinpoint the neurological activity that underlies these and other mental processes. This level of analysis can be useful to cognitive therapy theorists in providing neuroanatomical detail about the workings of mind, and in affirming and raising questions concerning the viability of cognitive assumptions about it (Damasio, 1999; Pliszka, 2003; Siegel, 1999).

3. It would be an exaggeration to say that psychology never considers context; some branches of psychology (social psychology, cultural psychology, community psychology) have focused on the person in interaction with other social units. More typically, however, the starting point and ending point of psychological inquiry is

what is happening within the person: for example, how is the individual's brain responding; what is the emotional tone; what are the conscious perceptions; what are the consistencies in cognitive, emotional, and behavioral reactions over time; and how can we help one alter the internal source of distress.

REFERENCES

Bandura, A. (1986). Social foundations of thought and action: A social cognitive theory. Englewood Cliffs, N.J.: Prentice-Hall.

Banks, A. (2001). *Post-traumatic stress disorder: Relationships and brain chemistry.* Victims of Violence Program, Jean Baker Miller Training Institute, Project Report 8. Wellesley, Mass.: Wellesley College.

Bargh, J. A. (1982). Attention and automaticity in the processing of self-relevant information. *Journal of Personality and Social Psychology,* 43, 425–436.

Barlow, D. H. (Ed.) (2001). Clinical handbook of psychological disorders, 3d ed. New York: Guilford Press.

Batson, C. D., & Marz, B. (1979). Dispositional bias in trained therapists' diagnoses: Does it exist? *Journal of Applied Social Psychology,* 9, 476–489.

Batson, C.D., O'Quin, K., & Pych, V. (1982). An attribution theory analysis of trained helpers' inferences about clients' needs. In T. A. Wills (Ed.), *Basic processes in helping relationships* (pp. 59–80). New York: Academic.

Beck, A. T. (2005). The current state of cognitive therapy: A 40-year retrospective. *Archives of General Psychiatry,* 62, 953–959.

Beck, A. T., Rush, A. J., Shaw, B. F., & Emery, G. (1979). *Cognitive therapy for depression.* New York: Guilford.

Beck, J. (1995). *Cognitive therapy: The basics and beyond.* New York: Guilford.

Berlin, S. B. (2002). *Clinical social work practice: A cognitive-integrative perspective.* New York: Oxford University Press.

Berlin, S. B. (2006). Review of R. L. Leahy (Ed.), *Contemporary cognitive therapy. Social Service Review,* 80, 194–196.

Bertalanffy, L. von. (1968). *General system theory: Foundations, development, and applications.* New York: Braziller.

Briere, S., & Scott, C. (2006). *Principles of trauma therapy: A guide to symptoms, evaluation, and treatment.* Thousand Oaks, Calif.: Sage Publications.

Bruner, J. (1990). *Acts of meaning.* Cambridge, Mass.: Harvard University Press.

Caspi, A. (1993). Why maladaptive behaviors persist: Sources of continuity and change across the life course. In D. C. Funder, R. D. Parke, C. Tomlinson-Keasey, and K. Widaman (Eds.), *Handbook of personality: Theory and research* (pp. 343–376). Washington D.C.: American Psychological Association.

Caspi, A. (2005). Personality development: Stability and change. *Annual Review of Psychology,* 56, 453–484.

Chambless, D. L., & Peterman, M. (2004). Evidence on cognitive-behavior therapy for generalized anxiety disorder and panic disorder. In R. L. Leahy (Ed.), *Contemporary cognitive therapy: Theory, research, and practice* (pp. 86–115). New York: Guilford Press.

DeRubeis, R. J., Gelfand, L. A., Tang, T. Z., & Simons, A. D. (1999). Medications versus cognitive behavioral therapy for severely depressed outpatients: Mega-analysis of four randomized comparisons. *American Journal of Psychiatry,* 156, 1007–1013.

Evans, M. D., Hollon, S. D., DeRubeis, R. J., Piasecki, J. M., Garvey, M. J., Grove, W. M., et al. (1992). Differential relapse following cognitive therapy, pharmacotherapy, and combined cognitive-pharmacotherapy for depression. *Archives of General Psychiatry,* 49, 802–808.

Gardner, H. (1987). Laying the foundation of cognitive science. In *The mind's new science: A history of the cognitive revolution* (pp. 10–27). New York: Basic Books.

Greenberg, L. S. (2002). Integrating an emotion-focused approach to treatment into psychotherapy integration. *Journal of Psychotherapy Integration,* 12, 154–189.

Hobfoll, S. E. (1989). Conservation of resources: A new attempt at conceptualizing stress. *American Psychologist,* 44, 513–524.

Hobfoll, S. E. (2003). Resource loss, resource gain, and emotional outcomes among inner city women. *Journal of Personality and Social Psychology,* 84, 632–643.

Hollon, S. D., & DeRubeis, R. J. (2004). Effectiveness of treatment for depression. In R. L. Leahy (Ed.), *Contemporary cognitive therapy: Theory, research, and practice* (pp. 45–61). New York: Guilford Press.

Jones, E. E. & Nisbett, R. E. (1971). The actor and the observer: Divergent perspectives of the causes of behavior. In E. E. Jones et al. (Eds.), *Attribution: Perceiving the causes of behavior* (pp. 79–94). Morristown, N.J.: General Learning Press.

Kemp, S. P., Whittaker, J. K., & Tracy, E. M. (2002). Contextual social work practice. In M. O'Melia and K. K. Miley (Eds.), *Pathways to power: Readings in contextual social work practice* (pp. 15–35). Boston: Allyn and Bacon.

Kitayama S. (2002). Cultural and basic psychological processes: Toward a system view of culture. *Psychological Bulletin,* 128, 89–96.

Klinger, E. (1996). Emotional influences on cognitive processing with implications for theories of both. In P. M. Gollwitzer & J. A. Bargh (Eds.), *The psychology of action: Linking cognition and motivation to behavior* (pp. 168–192). New York: Guilford.

Leahy, R. L. (Ed.). (2004). *Contemporary cognitive therapy: Theory, research, and practice.* New York: Guilford Press.

Magnusson, D. (1990). Personality development from an interactional perspective. In L. A. Pervin (Ed.), *Handbook of personality: Theory and research* (pp. 193–222). New York: Guilford.

Mahoney, M. M. (1995). Theoretical development in the cognitive and constructive psychotherapies. In M. M. Mahoney (Ed.), *Cognitive and constructive psychotherapies: Theory, research, and practice* (pp. 3–19). New York: Springer.

Markus, H. R., & Cross, S. (1990). The interpersonal self. In L. A. Pervin (Ed.), *Handbook of personality: Theory and research* (pp. 576–608). New York: Guilford.

Markus, H. R., & Kitayama, S. (1997). Models of agency: Sociocultural diversity in the construction of action. *Nebraska Symposium on Motivation,* 45, 1–57.

Markus, H. R., & Nurius, P. S. (1986). Possible selves. *American Psychologist,* 42, 954–961.

Masten, A. S., & Coatsworth, J. D. (1998). The development of competence in favorable and unfavorable environments: Lessons from research on successful children. *American Psychologist,* 53, 205–220.

Meyer, C. H. (1983). *Clinical social work in the ecosystems perspective.* New York: Columbia University Press.

Miller, G. A. (2003). The cognitive revolution: A historical perspective. *Trends in Cognitive Science,* 7, 141–144.

Miller, J. B. (2002). How change happens: Controlling images, mutuality, and power. Work in Progress 96. Wellesley, Mass.: Stone Center.

Mischel, W. (2004). Toward an integrative science of the person. *Annual Review of Psychology*, 55, 1–22.

Segal, Z. V., Williams, J. M. G., Teasdale, J. D. (2002). *Mindfulness-based cognitive therapy for depression*. New York: Guilford.

Smail, D. (2001). De-psychologizing community psychology. *Journal of Community and Applied Social Psychology*, 11, 159–165.

Teasdale, J. D. (1997). The mind in place in mood disorders. In D. M. Clark & C. C. Fairburn (Eds.), *Science and practice of cognitive behavior therapy* (pp. 26–47). Oxford, U.K.: Oxford University Press.

Teasdale, J. D., Scott, J., Moore, R. G., Hayhurst, H., Pope, M., & Paykel, E. S. (2001). How does cognitive therapy prevent relapse in residual depression: Evidence from a controlled trial. *Journal of Consulting and Clinical Psychology*, 69, 347–357.

Ungar, M. (2002). A deeper, more social ecological social work practice. *Social Service Review*, 76, 480–497.

Wachtel, P. L. (1993). Therapeutic communication: Knowing what to say when. New York: Guilford.

Wachtel, P. L. (2005). Anxiety, consciousness, and self-acceptance: Placing the idea of making the unconscious conscious in an integrative framework. *Journal of Psychotherapy Integration*, 15, 243–253.

Walsh, F. (2003). Family resilience: A framework for clinical practice. *Family Process*, 42, 1–18.

3 THE COGNITIVIZATION OF PSYCHOANALYSIS

Toward an Integration of Psychodynamic
and Cognitive Theories

JEROME C. WAKEFIELD AND JUDITH C. BAER

COGNITIVE THERAPY TENDS to focus on the internal thoughts of
the client and how those thoughts distort reality and lead to anxiety and
depression. But what if reality itself introduces stresses that would cause
anyone anxiety or depression? In her reformulations of cognitive approaches
to intervention, Sharon Berlin (2002; chapter 2, this volume) emphasizes the
need to consider real challenges in the outer world of the client in assessment
and treatment. The point is fundamental: the very notion that an individual's
cognition is "distorted" or "irrational" depends on a prior assessment of the
actual environment and whether the individual is reacting normally to it, so
cognitive assessment makes no sense without considering the individual's
relationship to the environment.

The problem of lack of attention to environmental context goes well
beyond cognitive-behavioral theory. One of us (Wakefield), in a recent book
with sociologist Allan Horwitz titled *The Loss of Sadness: How Psychiatry
Transformed Normal Sorrow into Depressive Disorder* (2007), argued that the
current, fourth edition of the American Psychiatric Association's *Diagnostic and Statistical Manual of Mental Disorders* (DSM; 2000) failed to consider the context of depressive symptoms, thus failed to distinguish normal
sadness due to environmental stressors from genuine depressive disorders
where something has gone wrong with an individual's functioning and they

are "stuck" in a pathologically deep or prolonged state of sadness and associated symptoms. Because sadness is biologically designed to be an emotion experienced in response to certain kinds of losses and other environmental stresses, one cannot infer that there is a biological or other internal dysfunction without evaluating the relationship between the environment and the individual's response to it.

The realization that cognitive-behavioral theory must be expanded to include assessment of environmental variables leads to the question: are there other limitations in the cognitive-behavioral perspective that unnecessarily constrain the therapist's understanding of and response to the client's problem? The answer, we believe, is that today's clinician must be an integrationist about theory and must incorporate defensible insights from a variety of theoretical perspectives into the basic cognitive-behavioral repertoire, including some of the insights of psychodynamic theory.

What follows in this chapter is, first, a discussion of the rationale for theoretical integration and a review of the types of integration. We then consider some deep conceptual and philosophical commonalities between the Freudian psychodynamic and cognitive perspectives that allow for unusual ease of integration. Aaron Beck's approach to cognitive-behavioral therapy and three recent psychodynamic theories are then reviewed to illustrate how psychodynamic theory itself is becoming more cognitivized and how it shares crucial theoretical framework principles with the most prominent form of cognitive theory. Finally, we identify other psychodynamic principles that lend themselves to incorporation into cognitive theory and practice.

LEVELS OF MEANING AND REASONS FOR INTEGRATION OF PSYCHOTHERAPY THEORIES

There are persuasive scientific and moral arguments for integration of clinical ideas in social work education and practice. (We consider the reasons for integration, not the "how to," which would require a different essay.) The scientific argument for an integrationist view of psychotherapy theory is simple: each of the extant major theories focuses on one aspect of human nature, and each gets at part of the truth. One might say that individuals operate at several levels of meaning, and all these levels are potentially involved in a psychosocial problem and in its treatment. To adhere to one theoretical perspective is thus to limit the options for one's client. An attempt to document each of the following statements is beyond the scope of this chapter, but we believe the levels of meaning-processing include at least the following:

1. Although not strictly in itself a level of meaning, people's meaning systems are rooted in biological structures that support the generation of meaning in the brain.

2. People are instrumentally conditioned by contingent reinforcers and classically conditioned as well. We know this not only from a vast empirical literature on learning, but also from recent neuroscientific discoveries that reveal the anatomy of learning; so people really do have conditioned behaviors subject to the principles of learning.

3. People have cognitive and representational mental contents, including conscious beliefs and desires, sometimes irrational, that motivate and guide their actions. We know this not only from our common-sense understanding of our own and others' minds, but also from the remarkable effectiveness of "folk psychology" (that is, the intuitive understanding of people in terms of beliefs and desires that cause their actions) that we use to interact with others in our everyday lives. For example, how is it that all the chapters that make up this volume converged at the editor at the right moment for publication? The only answer is that the various writers had certain beliefs about the deadline and what was required of them, and certain desires, such as to have their chapter included in the book, and thus their actions led to the convergence of the chapters. There is nothing in behavioral or psychodynamic theory that would begin to enable one to predict such events. Cognitive explanation in terms of beliefs and desires is firmly anchored in this folk-psychological understanding, which may itself be a biologically rooted way we have of interpreting one another. But beyond folk psychology, this level of conscious representations is also supported by a vast empirical research tradition in cognitive science.

4. People are also influenced by an extensive network of mental representations that are outside their awareness. We know this not only from everyday experience but also from a vast literature in cognitive science that demonstrates the unconscious activation of meanings, as well as from some reliable elements of the psychodynamic literature. These unconscious meanings can interact with conscious meanings out of our awareness.

5. People are shaped in ways of which they may not be aware by cultural and family rules, and other interpersonal processes that form the context and background for their actions and provide implicit rules, which may be followed without awareness. For example, when having a conversation, people from different cultures feel comfortable standing at different distances,

some closer, some farther away (at international conferences, this becomes apparent as people adjust themselves to others' comfort levels).

The moral case for integration is that it is in effect a form of malpractice to approach the client within one theoretical perspective when it is scientifically known that the truth is more complex and that the therapeutic options available are broader than those encompassed by any one theory. Informed consent requires that theoretically divergent intervention options be presented to the client, and that treatment not be limited by the therapist's theoretical persuasion. The moral argument is based on the scientific argument. It is, first, that research demonstrates that no one treatment works for everyone, and so to serve all clients, the practitioner must be prepared to be flexible and offer a change of treatment strategy when warranted by the client's lack of response or incomplete response to the initial intervention strategy. Moreover, because each individual is operating at all the meaning levels noted here, different sorts of interventions are often required in the course of treatment to get at aspects of the same problem. The different levels are so interconnected that, except for the biological level (which arguably requires an entirely different training to directly evaluate and treat, although all the levels are influencing and are influenced by biology), a clinician must be prepared to utilize any of them with a given client; referring out seems a cumbersome and inadequate response to such need for flexibility.

Traditionally, in what has been known as the "psychotherapy wars," universal claims were made by each theory as to its truth and therapeutic efficacy, and each theory competed with all the others. It seems fair to say that this strategy has not led to a scientific resolution in favor of one or another theory and has not yielded much progress. The reason for this failure is that the competition was based on a misconstrual of the relationship among the various theories. They were framed as mutually exclusive universal theories, but their relationship turned out to be complementary.

If one open-mindedly considers the evidence from research, clinical experience, and everyday life, it seems apparent that all the major theories of psychopathology have important elements of truth. The processes described by behaviorists, cognitivists, psychodynamicists, systems theorists, and biological researchers all shape behavior and are all necessary to explain disorder in some contexts. Moreover, a process may be useful in treating a disorder even when the etiology lies elsewhere. In other words, on the basis of the overall evidence available at this time, if there is any theory of etiology and treatment in which it is rational to believe, it is some version of integrationism. From this perspective, all the traditional theories, if framed as universal, exclusive alternatives, are pseudoscientific; their unjustifiably inflated claims are based on ideology rather than evidence.

For example, the many theories of depression—biological, behavioral, systems-theoretic, cognitive, and psychodynamic—appear each to capture some possible cases and thus to be about specific etiologic pathways rather than universal theories of etiology. These theories are not logically in competition— or at least to the extent they are formulated in a way that they are, the formulations are needlessly inflated and ignore reality. Rather, each theory attempts to capture one possible causal pathway that can—by itself or in conjunction with the others—lead someone to become disordered. Consequently, what is called for is not competition but cooperation to identify etiologically pure patients and to identify the role of each explanatory hypothesis in hybrid cases. In a multiple-etiology reality, a competition between single-etiology nosologies is not progressive and cannot yield a valid diagnostic manual.

There is much to criticize in the DSM's operationalized definitions of various mental disorders (Wakefield, 1996, 1997). However, one of the great contributions of the DSM has been to provide theory-neutral criteria that do not cite any etiology and, because they are based on manifest symptoms, can be used by adherents of all theoretical schools to identify individuals with a certain disorder. The DSM enabled representatives of the different schools to talk to one another and compare their theories in a way that had not been happening before. This subtle but historically important and beneficial contribution of the DSM to providing the conceptual infrastructure for theory integration has not been adequately recognized.

TYPES OF INTEGRATION

Traditionally there are four forms of psychotherapy integration (Gold, 1996; see Borden, chapter 1, this volume): technical eclecticism, the common-factors approach, theoretical integration, and assimilative integration, all of which combine theory and technique. Technical eclecticism has been considered the most clinical and technically oriented form of psychotherapy integration; however, it is the least conceptually or theoretically integrated (Stricker & Gold, 2003). In technical eclecticism clinical strategies and techniques from two or more therapies are applied sequentially or in combination. Techniques are chosen based on clinical match to the needs of the patient, without any systematic theoretical rationale, based on clinical skill and intuition as well as patient preference.

Common-factor integration is based on the idea that groups of therapies share similar change processes and techniques (Rosenzweig, 1936). Additionally, all therapies have certain commonalities, such as socially sanctioned rituals, or the provision of hope and encouragement to the patient (Frank, 1961). When using the common-factors approach, the therapist attempts to identify which of the common factors will be most important in interventions for specific cases. The goal is to provide the patient with the best possible unique combination of known therapeutic factors to ameliorate his or her problems. Common-factors integration often combines insight, new relational learning and experiences, and hope by way of the therapeutic relationship. The therapeutic relationship is now believed to be the most potent common factor.

Theoretical integration consists of a synthesis of central elements from two or more theories, potentially including the theories' models of personality, psychopathology etiology, and mechanisms of psychological change. By forming one consistent theoretical system incorporating different models, there is a logical coherence to theoretical integration, lacking in the other approaches, that allows the therapist to approach a case in a more systematic fashion. Different theoretical assumptions are placed within one overarching theory, so the therapist can make principled judgments.

Safran and Messer (1997) argue from a postmodernist position that different theories have such different ontological assumptions that in principle they can never be theoretically or technically integrated. This seems a dubious argument, if we are right that the theories capture different levels of the meaning system that does exist in human beings, and that the different levels interact in overall functioning. The parts of the theories that reflect the larger reality and do in fact interact ought to be able to be captured in some future theory. The postmodernist view seems a dead end intellectually that freezes us in a state of therapeutic ideology. The major theories as currently stated are incompatible in part because they each claim to have the exclusive truth and apply to all possible situations, which is false, and in part because each of the theories is just incorrect on many points. The point of theoretical integration is to evaluate which components of each theory deserve to be retained, to moderate the claims of each so they can be placed within a larger system, and to hypothesize how the overall system of interacting levels of meaning works so that intervention strategies can be devised accordingly.

However, there has as yet been no successful, superordinate integration that includes personality, psychopathology, worldview, meta-theoretical and epistemological assumptions, or a theoretically coherent and adequate technical eclecticism (Safran & Messer, 1997). One response, other than awaiting a future theoretical integration, has been to embrace theoretical pluralism. The pluralistic tradition falls within postmodernism, and holds that one theory cannot preempt an alternative organization of the evidence; therefore, the best way to approximate truth is to have multiple theories competing by way of evidence (see Borden, 2008; Safran & Messer, 1997).

Pluralist perspectives emphasize the limits of human understanding. As Borden explains in his account of pluralism in chapter 1, thinkers assume that no single framework captures the complexity of actual experience in the real world and approach concerns from multiple, independent perspectives, acknowledging that there are mutually exclusive descriptions of experience and equally valid points of view that inevitably contradict one another. Pluralist thinkers challenge notions of grand theory, which presume to set forth universal truths, and assume that theoretical formulations and empirical findings provide only partial, incomplete accounts of experience. "Each theoretical system has its own history, root metaphors, domains of concern, purposes, rules, methods, strengths, and limits" (Borden, chapter 1, this volume, p. 7). Such a pluralist sensibility has many strengths as a strategy for the medium term given the immaturity of psychological science. However, we would caution that over the long run, as a fuller picture of the complexities of the human mind emerges, pluralism should gradually give way to a single more multifaceted account, as in other mature sciences.

Another answer to the challenges of integrating diverse theoretical approaches is assimilative integration. Stanley Messer (2001) argues that theories of therapy are grounded in observation and evidence, but contain multiple truths defined and contained by the interpersonal, historical, and physical context in which interventions occur. Theoretically integrative approaches are assimilative when they start from one approach as fixed and primary, and open themselves to incorporate new techniques into the existing conceptual model of therapy. When the therapeutic context differs from the context in which the new techniques were developed, the meaning, impact, and use of the interventions may be modified and reinterpreted to fit the primary model. The psychodynamically based integrative therapy developed by Stricker and Gold (1996) is an example of assimilative integration, according to Messer, because the therapy proceeds along standard guidelines, but other methods are used as needed, and these may advance psychodynamic goals while affecting the target problem. Again, we would emphasize that assimilative integration may be the best strategy for integrative widening of the scope of each theory within its own assumptive framework in the short run, but in the longer run a critical integrationism should allow no one theory to be an unquestioned base from which to expand but rather should portray the complex reality independent of the starting point.

CONCEPTUAL COMMONALITIES BETWEEN PSYCHOANALYSIS AND COGNITIVE THEORY

There are remarkable conceptual affinities between cognitive and psychodynamic approaches that allow for easy integration. We now survey some of the points at which there is conceptual commonality and contact—actual or potential—at a theoretical level between Freud's classic psychoanalytic theory and contemporary cognitive science and cognitive-behavioral theory.

MENTAL REPRESENTATIONS (OR "INTENTIONALITY") AS THE ULTIMATE ELEMENTS OF THE MIND

Freud called his new science "psycho-analysis." But what are the units into which the psyche is to be analyzed? Freud's answer is that the mind is ultimately composed of—and is to be analyzed into—mental representations, which interact with each other according to associative principles (Wakefield, 1992). Mental representations, or "ideas," whether in the form of mental images (analogous to pictures in the head) or thoughts (analogous to sentences being spoken in the head) are otherwise known as "intentionality" and are brain states of some unknown kinds that, like a picture or a sentence, represent some actual or possible state of affairs outside of themselves through their structure. *Intentionality* refers particularly to the way in which mental states, in virtue of their structure, are intrinsically directed at some real or possible objects or states of affairs (Brentano, 1973/1874; Searle, 1983). For example, a belief is always a belief that something is the case, a desire is always a desire for something, and a fear is always a fear of something. The standard account of how mental states can be directed in this way is that they consist in part of representations of their objects. For example, beliefs, desires, and fears involve mental representations of what is believed to be true, desired, or feared, respectively. Just like cognitive psychologists today, Freud emphasized representations in the form of thoughts and mental images, which represent states of affairs in the world through their pictorial or grammatical structures, respectively, analogous to nonmental pictorial or linguistic representations (Freud, 1957c/1923; Kosslyn, 1980; Paivio, 1986; Rollins, 1989). Such representations form the essence of cognitivism.

The representation is said to provide the *content* of the intentional state, and the thing or state of affairs in the outside world at which a mental state is directed through its content is the *object* of the mental state (hence "object relations"). The kind of relationship the person has to the object through the representation, such as one of belief, desire, or fear, is often called the *mode* of the intentional state. Freud's case histories can be conceptualized as analyses of the changing contents, objects, and modes of a person's intentional states over time.

The idea that the mind consists of a system of mental representations is arguably the currently received view in academic psychology and related fields based on cognitive theory. As a glance at the titles of cognitive science books demonstrates (e.g., Brand & Harnish, 1986; Chomsky, 1980; Fodor, 1981; Paivio, 1986; Putnam, 1988), mental representation is certainly the core concept of that influential discipline. Indeed, Gardner (1987), in his history of cognitive science, states that "to my mind, the major accomplishment of cognitive science has been the clear demonstration of the validity of positing a level of mental representation" (p. 112). So, in acknowledging the centrality of representationality in any account of the mind, Freud was being thoroughly modern.

THE EXISTENCE OF UNCONSCIOUS MENTAL STATES

One hundred years ago, psychology was by and large the science of consciousness. Most eminent psychologists, as well as most philosophers, held quite explicitly the traditional Cartesian view that *consciousness* and *mental* refer to the same things. William James, for example, titled a section of his *Principles of Psychology,* "Do Unconscious Mental States Exist," and after reviewing and rejecting all the arguments known to him for the existence of such states, he answered his question with a resounding *no.*

Freud argued for the contrary and at the time radical thesis that representationality can be realized in nonconscious brain structures and that, therefore, there can be mental states that are unconscious. Freud thus separated mental representation from consciousness.

It is truly remarkable that, a century later, the very subject matter of psychology has changed. The focus now—manifested in the "cognitive revolution " (Baars, 1986)—is on mental representation: that is, on the way that internal brain states represent or model external states of affairs, and how those representations function to organize behavior, sustain reasoning, trigger affects, and so on. As the cognitive scientist George Mandler (1988) puts it, "Theoretical cognitive psychology of the past quarter century—in contrast to the psychologies of the nineteenth century—has assumed the dominance of unconscious processes in the explanation of thought and action" (p. 21). Freud's view has now become routinely accepted in cognitive science, and indeed might be considered the foundation stone upon which modern cognitive psychology rests. Ample experimental evidence shows that unconscious meanings do exist and are routinely accessed by one's mind outside of awareness (see Gardner [1985] for a review of some of these studies).

Unconscious brain states can be mental in virtue of their being representations, and they are representational in virtue of their being structured so as to represent and thus refer to outside objects. Just like sentences in a book on the shelf, or paintings stored in a vault, representational states need not be consciously accessed for them to be true representations, according to this line of argument. Contemporary cognitive scientists follow Freud in rejecting the consciousness criterion for the mental and assuming that intentional states can be unconscious. They, too, analyze the mind as a system of interacting conscious and unconscious mental representations.

If we put together the first thesis, that the mental is the representational, and this second thesis, that unconscious mental states exist, we get the thesis that the mental encompasses conscious and unconscious representations. Indeed, Freud is the pivotal figure in nothing less than the transformation of psychology from a science of consciousness to a science of conscious and unconscious mental representations.

Of course, it is now understood that Freud did not "discover" the unconscious (Ellenberger, 1970; Whyte, 1960); rather, he is one in a long line of thinkers who postulated unconscious mental states. Nonetheless, Freud played a critical role in the transformation of psychology from a science of consciousness to a science of mental representations because he offered the most sustained, systematic, and persuasive argument for the change.

An important caveat is that we are referring here just to the basic property that a cognition can be unconscious even as it interacts in significant ways with conscious meanings. Freud went beyond the argument that mental representations can be unconscious to argue for what he called the "dynamic unconscious": states that are unconscious because of having been forced away from consciousness due to their painful or threatening content—that is, repressed, or otherwise defended against. This thesis has not been embraced by contemporary cognitive science and is generally eschewed by cognitive therapists. However, cognitive therapists, like cognitive scientists, have been driven to postulate that unconscious representations or schemas exist that influence conscious thoughts and feelings, as we shall see.

CAUSAL POWERS OF IDEAS: HOW TO INTEGRATE
MOTIVATION INTO COGNITIVISM

If the mind is a system of interacting intentional states, then how does motivation come into the picture? The problem of motivation is one that bedevils contemporary cognitive approaches. Freud provided a very elegant solution to the problem of how to conceptualize motivation within a systematic cognitive psychology. Cognitive accounts of the mind tend to focus on the processing of evidential, logical, deductive, inductive, associative, means-end, and other such relationships among representations. Perception and memory can be considered inputs to the flow of mentation that provide additional premises from which the inferential engine that constitutes the mind can derive new propositions. Cognitivists typically link all this thought to action by means of Davidson's (1963) account of action as "behavior caused by reasons." That is, cognitions cause people to act to accomplish their goals. But even on Davidson's account, a belief *and* a desire are necessary to cause action. Each person has many beliefs about what they could accomplish by performing various actions; the desire is necessary to explain why the person acts on one belief rather than another.

What is a desire on a cognitivist approach? Freud interprets desire as a property of representations, and specifically as a property of how they interact. This allows the cognitivist to retain the claim that the mind is a system of representations, while also allowing for some difference between desires and other cognitions that do not have the special motivational properties. The problem, then, is to specify the kind of property that makes an idea a desire.

For example, exactly the same idea of water may be more or less active— that is, may exert more or less pressure and demand more or less work— depending on the bodily state with respect to hydration, so the content of the idea, which is the same, is not what determines the causal powers or the intensity of the activity. Rather, one might argue, the idea takes on new dynamic properties depending on other factors, such as the relation of the idea to bodily processes that make it more or less salient. These new properties include new causal relations of the idea to other ideas, to emotion, and to action. In sum, when one is thirsty, the idea of water takes on entirely new causal properties than when one is not thirsty, and that is the essence of the instinctual impulse of thirst. The acquisition of such causal powers is what Freud has in mind when he writes of the "cathexis" of an idea by instinct. Seen in this way, the technical concept of cathexis is not, as many have claimed, rooted primarily in outmoded nineteenth-century biology, but rather is a formalization of the essential, common-sense notion of the intensity of desire. And the preservation of cathectic energy across transformations is also rooted in a common-sense understanding that motivational powers are communicated from idea to idea under a variety of circumstances; for example, "to desire the end is to desire the means" is an idea about what is technically an energic transformation.

PSYCHIC ENERGY AS SCHEMA ACTIVATION

Cognitivists understand that, with all the representations that are in the mind, one has to explain why only some are having an impact on functioning at any given moment. Generally, they slip by this problem by use of a term such as *activation*, as in *schema activation*, meaning that a certain cognitive schema was activated and became influential in mental processing at a certain time. This, of course, describes the phenomenon but in no way explains it.

Freud's notion of psychic energy is best considered a way of talking about schema activation and the intensity of such activation. Here Freud was a step ahead of contemporary cognitivists in two respects. First, he understood that sometimes activation moved along associative pathways, and thus that the history of activation could be useful in explaining why certain schemas came into influence. This is in principle a simple point: for example, to understand why my "go to sea" schema is activated, one might have to understand that, say, my "desire to make money by trading internationally" schema was activated beforehand and led to going to sea as an instrumental action believed to satisfy my desire. Second, Freud saw that activation is not just a yes/no matter, but a matter of degree or intensity. Some desires are much more intense than others and thus have the power to influence mental processing more widely and more definitively, and this difference can be important in understanding why people do what they do.

THE ASSOCIATIONIST BASIS OF PATHOGENESIS

Like many cognitive-behaviorists, Freud plays down the rational-processing modes of the mind and emphasizes instead the web of mental representations and how activation of ideas spreads throughout this web by means of nonrational linkages of all sorts, such as similarity and sensual arousal. Freud, unlike most cognitive-behaviorists, attempts to decipher the process of associational linkages by which a certain pathogenic set of ideas and symptoms emerged. But in its structure, the process is cognitivist/

associationist. Consider, for example, Freud's explanation of why five-year-old Little Hans (Freud, 1909) developed a horse phobia. The child witnessed a horse fall down in the street, but Freud sees the horse accident as important, not because of classical fear conditioning, but because of the way the accident brought together a converging set of ideas. He says that the chance event "acquired its great effectiveness only from the fact that horses had formerly been of importance to him as objects of his predilection and interest, from the fact that he associated the event in his mind with an earlier event at Gmunden which had more claim to be regarded as traumatic, namely, with Fritzl's falling down while he was playing at horses, and lastly from the fact that there was an easy path of association from Fritzl to his father." According to Freud, "even these connections would probably not have been sufficient if it had not been that, thanks to the pliability and ambiguity of associative chains, the same event showed itself capable of stirring the second of the complexes that lurked in Hans's unconscious, the complex of his pregnant mother's confinement" (1909, pp. 136–137). These Oedipal-related linkages are like unconscious "automatic thoughts" in that they are activated each time the thought of the horse accident is activated. Freud's approach to mental linkages of ideas resembles the associationist psychologies of the English empiricists, such as Hume and Locke (note that Freud translated one of Hume's works for publication), and these associationist psychologies formed the basis for some later cognitivist learning theories based on associations of ideas. One can reject the specific content (e.g., Oedipal) of Freud's clinical interpretations while embracing the associationist framework he shares with cognitivism.

EMOTION AS COGNITION PLUS BODILY AROUSAL

One of the hallmarks of contemporary cognitive therapy theories, including those of Beck and Ellis, is the view that emotion is caused by cognition—that is, that an emotion is a thought that causes an associated bodily arousal. Consequently, to understand a problematic feeling like anxiety, one always looks for the thought underlying the feeling. It can be argued that everything except the feeling in an emotional experience is simply cognition, along with motivational properties of the cognition. Fear is based on belief in impending harm or danger and the motivational properties of such beliefs; guilt, on belief that one has transgressed and the associated motivational properties; and so on. The rest of an emotion, it might be argued, is bodily feeling. This approach to the relation between cognition and emotion was taken, for example, by Schachter and Singer (1962) in their classic studies, which were instrumental in putting a cognitive spin on emotion for contemporary psychologists. Those studies claimed to show that emotion consists essentially of bodily arousal conjoined with cognition about the cause of the arousal. Similarly, other cognitivists—such as Albert Ellis (1962), who considers negative emotion to consist primarily of irrational belief (a view that goes back to the Stoic philosophers), and Richard Lazarus (see Lazarus, Averill, & Opton, 1970), who asserts that emotion is essentially an evaluative judgment—attempt to explain emotion as essentially a variant of cognition, perhaps conjoined with some other bodily element. This emphasis on the cognitive component in emotion has become standard in the field (e.g., Ortony, Clore, & Collins, 1988). Freud, too, takes a "cognition plus bodily arousal" approach to emotion. However, more than cognitivists, Freud emphasizes that the idea may be separated from the arousal, such that the arousal is experienced as, for example, "free-floating anxiety."

CONVERGENCE OF COGNITIVE AND PSYCHODYNAMIC APPROACHES: THEORY AND PRACTICE

We believe that there has been a cognitivization of psychodynamic theory as well as a psychodynamicization of cognitive theory, yielding a gradual convergence of the two approaches. There is a long way to go in integrating these two theoretical approaches. We review some of the major approaches within these two theoretical camps to illustrate the degree to which certain common themes and views are emerging and merging.

OVERVIEW OF AARON BECK'S COGNITIVE THERAPY

Aaron Beck is one of the chief architects of cognitive-behavioral theory and therapy. Beck originally formulated his ideas while working from a psychoanalytical perspective. During treatment he noticed that depressed patients experienced specific types of thoughts that were on the periphery of the patients' stream of consciousness. The thoughts arose quickly and automatically, almost reflexively; they were outside of conscious control, were quite plausible to the patient, and usually generated negative affect. While the patients were aware of the unpleasant affect, they were mostly unaware of the preceding automatic thoughts. When probed about their thoughts related to the affect, patients responded with a string of negative thoughts that had a theme, such as deprivation, disease, or defeat, resulting in a negative view of the past, present, and future. The internal communications of the patients were permeated by negativity, which in turn affected self-evaluation, attributions, expectancies, inferences, and recall. Negative interpretations resulted, including low self-esteem, self-blame, and self-criticism, as well as negative predictions of the future. Beck noticed that patients did not report these types of thoughts during free association; the thoughts required a cognitive probe. However, once the patients' focused on the thoughts, changes in affect became apparent.

Beck believed that his recognition of automatic thoughts signified that he had tapped another level of consciousness, analogous to Freud's proposition of the preconscious. Beck's new level of consciousness involved self-monitoring and concerned what people say to themselves. Thus, he concluded that automatic thoughts were part of an internal communication system (Beck, 1976, pp. 24–46) According to Beck (1979), change in the patient occurred when he or she came to recognize evidence that disconfirmed his or her existing paradigm or when an anomaly could not be accommodated.

Beck noticed that the patients' concerns were primarily social and involved issues such as success or failure, acceptance or rejection. Furthermore, these meanings were accessible to introspection. Beck reported that when the therapist picked out a common theme across the patient's discourse, the patient consequently provided a rich set of responses. Furthermore, it was notable that the meanings the patient attributed to discrete stimuli were fixed. For example, a man always reacted with the thought, "She does not respect me" when his wife did not respond to him. Thus, Beck concluded that the evoked meanings were powerful, invariant, and emanated from a network of beliefs, assumptions, formulas, and rules that were connected to memories relevant to the development and formation of the beliefs (Beck, 1964). Although cognitive processing is unconscious, its products may be conscious (Beck, 1987).

As Beck elaborated his theory, he proposed that schemas were learned in childhood in response to life events and circumstances. Once learned, the schemas were not readily changeable, because they make the world comprehensible and predictable. Using principles of information processing, Beck postulated that relevant beliefs interact with symbolic situations to produce "automatic thoughts." The therapy consists of a formulation of the patient's dysfunctional ideas and beliefs about himself, his experiences, and his future into hypotheses that are tested by the therapist and the patient in a systematic way. Imagery interventions are also used. Just as the therapist interprets symbols and images in classical psychoanalysis, the cognitive therapist uses the content of spontaneous images to point to the cognitive distortions in areas where the client is having problems.

For example, a middle-aged woman initiated psychotherapy in order to address symptoms of chronic anxiety about her children that escalated into panic attacks. On one occasion she had severe anxiety over a cross-country trip that her son had taken. The usual questioning of automatic thoughts (examining the probability of a mechanical breakdown or accident) did not affect her symptoms. However, when the therapist asked her to picture her son on his trip and relate as much information about the image with as much detail as she could, she was able to provide a wealth of information about the content of her anxiety.

She pictured her son sitting in a stalled car surrounded by hostile strangers, without any idea of what to do or where to look for help. She described a series of horrible scenes that might take place and imagined her son's feelings of helplessness and despair. It was as thought she were watching a movie of the feared event (Beck, Emery & Greenberg, 1985).

As is illustrated in this case example, when her anxiety became very intense, she patient began to catastrophize and lost her ability to reason about the problem. The therapist modified her thinking—both her automatic thoughts and ultimately her underlying schema—using cognitive techniques such as decatastrophizing the image, using the turn-off technique, substituting positive imagery, and so on. A large body of outcome studies using a randomized control design has shown the model to be efficacious across a wide variety of patients who suffer from depression, anxiety, and other affective disorders.

JOHN BOWLBY'S ATTACHMENT THEORY

Within the broad scope of psychoanalytic theory, "object relations theory" includes those theories that reject Freud's notion that people ultimately are driven by the need for sensual gratification in relating affectionately to others, and instead postulate an inherent need to relate to other individuals independent of sensual pleasure. Out of a complex tradition of such object-relational theories, one theory, Bowlby's theory of attachment, has had a dominant influence recently because it is anchored in a vast amount of empirical research, unlike any other such theory (De Ruiter & van Ijzendoorn, 1992 Main, 1983; Spieker, Nelson, Petras, Jolley & Barnard, 2003; van Ijzendoorn et al., 1995; van Ijzendoorn & Vliet-Visser, 1988; van Ijzendoorn, Sagi, & Lambermon, 1992).

Bowlby's (1969/1973, 1980, 1988) formulation of attachment theory proposes that children have an instinctual need to remain in proximity to a primary caregiver for safety or to seek out the caregiver for soothing when anxious, and that the formation of a sense of security about the caregiver's potential availability offers the child a "secure base" that allows the child to explore the environment. According to Bowlby attachment has an evolutionary function of safety, for example, protecting the child from predators.

Later theorists have suggested that the attachment relationship has further developmental functions, beyond safety and a secure base for exploration. The intense and focused interactions of early object relations equip the very young child with an environment within which the child develops an understanding of mental states in others and in himself (Fonagy & Target, 2004).

The detailed nature of the child's primary attachment relationship is, according to Bowlby, important for longer term development as well. Bowlby postulates that the child's early experiences in the parent-child relationships produce internal "working models" that shape later social relationships. The working model is understandable as fundamentally a cognitive notion in which the features of early relationships remain internally represented as a template for understanding and shaping future interactions—not unlike Beck's "schemas," Weiss's "unconscious pathogenic beliefs," or Luborsky's "core conflictual relationship theme" (for the latter two, see below). Internal working models of social relationships, based on memories of early caregiving relationships, include thoughts and feelings that establish expectations about the behavior of others toward the self, the self's strategies for coping with the responses of others, and the individual's behavior toward self. Affect regulation, the capacity to modulate affect states, is also importantly involved. Bowlby's central hypothesis that the quality of attachment is dependent upon the quality of the caregiver-child relationship has been replicated with diverse samples as well as in laboratory studies (Bates, Maslin, & Frankel, 1993; Egeland & Farber, 1984; Meins, Fernyhough, Russel & Clark-Carter, 1998; Waters, Wippman & Sroufe, 1979).

The patterned dyadic interactions between the caregiver and child lead the child to develop an attachment style (Ainsworth, Blehar, Waters & Wall, 1978). For example, in the case of disorganized attachment style, there is not an organized strategy to deal with stress, the child is afraid but does not know what to do. Maltreating caregivers create disorganized attachment schema in infants when they confront the infant with a pervasive paradox where the parent/caregiver is potentially the only source of comfort, while at the same time he or she frightens the child through unpredictable abusive behavior.

By way of illustration, Sam, a ten-year-old boy, was treated in a residential facility for eight months. He was admitted because of aggressive and dangerous behavior in his therapeutic foster home and at school. His early childhood included neglect and physical, sexual, and emotional abuse. He lived with his biological mother for the first two years of his life, but was subsequently removed and placed with relatives. Unfortunately, he was sexually abused by the relatives, which led to his placement in the residential treatment facility.

Sam was unable to discuss any of these issues, and he refused to participate in the assessment and evaluation. During his time in residential treatment he had no emotional engagement with his therapist or with any of the staff. Sam's presentation was notable for impulsivity, intrusiveness, and argumentative behavior. He vacillated between being oppositional with adults and protecting them from perceived injustices by other residents. At times he was affectionate toward some adults and expressed pleasure in their presence. Yet at other times he was dismissive or neutral toward the same adults. He referred to his foster parents as "mom and dad" but never asked to see them or contact them. When they visited, he expressed displeasure or was neutral. He would initiate contact with peers, but then sabotaged his relationships by stealing the peer's property.

He was quick to become aggressive, especially if anyone came near him. He had some sexualized behaviors, such as touching peers' genitals or disrobing in public. He typically did not express regret for his behavior or respond to the efforts of staff to engage with him about the meaning of his behavior.

Several attachment themes are present in Sam's behavior that are typical of the disorganized-disoriented pattern of attachment associated with maltreatment. Sam exhibits conflicted behaviors toward others in accordance with the disorganized-disoriented pattern. Sam displays approach/avoidant behavior as at times he seeks proximity to and interaction with adults, and at other times he actively attempt to distance himself from them. His attempts at peer socialization are interspersed with socially unacceptable behavior that causes peers to distance themselves from him. He does not seek comfort from adults and refuses it when offered during periods of distress. However, he expresses reproach when his needs are not met.

Overall, Sam's disorganized relational schema prevents him from forming close, emotionally connected relationships to others. He is disinhibited in his immediate attempts to engage with anyone he encounters, which is typical of disorganized attachment. Sam's internal working models for interpersonal relationships were defined by his experiences with caregivers who were neglectful and who actively harmed him.

LESTER LUBORSKY'S THEORY OF CORE
CONFLICTUAL RELATIONSHIPS

Inspired by Freud's psychoanalytic theory of transference and of repetitive maladaptive styles of relating as central to people's psychological problems, Lester Luborsky (1997) has developed a supportive-expressive type of brief therapy titled the Core Conflictual Relationship Theme (CCRT). In CCRT the focus of treatment consists of an expression of the patient's central relationship pattern, which forms the basis for the patient's relational interactions. The central relationship pattern is hypothesized to derive from an internalized schema developed in early childhood about how relationships function that is partially unconscious and partly conscious. Problematic relational schemas are manifest in the patient's core conflictual relationship theme, which has three main components:

1. The patient's wishes, needs, or intentions as experienced toward others, such as a desire to be liked or loved or the need to be honest and known to the other.
2. The expected response from others—perceptions or beliefs about the consequences of wishes or needs, often consisting of potentially negative and distressing responses that are rejecting, humiliating, or otherwise feared.
3. Response of the self, which includes affective reactions, such as fear, humiliation, anger, or sadness, as well as behavioral and psychological responses that enable the patient to avoid the feared consequences (withdrawal, pretending not to care, and other "defensive" reactions).

The CCRT is made up of the most frequent of each of the three components as expressed in the patient's narrations across the relationship episodes in each session (Luborsky, 1997). The therapist attends to the pervasiveness of each component with attention to repetition in the three areas. Additionally, the therapist uses the "symptom-context method" to locate the patient's symptoms within the relational pattern by examining the natural temporal sequence that includes the context before, during, and after the patient's symptoms appear.

CCRT therapy is centered on the core conflictual relationship theme, which is identified from the central relationship patterns that emerge from relationship narratives. Narratives are parts of the sessions in which the patient tells episodes about relationships (relationship episodes, or REs), whether to others in the patient's current life outside of therapy, to family members or others earlier in life, or to the therapist. Ten REs is considered the lower limit to provide a basis for CCRT. From each RE in a session, the therapist makes inferences about three types of components: wishes, responses from other, and responses of self. Using this information, the therapist identifies one primary pattern and formulates the patient's core conflictual relationship theme.

The CCRT treatment is manualized and is structured around several principles. These include, first, understanding: The therapist attempts to understand the patient's symptoms in the context of his or her relationships; attends to shifts in the patient's states of mind; formulates the core conflictual relationship theme by clinical methods; attends to each sphere of the relationship triad (the patient's wishes, response from others, response from self); reviews trends to produce further understanding; views the symptoms as problem-solution or coping attempts; and attends to the patient's perception of therapist's behavior. Once the therapist has formulated the patient's core conflictual theme, the therapist encourages the patient to make the unspoken components of the CCRT explicit. This is done by asking exploratory questions that encourage the patient to state explicitly what he or she wants or to ask what he or she was thinking or had in mind.

For example, Mrs. Hines, was a forty-two-year-old divorced secretary who entered treatment because of episodic anxiety concerning her relationship with John, a man she had recently started dating. She reported the following relationship episode: " I was looking forward to dinner with John. We were at a great restaurant. The wine had been poured, and I was just telling him about a movie I saw when an old friend of John's walked up. He talked to him and introduced me and then I lost interest in what I was saying."

Using this information, the therapist attempts to make sense of Mrs. Hines's unspoken desires: to be close to John, to be exclusive with John, to be attended to without interruption, to be the center of John's attention, to be taken seriously by John, to be admired and acknowledged. The therapist similarly proceeds to make the response of other and response of self explicit. The goal of treatment, in addition to symptom relief, is to help the patient actualize his or her wish. This is accomplished by working through the patient's response from others as either a transference distortion or a repetition disorder (Book, 1998).

JOSEPH WEISS'S CONTROL-MASTERY THEORY

Joseph Weiss has developed a model of psychotherapy, often called "control-mastery theory," that is based on the premise that the main goal of therapy is to disconfirm a set of idiosyncratic beliefs about feared consequences of adaptive action that impede the client from acting successfully to achieve desired goals. A basic tenet of control-mastery theory is that, contrary to the classical view that the patient's rising anxiety leads to a breakthrough of unconscious content, the patient is able and willing to reveal underlying beliefs when he or she feels safe, and thus feels capable of taking a chance and of mastering the consequences of his or her actions, if things should become painful. Thus, the process of treatment involves the demonstration that the patient's fears are groundless, allowing the patient to reveal more of the fears. The concept of pathogenic beliefs is a central organizing theme, just as it is in cognitive therapy; however, Weiss's theory comes under the rubric of psychodynamic in part because it was derived directly from some of Freud's major ideas. Weiss developed his theory with the assistance of Harold Sampson while Weiss was an analyst associated with the San Francisco Psychoanalytic Institute.

According to Weiss, psychopathology arises from false and maladaptive pathogenic beliefs. As in cognitive theory, these beliefs are formed in childhood from traumatic experiences with parents or primary caregivers and become part of the patient's unconscious mental operations. When activated, these beliefs generate a warning system to the patient that if he or she attempts to gratify certain impulses or seek certain developmental goals, the result will be the disruption of parental affective ties. The pathogenic beliefs generate fear, anxiety, guilt, shame, and remorse, from which repression, symptoms, inhibitions, and faulty object relations may occur. They often involve fears such as that if one is successful or independent, one will damage and/or be rejected by the other.

As in cognitive therapy, the treatment targets the pathogenic beliefs. However, rather than directly disputing the beliefs, the therapist, working in the psychodynamic tradition, primarily uses transference, interpretation, and the therapeutic relationship to affect change. But the reaction to transference and the very notion of therapeutic neutrality differ within Weiss's framework from Freud's original ideas. According to the theory, the client comes into treatment with a desire to get over the problem and thus with an unconscious plan to test the pathogenic beliefs by trial actions with the therapist in the hopes of disproving them or having them disconfirmed. In testing the therapist, the client unconsciously expresses impulses or seeks certain goals that involve the pathogenic beliefs. The client's testing of the therapist is done through experimental actions. For example, if the client's fear is that she will be abandoned if she acts against the rules, then she may come late to therapy, not so much as classical resistance to treatment, but as a way to test her fear that acting against the rules will bring criticism and abandonment down upon her. Dealing with this instance of "transference" requires therapeutic neutrality in the following special sense: the therapist must act in accordance with the patient's plan and must disconfirm the patient's fear. In this instance, rather than doing the usual thing and asking about the lateness, the therapist might accept and ignore it until raised by the patient, for to raise the lateness as an issue would be to imply to the patient that the therapist was disapproving and that the patient had done something notably incorrect. If the client can see that his or her actions do not threaten the therapeutic relationship, as the pathogenic belief implies, then he or she moves forward in the therapy, becomes less anxious, more conscious of the belief, and closer to disconfirmation of it.

Extensive empirical studies of the hypotheses of control-mastery theory and therapy have been conducted by the San Francisco Psychotherapy Research Group (Bush & Gassner, 1986; Caston et al., 1986; Fretter, 1984; Silberschatz et al., 1989 and by others associated with the group. These studies focused on the relationship between accurate interpretations of the patient's plan (plan congruent) and the patient's progress. Findings indicated that the cases with the highest proportion of accurate interpretations, in accordance with theory's definition of accurateness, achieved the best outcome.

AFFINITIES AMONG THE FOUR COGNITIVE AND PSYCHODYNAMIC THEORIES

The dramatic similarities in deep structure of all four of these outlined clinical theories should be apparent, both in the representational basis for behavior in relatively automatic cognitions and in the existence of deeper schemas shaped by early experience that generate the immediate thoughts. Within Luborsky's approach, the patient's sequence of (1) wish, (2) feared response from other and inability to cope with it, and (3) consequent defensive compromise (symptom) in response to the expected dangerous response from the other is claimed to be based on previous negative experiences that have formed a pattern of behavior. One can see here the resemblance to both Bowlby and Beck, as well as to Weiss. While Luborsky focuses more exclusively than Beck on the relationship schemas of the patient, it is clear that what for Luborsky is a CCRT is for Beck a deep schema that shapes the patient's view of relationships and thus the automatic thoughts the patient is likely to experience—which for Luborsky are the automatic thoughts of the feared responses of the other and the automatic internal responses of the self to that fear.

For Bowlby, Luborsky's core conflictual relationship theme will likely be precisely the one established in a problematic working model possessed by the patient from early relationships and now repeated in other relationships due to this template. Although Bowlby does not emphasize that the reaction to a problematic working model of attachment will yield a classic-type wish-fear-defense approach as in Luborsky's account, the need to adjust to the pain of unfulfilled attachment longings seems inevitably to lead to such defenses and self-responses. Indeed, the various strategies of the insecurely attached that have been described by Bowlby and those attachment researchers who followed him—such as aloofness from the object, or chronic monitoring of the object, and so on—would in some cases seem to be exactly the sort of defensive reaction that Luborsky describes.

Analogously, for Weiss there are ingrained pathogenic beliefs about relationships that are anchored in early experience and resonate widely in the individual's relational life. These beliefs yield fears mostly about the responses of others, and the patient's symptoms are a result of defensive strategies to avoid these feared outcomes. Therapy is useful to the patient, according to Weiss, because he or she has an opportunity to test these ideas on the therapist; Luborsky, like Weiss, sees such processes, although not explicitly as "testing," which brings in ego-psychological notions beyond those embraced by Luborsky, at least as the use of transference to correct and "disconfirm" the patient's CCRT distortions, especially the beliefs about the response of the other to the patient's wishes.

NEXT STEPS IN INTEGRATION: WHAT COGNITIVE THEORY MIGHT ASSIMILATE FROM PSYCHODYNAMICS

We have discussed some conceptual framework principles by means of which cognitive and psychodynamic approaches tend naturally to go together. We now proceed to some further features of the psychodynamic approach that are not currently as congenial to cognitive approaches but which seem to us to be essential to an accurate overall view of human mental functioning, and easily assimilated.

Cognitivism attributes problems to irrational or distorted cognitions, and thus holds that the solution is to correct beliefs through disputation or learning, the latter including, for example, extinction or disruption of negative thoughts and reinforcement of positive thoughts. What might such cognitive theory still learn from the psychodynamic tradition?

One lesson—that cognitions can be unconscious—has already been learned, with respect both to the individual's initial lack of awareness of automatic thoughts and to the deeper lack of awareness of the meaning schemas that generate the automatic thoughts. With respect to the existence of mental representations outside of awareness, there has been a convergence to some extent of cognitive-behavioral and psychoanalytic views. To take one example: The cognitive-behavioral theorist Aaron Beck (1976) posits deep schemas derived from childhood experiences that shape and generate the automatic negative thoughts that people have about their relationships and other aspects of their lives. John Bowlby (1958), the object-relations theorist responsible for attachment theory, similarly posits mental representations outside of awareness that are derived from childhood attachment patterns and constitute an "internal working model" of attachment that shapes expectations in relationships throughout life. These views are in many ways quite congruent. But there are other aspects of psychodynamic theory that could be usefully assimilated to cognitive theory, in our view.

THE MODULARITY OF MIND

Starting with Socrates, there were those psychologists who argued that the mind is essentially one unified system of rational thought. Beginning with Plato, there were those who with equal conviction argued that the mind is a set of subagents and subprocesses that often conflict with each other, some of which can hardly be called rational. Freud states the case elegantly for the "divided mind" view. He offers careful and persuasive accounts of how individuals who fail to integrate conflicting tendencies of motivational subunits often suffer as a result. Any evolutionist like Freud will be drawn to the "modularity" thesis (Fodor, 1983) that the mind is composed of many different mental "organs," analogous to the body, the parts of which have evolved to fulfill distinct functions. Freud's vivid clinical accounts, and his simple yet powerful account of the divisions in the mind that can lead to fundamental conflicts, have provided a background to the current move to envision the mind as a set of competing subselves or submechanisms (Elster, 1985), and have made "integration" a central concept in contemporary psychology.

INTENTIONAL SELF-MANIPULATION OF COGNITIONS (DEFENSE)

A final Freudian contribution to cognitive psychology is related to Freud's theory of defenses, which is often cited as a clear contribution of Freud to substantive psychological theory. However, we believe that an equal or greater contribution lies in a meta-theoretical assumption underlying the theory of defenses—namely, that people intentionally manipulate their own cognitive states. This general principle has implications that are much more far-reaching than the theory of defense in the specific form that Freud or his followers developed it, and stands as a major contribution even if the theory of defense, in any specific form, should ultimately fail to be confirmed. Indeed, it may well be that the theory of defense is really just an account of one way of using mechanisms for intentional self-manipulation that have much more general functions.

The meta-level assumption that people are cognitive self-manipulators underlies various literatures that deal both with how people manipulate themselves in order to have desired effects on others, as in the "self-presentation" literature (for example, Baumeister, 1982), and in how people manipulate their cognitive states in order to have desired effects on their own internal cognitive, affective, and motivational states, as, for example, in the "defensive pessimism" literature (for example, Norem, 1989). Intentional self-manipulation of cognitions is at the heart of recent interpretations of Freud's concept of repression (Erdelyi, 1990). The growing emphasis on cognitive self-manipulation both as a matter of normal psychology and as a potentially valuable clinical interventive technique is, I think, indebted to Freud for a general approach to the mind in which such internal self-manipulation makes sense.

WEAKNESS OF WILL AND CONFLICT

There is a sense in which the intellectual apparatus of psychoanalysis is aimed at understanding how human problems go beyond what can be accounted for by routine cognitivist interpretation in terms of distorted cognition. The two most essential problems not dealt with by cognitive theory are weakness of will and conflict. Weakness of will is the single most basic challenge to the cognitivist position. For example, if the patient is having a problem overeating cake, the cognitivist looks for the irrational or distorted beliefs that lead to the self-defeating behavior. However, what psychodynamicists see is that even if all the beliefs are lined in the right direction, and even if the patient clearly, rationally, and undistortedly understands that it is better not to eat the cake, the patient still may eat the cake. The psychodynamic insight is that the problem is not always essentially one of cognition at all; rather, action may flow from a desire other than the one attached to the preferred cognition. Cognitivists, like the philosopher Socrates, tend to see humans as having rational thoughts that lead to action; psychodynamicists see that thoughts are often in competition with each other and that the rational thought does not always win in the competition to cause action. Thus, no amount of adjustment of thought ensures the solution to a problem of impulsive or self-defeating action.

Weakness of will occurs when there is conflict between desires and the best desire doesn't win. Thus, to deal with symptoms, psychodynamicists attend to internal conflict. One problem in resolving conflict is that desires are not always integrated and rationally judged one against the other. Thus, psychodynamicists work on helping people to recognize their conflicted desire and to integrate them within their rational calculus to the degree possible. Because conflict is not recognized as basic by cognitivists, this aspect of mental functioning is essentially ignored. We believe an enlarged cognitive viewpoint that assimilates selected insights from the psychodynamic approach in this way offers a fruitful step toward the grander synthesis for which the field is waiting.

CONCLUDING REMARKS: FUTURE CHALLENGES

There are limits to cognitivism. The integration proposed here is needed, but even if effected, faces important further challenges from wholly different points of view. Both psychoanalysis and cognitivism, as they converge, face their major threat from the outside in new, noncognitive approaches. Much of the working of the mental system is contained in the ways that the representations are connected and processed, rather than in the representational contents themselves. The distinction between intentional contents and processing principles is often blurred or left ambiguous, as in talk of defenses (Gillett, 1987). Moreover, many phenomenologically oriented thinkers, such as Heidegger (1962), Merleau-Ponty (1962), and Searle (1983), have argued that a goodly portion of what we should call "meaning" is contained in the background way in which the mind and body function, rather than in explicit mental representations, so that the mental might be argued to go beyond the representational (for reviews of these arguments, see Dreyfus & Wakefield,

1988; Wakefield, 1988). Rather than entering into these complex issues, suffice it to say that both Freud's approach and the closely related approaches of cognitivists will be challenged by such noncognitive views. These views are getting a boost from the recent discovery of mirror neurons, which seem to show direct, precognitive connections between human beings. But at this point, intentional states as the medium of meaning remains favored by contemporary cognitivists.

But more immediately, in terms of the challenges of integrating the legitimate insights of current cognitive and psychodynamic views, we have argued that there is a remarkable and sometimes hidden conceptual affinity between Freud and cognitive psychology that makes such an integration feasible. Interpreted in the right way, psychoanalysis can be seen as an applied, idiographic branch of cognitive science, engaged in the intentional mapping of individuals' minds within a cognitivist framework. The increasingly recognized implausibility of much of the content of Freud's interpretations should not blind us to the enduring plausibility of the very elegant framework within which Freud pursued the construction of such interpretations. It may well be certain of Freud's meta-psychological assumptions—understood sympathetically as attempts to incorporate various necessary features into a systematic theory of intentionality—rather than his specific clinical hypotheses that serve to make Freud a theorist from whom one can still learn, and whose insights may become an integral part of a future hybrid cognitive-psychodynamic theory.

REFERENCES

Ainsworth, M. D., Blehar, M. C., Waters, E., & Wall, S. (1978). *Patterns of attachment: A psychological study of the strange situation.* Hillsdale, N.J.: Lawrence Erlbaum Associates.

American Psychiatric Association. (2000). *Diagnostic and statistical manual of mental disorders.* 4th ed., text revision. Washington, D.C.: American Psychiatric Association.

Baars, B. J. (1986). *The cognitive revolution in psychology.* New York: Guilford.

Bates, J., Maslin, C., & Frankel, K. (1985). Attachment security, mother-child interactions, and temperament as predictors of behavior problem ratings at age three years. In I. Bretherton & E. Waters (Eds.), *Growing pains in attachment theory and research* (pp. 167–193). Monographs of the Society for Research in Child Development 50 (Serial 209, 1–2).

Baumeister, R. F. (1982). A self-presentational view of social phenomena. *Psychological Bulletin, 91,* 3–26.

Beck, A. T. (1964). Thinking and depression: Theory and therapy. *Archives of General Psychiatry, 10,* 561–571.

Beck, A. T. (1976/1979). *Cognitive therapy and the emotional disorders.* New York: International Universities Press.

Beck, A. T. (1987). Cognitive therapy. In J. K. Zeig (Ed.), *The evolution of psychotherapy.* (pp. 149–163). New York: Bruner/Mazel.

Beck, A. T., Emery, G., & Greenberg, R. L. (1985). *Anxiety disorders and phobias: A cognitive perspective.* New York: Basic.

Berlin, S. (2002). *Clinical social work practice: A cognitive-integrative perspective.* New York: Oxford University Press.

Borden, W. (2008). Comparative theory and integrative perspectives in psychosocial intervention. In A. Roberts (Ed.), *Social workers' desk reference* (pp. 259–264). New York: Oxford University Press.

Book, H. E. (1998). *How to practice brief psychodynamic psychotherapy: The core conflictual relationship theme method.* Washington, D.C.: American Psychological Association.

Bowlby, J. (1958). The nature of the child's tie to his mother. *International Journal of PsychoAnalysis,* 39, 1–23.

Bowlby, J. (1969). *Attachment and loss, Vol. 1: Attachment.* New York: Basic.

Bowlby, J. (1973). *Attachment and loss, Vol. 2: Separation.* New York: Basic.

Bowlby, J. (1980). *Attachment and loss, Vol. 3: Loss, sadness and depression.* York: Basic.

Bowlby, J. (1988). *A secure base: Parent-child attachment and healthy human development.* New York: Basic.

Brand, M., & Harnish, R. M. (1986). *The representation of knowledge and belief.* Tucson: University of Arizona Press.

Brentano, F. (1973/1874). *Psychology from an empirical standpoint.* New York: Humanities Press.

Bush, M., & Gassner, S. (1986). The immediate effect of the analyst's termination interventions on the patient's resistance to termination. In J. Weiss, H. Sampson, & The Mount Zion Psychotherapy Research Group (Eds.), *The psychoanalytic process: Theory, clinical observation, and empirical research* (pp. 299–320). New York: Guilford.

Caston, J., Goldman, R. K., & McClure, M. M. (1986). The immediate effects of psychoanalytic interventions. In J. Weiss, H. Sampson, & The Mount Zion Psychothrapy Research Group (Eds.). *The psychoanalytic process: Theory, clinical observation, and empirical research* (pp. 277–298). New York: Guilford.

Chomsky, N. (1980). *Rules and representations.* New York: Columbia University Press.

Davidson, D. (1963). Actions, reasons, and causes. *Journal of Philosophy,* 60, 684–700.

De Ruiter, C., & van Ijzendoorn, M. H. (1992). Agoraphobia and anxious ambivalent attachment: An integrated review. *Journal of Anxiety Disorders,* 6, 365–381.

Dreyfus, H. L., & Wakefield, J. C. (1988). From depth psychology to breadth psychology: A phenomenological approach to psychopathology. In S. Messer, L. Sass & R. Woolfolk (Eds.), *Hermeneutics and psychological theory: Interpretive approaches to personality, psychotherapy, and psychopathology* (pp. 272–288). New Brunswick, N.J.: Rutgers University Press.

Egeland, B., & Farber, E. A. (1984). Infant-mother attachment: Factors related to its development and change over time. *Child Development,* 55, 753–771.

Ellenberger, H. F. (1970). *The discovery of the unconscious.* New York: Basic Books.

Ellis, A. (1962). *Reason and emotion in psychotherapy.* New York: Lyle Stuart.

Elster, J. (1985). *The multiple self.* Cambridge, U.K.: Cambridge University Press.

Erdelyi, M. H. (1985). *Psychoanalysis: Freud's cognitive psychology.* New York: W. H. Freeman.

Erdelyi, M. H. (1990). Repression, reconstruction, and defense: history and integration of the psychoanalytic and experimental frameworks. In J. L. Singer (Ed.), *Repression and dissociation: Implications for personality theory, psychopathology, and health* (pp. 1–32). Chicago, Ill.: University of Chicago Press.

Fodor, J. A. (1981). *Representations: Philosophical essays on the foundations of cognitive science*. Cambridge, Mass.: MIT Press.

Fonagy, P., & Target, M. (2004). The roots of borderline personality disorder in disorganized attachment. In P. Fonagy, G. Gergely, E. Jurist & M. Target (Eds.), *Affect regulation, mentalization, and the development of the self* (pp. 343–373). New York: Other Press.

Frank, J. (1961). *Persuasion and healing*. Baltimore: Johns Hopkins University Press.

Fretter, P. B. (1984). *The immediate effects of transference interpretations on patients' progress in brief, psychodynamic psychotherapy*. Ph.D. diss., University of San Francisco, 1984. *Dissertation Abstracts International*, 46, 1519A.

Freud, S. (1909). Analysis of a phobia in a five-year-old boy. In J. Strachey (Ed.), *The standard edition of the complete psychological works of Sigmund Freud* (Vol. 10, pp. 5–149). London: Hogarth Press.

Freud, S. (1957c/1923). The ego and the id. In J. Strachey (Ed.), *The standard edition of the complete psychological works of Sigmund Freud* (Vol. 19, pp. 12–59). London: Hogarth Press.

Gardner, H. (1987). *The mind's new science: A history of the cognitive revolution*. New York: Basic Books.

Gillett, E. (1987). Defense mechanisms versus defense contents. *International Journal of Psycho-Analysis*, 68, 261–269.

Gold, J. (1996). *Key concepts in psychotherapy integration*. New York: Plenum.

Heidegger, M. (1962). *Being and time*. Trans. J. Macquarrie & E. Robinson. Oxford: Basil Blackwell.

Horwitz, A. V., & Wakefield, J. C. (2007). *The loss of sadness: How psychiatry transformed normal sorrow into depressive disorder*. New York: Oxford University Press.

Kosslyn, S. M. (1980). *Image and mind*. Cambridge, Mass.: Harvard University Press.

Lazarus, R. S., Averill, J. R., & Opton, E. (1970). Towards a cognitive theory of emotion. In M. B. Arnold (Ed.), *Feelings and emotions* (pp. 207–232). New York: Academic.

Luborsky, L. (1997). The convergence of Freud's observation about transference and the CCRT evidence. In L. Luborsky & P. Crits-Christoph (Eds.), *Understanding transference: The core conflictual relationship theme method*, 2d ed. (pp. 307–325). Washington, D.C.: American Psychological Association.

Main, M. (1983). Exploration, play, and cognitive functioning related to infant-mother attachment. *Infant Behavior and Development*, 6, 167–174.

Mandler, G. (1988). Problems and directions in the study of consciousness. In M. J. Horowitz (Ed.), *Psychodynamics and cognition* (pp. 21–45). Chicago: University of Chicago Press.

Meins, E., Fernyhough, C., Russel, J., & Clark-Carter, D. (1998). Security of attachment as a predictor of symbolic and mentalizing abilities: A longitudinal study. *Social Development*, 7, 1–24.

Merleau-Ponty, M. (1962). *Phenomenology of perception*. Trans. Colin Smith. London: Routledge & Kegan Paul.

Messer, S. B. (2001). Assimilative integration. *Journal of Psychotherapy Integration*, 11 (1), 1–4.

Norem, J. K. (1989). Cognitive strategies as personality: Effectiveness, specificity, flexibility, and change. In D. M. Buss & N. Cantor (Eds.), *Personality psychology: Recent trends and emerging directions* (pp. 45–60). New York: Springer-Verlag.

Ortony, A., Clore, G. L., & Collins, A. (1988). *The cognitive structure of emotions.* Cambridge, U.K.: Cambridge University Press.

Paivio, A. (1986). *Mental representations: A dual coding approach.* New York: Oxford University Press.

Putnam, H. (1988). *Representation and reality.* Cambridge, Mass.: MIT Press.

Rollins, M. (1989). *Mental imagery: On the limits of cognitive science.* New Haven, Conn.: Yale University Press.

Rosenzweig, S. (1936). Some implicit common factors in diverse methods of psychotherapy. *American Journal of Orthopsychiatry,* 6, 412–415.

Safran, J. D., & Messer, S. B. (1997). Psychotherapy integration: A postmodern critique. *Clinical Psychology: Science and Practice,* 4, 140–152.

Schachter, S., & Singer, J. (1962). Cognitive, social and physiological determinants of emotional states. *Psychological Review,* 69, 379–399.

Searle, J. (1983). *Intentionality: An essay in the philosophy of mind.* Cambridge, U.K.: Cambridge University Press.

Silberschatz, G., Curtis, J. T., & Nathans, S. (1989). Using the patient's plan to assess progress in psychotherapy. *Psychotherapy,* 26, 40–46.

Spieker, S. J., Nelson, D. C., Petras, A., Jolley, A., & Barnard, C. (2003). Joint influence of child care and infant attachment security for cognitive and language outcomes of low-income toddlers. *Infant Behavior & Development,* 26, 326–344.

Stricker, G., & Gold, J. R. (1996). An assimilative model for psychodynamically oriented integrative psychotherapy. *Clinical Psychology: Science and Practice,* 3, 47–58.

Stricker, G., & Gold, J. (2003). Integrative approaches to psychotherapy. In A. S. Gurman and S. B. Messer (Eds.), *Essential psychotherapies,* 2d ed. (pp. 317–349). New York: Guilford Press.

van Ijzendoorn, M., Dijkstra, J., & Bus, A. (1995). Attachment, intelligence, and language: A meta-analysis. *Social Development,* 4, 115–128.

van Ijzendoorn, M. H., Sagi, A., & Lambermon, M. W. E. (1992). The multiple caretaker paradox: Data from Holland and Israel. In R. C. Pianta (Ed.), *Beyond the parent: The role of other adults in children's lives* (pp. 5–24). New Directions for Child Development 57. San Francisco: Jossey-Bass.

van Ijzendoorn, M. H., & Vliet-Visser, S. (1988). The relationship between quality of attachment in infancy and IQ in kindergarten. *Journal of Genetic Psychology,* 149, 23–28.

Wakefield, J. C. (1988). Hermeneutics and empiricism: Commentary on Donald Meichenbaum. In S. Messer, L. Sass & R. Woolfolk (Eds.), *Hermeneutics and psychological theory: Interpretive approaches to personality, psychotherapy, and psychopathology* (pp. 131–148). New Brunswick, N.J.: Rutgers University Press.

Wakefield, J. C. (1992). "Freud and the intentionality of feeling." *Psychoanalytic Psychology,* 9, 1–23.

Wakefield, J. C. (1996). DSM-IV: Are we making diagnostic progress? *Contemporary Psychology,* 41, 646–652.

Wakefield, J. C. (1997). Diagnosing DSM-IV: Part 1: DSM-IV and the concept of mental disorder. *Behavioral Research and Therapy,* 35, 633–650.

Waters, E., Wippman, J., & Sroufe, L. A. (1979). Attachment, positive affect, and competence in the peer group: Two studies in construct validation. *Child Development,* 50, 821–829.

Whyte, L. L. (1960). *The unconscious before Freud.* New York: Basic.

4 SOCIAL WORK, PSYCHOBIOGRAPHY, AND THE STUDY OF LIVES

JAMES J. CLARK

IN EARLY 1940 Walter Benjamin wrote a series of meditations in which he attempted to come to terms with the encroaching reality of Nazi victories across Europe. Soon after completing his "Theses on the Philosophy of History," he would flee Paris, just hours before it fell to the invaders. As a radical theorist and German Jew, he faced arrest and deportation to a concentration camp if apprehended. Like many of the intellectuals Hitler drove from Europe, Benjamin's theoretical reflections on the press of history were wrought from personal narratives of flight, exile, internment, and despair. His ninth meditation—on the "angel of history"—depicted the flesh-and-bones terror known by those who were experiencing history's unfolding:

> This is how one pictures the angel of history. His face is turned toward the past. Where we perceive a chain of events, he sees one single catastrophe which keeps piling wreckage and hurls it in front of his feet. The angel would like to stay, awaken the dead, and make whole what has been smashed. But a storm is blowing in from Paradise; it has got caught in his wings with such a violence that the angel can no longer close them. The storm irresistibly propels him into the future to which his back is turned, while the pile of debris before him grows skyward. (Benjamin, 1968, pp. 257–258).

This meditation foreshadowed Benjamin's own fate. After hours of hard climbing on a mountain trail, a journey prolonged by his serious cardiac illness, he escaped across the border into Spain, where the refugees were informed that their visas had been revoked. While the details are still only partially known, his biographers agree that he committed suicide to escape Gestapo agents who were patrolling the border region (Broderson, 1996; Ecland & Jennings, 2003). The following morning, Benjamin's companions were allowed to continue their flight when the same authorities informed them that their visas were, after all, acceptable. Walter Benjamin's life story ended as if designed by his favorite writer, Franz Kafka. This deluge of war and genocide—what some Jewish theologians have come to call the "Shoah" and others have called the "Great Interruption"—effectively impeached the Enlightenment view of history-as-progress (Fiorenza & Tracy, 1984).

Bereft of classical, theistic systems of understanding, it is striking how powerless and ineffectual Benjamin's "angel of history" had become. The angel is frozen in all but traumatic perception, as it pierces the illusion of long decades of complex causal chains. Unlike us mortals, it witnesses all that occurs as that "one single catastrophe which keeps piling wreckage" (Benjamin, 1968, p. 57). From our vantage point many years later, we know that the "wreckage" includes all who were, are, and shall be destroyed in the firebombed cities, the concentration camps, and on the fields of "total war" (Ferguson, 2007; Gellately, 2007; Wasserstein, 2007). The wreckage includes all human beings no longer seen as persons but viewed as the expendable materiel of history, an intellectual perspective that "carries the threat of a quick and stormy death" (Solzhenitsyn, 1972, p. 17).

Marx, Hegel, and Kant presented their worldviews in grand philosophical systems and developed their theoretical systems with existential urgency (Breazeale, 2006), creating models of understanding of how the world worked and how it should run (Boundas, 2007). For their disciples, such theories provided viable blueprints for personal and social change, such as those found in Lenin's revisions of Marx and Engels. Indeed, Lenin famously pronounced that there could be no revolution without a *theory* of revolution (Malia, 2008). The twentieth century has punitively taught that theories guide and empower those who hold the power to make crucial decisions (Kershaw, 2007).

In this chapter I argue, first, that it is crucial to centralize persons in our theorizing, and second, that to do so effectively we must engage historical and biographical understanding. I will show that historical and biographical approaches can help us theorize about persons-in-situation in a manner that enhances theoretical and clinical understanding. While I attempt to support the claim that our theorizing must centralize the dignity of the human person, I also explain how this is a moral and philosophical choice, and not one that can be primarily defended as "scientific."

Next, I discuss the work of personality theorists who argue for theoretical attention to the study of lives, and then briefly review contemporary issues that face psychobiography and the study of lives. To clarify our terms, *psychobiography* is usually defined as the biographical study of an important historical or contemporary figure, which explicitly utilizes psychological theories. For example, the Central Intelligence Agency (CIA) routinely develops psychobiographies of figures like Osama bin Laden and other persons of concern in order to explain and predict their dangerous behaviors. More routinely, psychobiographies of major writers, poets, artists, musicians, scientists, and psychologists attempt to penetrate the creative process or the development of scientific breakthroughs (Nassar, 1998; Runyan, 2006; Schultz, 2005).

The term *study of lives* usually refers to the personality profiles or biographical portraits of "everyday people"; this branch of inquiry has been utilized to study children facing major psychosocial crises (Coles, 2003); children and adults struggling with neurological disorders (Sacks, 1973, 1996); persons with schizophrenia (Strauss, 2008); and violent offenders (Athens, 2005; Reamer, 2002, 2005). For purposes of this chapter, which introduces the overall approach, I reference both terms under the rubric of "biographical approaches" or even "historical-biographical approaches."

I then turn to a discussion of representative challenges to the validity of biographical and historical narrative, and their respective counterarguments and remedies. Following this, I present and analyze three cases—two treatment cases and a description of a multidisciplinary assessment program utilizing historical and biographical data. The purpose of the case presentations is to illustrate the uses of biographical and historical approaches for enhancing clinical theorizing and practice. Finally, I close with remarks about the study of lives and the data of human individuality.

STUDYING THE PERSON

In 1971 Rae Carlson raised the crucial question: "Where's the person in personality research?" She was sounding the alarm that in the pursuit of empiricism and internal validity, the scientific project known as personality and social psychology research had been splintered into disconnected and competing reports about traits, cognitions, perceptions, and other micro-phenomena (Carlson, 1971). Karl Popper's (1976) argument was that the social sciences could ultimately build valid and multidimensional models of the human person by some type of meta-analytic summing, or integration, of valid component studies. This approach certainly reflected academic psychology's employment of the reductionist approach in which complex scientific problems were reduced to models that could be controlled and accounted for. Instead of building grand unified theories (GUTs) and meta-psychologies composed of nonempirical, meta-psychological, and some-times metaphysical assertions, the leaders of academic psychology strove for an operationism that analytically divided the person into components that could be modeled and studies in laboratory settings (Nicholson, 2005). While some have argued that this move was a colossal mistake or even an inhumane project, it is probably wiser to see reductionism as a viable approach to studying components of human beings, which seeks to answer very specific questions.

For example, Eric Kandel (1998, 2006) describes his scientific work as having commenced with a set of psychoanalytic questions about the human personality. While he began with a naïve desire to explore the Freudian geography of the ego, id, and superego in the human brain, he ultimately realized that he needed to investigate the organic structures of human memory. Indeed, Freud himself had identified the neuroses as suffering that originated in "reminiscences" (Breuer & Freud, 1895/1957). Kandel soon dis-covered that his study of the biological substrates of human memory could not be successful if he chose to study human brains—in 1955 the compo-nents of human memory were visually and technologically inaccessible, and therefore inextricable from large neuroanatomical structures. Employing a reductionist approach, he initially moved to studying cats, and found even this animal model far too complex. Fortunately, he found the perfect animal model in *Aplysia*, a species of sea snail that presented with a simple neural structure whose stimulation and memory development could be observed nonmicroscopically and whose changes in neural structure could be experi-mentally manipulated and measured.

These experimental results allowed Kandel and his colleagues to develop a complex understanding of a simple neural structure, which then enabled the development of testable models of human memory. Kandel and other work-ers in this field deservedly won the Nobel Prize for this achievement. At the same time, he remained careful not to equate applications of animal models or component studies of human brain functioning as supporting any defini-tive, covering law about human selfhood. In a frustrating move for some observers, Kandel instead has insisted that other professions and branches of knowledge will be essential to integrate and understand the meaning of component findings for an understanding of the person. "The goal of this merger is to join radical reductionism, which drives basic biology, with the humanistic effort to understand the human mind, which drives psychiatry and psychoanalysis" (2006, p. 375).

Kandel demonstrates an unusual desire to integrate reductionism and humanism. In contrast, many *social* scientists have chosen reductionism *over* humanism. But this choice cannot be justified by any knowledge generated from doing the natural or social sciences. Such justification requires *philosophical* warrants, such as those found in the philosophy of naturalism, which assumes that valid knowledge can only be developed through inquirers guided by objectivist, materialist, hedonist, atomistic, and universalistic perspectives (Slife, 2004).

The perspective of human beings as another organism in a neutral or meaninglessness world underlies the philosophical anthropology required to approach person, self, and mind as entities that can be understood as mechanisms composed of particular components—for example, "Turing machines" or even computer hard drives. While this has been a fruitful method for developing the cognitive sciences, it sometimes represents a purposeful rejection of teleological and moral formulations of person or self. Indeed, Margaret Boden (2006) has argued, "The common-sense view is that . . . *life* is a precondition of . . . *mind*. But there's no generally accepted way of proving that to be so" (p. 1443, original emphasis).

Another interesting example of this line of thinking is the so-called "brain in a vat" (BIV) thought experiment. In the BIV scenario, a viable, functioning brain rests in a pool of nutrients and is hooked up to a supercomputer delivering electrical impulses that replicate the processes of normal human perception (Putnam, 1981). The skeptical formulation suggests that this brain will not be able to distinguish its state from that of an embodied perceiver. While there are significant philosophical objections to this position (e.g., Putnam, 1999), BIV is representative of the inclination to equate self or personhood with brain functioning. Analytic philosophies of mind are not unique in their inclusion of such approaches. Continental philosophies include many theories that argue for the decentering of the personal subject, most famously in Heidegger's work, as well as subsequent postmodern theories, as in the early work of Foucault. These approaches see the subjective experience of personhood as impossible, illusory, and derivative of more significant historical, cultural, class, linguistic, and social forces (Boundas, 2007; Pippin, 1999).

In contrast, Charles Taylor argues for a formulation of self that is closely tied to the centrality of the person:

> But if my position here is right, then we can't think of human persons, of selves in the sense that we are selves, in this light at all. They are not neutral, punctual objects; they exist only in a certain space of questions, through certain constitutive concerns. The questions or concerns touch on the nature of the good that I orient myself by and on the way I am placed in relation to it. *But then what counts as a unit will be defined by the scope of the concern by just what is in question.* And what is in question is, generally and characteristically, the shape of my life *as a whole.* It is not something up for arbitrary determination. (1989, p. 50)

At bottom, all theorizing about persons presupposes strong philosophical positions about what it means to be a person (Pomper, 1985) and how persons should be categorized and studied (Horwitz & Wakefield, 2007). Further, these beliefs become the schemata that guide choices about theoretical and research programs—including which questions are significant or trivial, permitted or forbidden, scientific or unscientific.

PERSONALITY PSYCHOLOGY AND THE STUDY OF LIVES

It is tempting to depict the philosophical discussion of personhood as a bipolar alternative between Putnam's BIV and Taylor's "narrative self." However, the intellectual history of this discussion has cut across philosophy, the natural sciences, and the social sciences. Avoiding a dichotomous analysis would require pluralist and integrative perspectives (Berlin, 2000; Borden, 2009; Clark, 2008; Wakefield & Baer, 2008).

One recent attempt to come to grips with these concerns is that of Dan McAdams and Jennifer Pals, "A New Big Five: Fundamental Principles for an Integrative Science of Personality," which claims that "personality psychology has yet to articulate clearly a comprehensive framework for understanding the whole person" and sees as necessary the development of "an integrative science of the whole person" (2006, p. 204). In the past grand unified theory personologies presented models that were difficult to test, and for the most part could not be falsified. Advances in many branches of psychology have now made it possible to try to assemble important theoretical approaches that have strong empirical support. While McAdams and Pals may not yet have achieved a design for an optimized integration, I would argue that they make a compelling case for lining up different perspectives that offer rich insights about persons and personality.

Their approach brings to mind a compelling demonstration advanced by the mathematician, poet, playwright, and humanist Jacob Bronowski (1973 in his seminal work, *The Ascent of Man.* In his chapter "Knowledge or Certainty," Bronowski showed how our understanding of a particular person is determined by the wavelength of light or sound utilized to perceive him or her, and he proceeds to collect data using radar, infrared, and white light telescopes, a simple camera, and then an impressionistic portrait painted by an artist using the naked eye. Bronowski points out that each image is a valid rendering of the person, but also that each presents the observer with very different kinds of knowledge. There is no hope of final integration or the unassailable predominance of one perspective, because the physics of perception will not allow it. If one perspective cannot be truer than another, then "tolerance" rather than "absolute certainty" is the best we can hope for. There is no cause for grief here: A line-up of veridical perspectives is not the "God's eye" view, but it seems a potentially rich way to approach the science of understanding human beings.

In this vein I find McAdams and Pals's strategy compelling: "Personality is conceived as (a) an individual's unique variation on the general evolutionary design for human nature, expressed as a developing pattern of (b) dispositional traits, (c) characteristic adaptations, and (*d*) *self-defining life narratives, complexly and differentially situated* (e) in culture and social context. The 5 principles suggest a framework for integrating the Big Five model of personality traits with those self-defining features of psychological individuality constructed in response to situated social tasks and the human need to make meaning in culture" (2006, p. 204, emphasis added). In this model they claim that

> contemporary narrative approaches have made much more explicit the ways in which storytelling shapes self-making, the kinds of stories that are commonly told, the relations between life stories and other features of human individuality, the impact of narrative processing on growth and well-being, and the complex interplay between narrative identity and culture. It is with respect to narrative identity, furthermore, that personality psychology's commitment to showing how every person is like no other person is most readily accomplished. Every life story is unique. The rich texture of human individuality is best captured in the intensive examination of the individual life story. . . . At the same time, common patterns across life stories,

especially within given cultures, can be identified, and these common patterns can speak to important and measurable individual differences between
people. Individual differences in narrative identity are not reducible to differences in dispositional traits or characteristic adaptations. But research
has documented important empirical relations between the levels—ways
in which traits and motives, for example, relate to narrative identity. . . .
A full accounting of a person's life requires an examination of the unique
patterning of dispositional traits, characteristic adaptations, and life narratives that characterize that life, all grounded ultimately in the evolutionary demands of the species and, at the same time, complexly influenced by
culture. (2006, p. 210)

In sum, life narratives contribute uniquely and significantly to the science
of the person, as one Bronowskian lens among others, enhancing the understanding produced by the others, while simultaneously constrained by those
other approaches from any claim of singular validity. This approach is certainly in line with Clyde Kluckhohn and Henry Murray's famous claim that
the human sciences should address the fact that any human being is (a) like
all other persons, (b) like some other persons, and (c) like no other person
(1948). On this last point, Kluckhorn and Murray emphasized that

Each individual's modes of perceiving, feeling, needing, and behaving have
characteristic patterns which are not precisely duplicated by those of any
other individual. . . . More exactly, the ultimate uniqueness of each personality is the product of countless and successive interactions between the matur-
ing constitution and different environing situations from birth onward. An
identical sequence of such determining influences is never reproduced. In this
connection it is necessary to emphasize the importance of "accidents," that is,
of events that are not predictable for any given individual on the basis of generalized knowledge of his physical, social, and cultural environments. A child
gets lost in the woods and suffers from exposure and hunger. Another child is
nearly drowned by a sudden flood in a canyon. Another loses his mother and
is reared by an aged grandmother, or his father remarries and his education
is entrusted to a stepmother with a psychopathic personality. Although the
personalities of children who have experienced a trauma of the same type will
often resemble each other in certain respects, the differences between them
may be even more apparent, partly because the traumatic situation in each
case had certain unique features, and partly because at the time of the trauma
the personality of each child, being already unique, responded in a unique
manner. Thus there is uniqueness in each inheritance and uniqueness in each

environment, but, more particularly, uniqueness in the number, kinds, and temporal order of critically determining situations encountered in the course of life. (1948, p. 37)

The foregoing arguments justify a careful exploration of the value of psychobiography and life studies, with the caveat that this will require conceptual clarity, methodological rigor, and epistemological humility.

PSYCHOBIOGRAPHY AND THE STUDY OF LIVES

Social work has not been greatly involved in the debates about personhood, but the field has shared the problematic search for research epistemologies consistent with its professional missions. Over the last century the profession has generated practice models that have reflected various meta-psychological paradigms—for example, psychoanalysis, Rankian psychology, behaviorism, and cognitive psychology. Additionally, the profession has proliferated models that have come from the various settings and tasks, including medical-psychiatric approaches to individuals, group work that emphasizes therapeutic activities over rumination, and community activism emphasizing social change. Recently, the widespread interest in evidence-based practice has centralized scientific validity concerns. Despite social work's value system prioritizing the person, conceptions of how to animate practice approaches with this concern, while still drawing on theoretical and scientific conceptions that carry particular views (and sometimes contrary views) of personhood and truth, have created tensions and confusion. Jerome Wakefield (1995) has meticulously described the archaeology of this contemporary conflict, which is found in ancient philosophies of knowledge, meaning, and personhood. He argues for the development of methodologies that can address some of the enduring epistemological problems that continue to challenge social work research and theory.

One approach that moves toward addressing these problems is found in psychobiography and the study of lives. At its best, biography is about "life and times" and "person in situation." Psychobiography and the study of lives encourage the kind of integrative approaches that could be very relevant for social work theorizing. It seems to be one way of exercising Mills's (1956) "sociological imagination." A close reading of Mills's approach to biography and history suggests that this perspective would significantly contribute to clinical social work theorizing:

The first fruit of this imagination—and the first lesson of the social science that embodies it—is the idea that the individual can understand his own experience and gauge his own fate only by locating himself within his period, that he can know his own chances in life only by becoming aware of those of all individuals in his circumstances. In many ways it is a terrible lesson; in many ways a magnificent one. We do not know the limits of man's capacities for supreme effort or willing degradation, for agony or glee, for pleasurable brutality or the sweetness of reason. But in our time we have come to know that the limits of "human nature" are frighteningly broad. We have come to know that every individual lives, from one generation to the next, in some society; that he lives out a biography, and that he lives it out within some historical sequence. By the fact of his living he contributes, however minutely, to the shaping of this society and to the course of its history, even as he is made by society and by its historical push and shove. The sociological imagination enables us to grasp *history* and *biography* and the relations between the two within society. That is its task and its promise.... No social study that does not come back to the problems of biography, of history and of their intersections within a society has completed its intellectual journey. (1956, p. 12, original emphasis)

This last sentence presents a particularly daunting claim for the social sciences, and proposes fundamental reconsiderations for contemporary theoretical and empirical work. William Todd Schultz (2005) proposes a renewed attention to psychobiography that might address some of Mills's concerns. "[Psychobiography] has chiefly to do with the subject's interior world, the effects of the life history on his mind and actions" (1956, p. 9). In effect, psychobiography involves the explicit and sophisticated use of psychological and social psychological theories to intensively study particular persons living in specific social surroundings during defined historical periods. When such studies are effectively developed, they can also contribute to theory, suggesting a translational research process.

Psychobiography—often caricatured by its critics as sloppy, muckraking, and epistemologically naïve—should instead be contrasted with "bad psychobiographies," which are characterized by pathographical, speculative, and retrospective reconstructions of their subjects. (See Clark [2007] for an extended review of Schultz [2005]; see Pietikainen and Ihanus [2003] for an informative, critical history of psychoanalytic psychohistory.)

William McKinley Runyan, professor in the School of Social Work at the University of California—Berkeley and scholar of psychology, history, psychobiography, and the study of lives, has observed that the study of lives was a priority for the founders of personality psychology, especially Henry A. Murray and Gordon Allport. For example, John Dollard's (1934) *Criteria for the Life History* promised a social science that synthesized culture, society, and personality through intensive and theoretically pluralistic studies of human lives. Unfortunately, this agenda lost academic respectability with the "changing intellectual fashions of what it meant to be scientific, personal and temperamental preferences for particular types of research, the kinds of graduate students attracted to the field . . . after World War II, patterns of funding and grant support, and institutional processes determining who was hired at [the major universities]" (Runyan, 1997, p. 42). The shift was remarkable and decisive.

While there was a resurgence of interest with the important work of Robert W. White (1952, 1963) and Erik H. Erikson (1958, 1969), the field was and continues to be marginal to mainstream personality psychology, which has devalued personology, while instead favoring hard sciences approaches found in trait and other component theories. Some observers have noted that, despite promising beginnings, psychobiographical scholarship has not progressed because too few scholars have pursued the work, and even exemplary investigations have not generated sustained critique and discussion. In effect, while psychobiography has drawn on various psychological theories to understand lives, psychobiographical findings have rarely flowed back into psychological theory. Academic psychologists have generally not attended to this type of "soft," idiographic scholarship, preferring the pursuit of "rigorous" experimental methods addressing nomothetical problems (Mazlish, 1975).

The progress of psychobiography and the study of lives has been impeded by the ambivalence of biographers themselves. For example, psychobiography was invigorated when Erikson produced *Young Man Luther* (1958) and *Gandhi's Truth* (1969), which were studies applying and extending his psychosocial theory of the human life cycle. Despite such successes, Erikson believed that psychobiography should probably not be developed as a field distinct from historical biography. His hope, apparently, was that historians and biographers, guided by "disciplined subjectivity," would integrate psychosocial theory into their existing historiographical approaches.

Unfortunately, historians understandably remain suspicious of psychobiographical approaches, and are often quick to distance themselves from these methods, while simultaneously offering their own, usually implicit and sometimes incomplete working models of their subjects' inner lives. The psychobiographer argues that it is necessary for the biographer to grapple with his or her subject's motives in order to understand complex decisions and behaviors over a lifetime (Elms, 1994). Not so, counters the biographer and military historian John Lukacs, who disparages any psychobiographical search for motives precisely because they are irremediably unconscious and inaccessible. In his brilliant historiographical volume *The Hitler of History*, Lukacs (1998) argues that psychoanalytic models of Hitler developed by consultants to the Office of Strategic Services during World War II led analysts down a blind alley, in effect, infantilizing Hitler rather than grappling with his ingenious ascent to political dominance in Germany. They thereby underestimated his capacities as a statesman and military strategist. Lukacs's solution is to study Hitler's *purposes,* which can be derived from studying his decisions and strategies, which are fully understandable at the conscious level. Lukacs also preserves the right to consider Hitler an example of evil intelligence operating in the world, and finds this *moral* framework superior to any psychobiographical model.

To illustrate the complexity of these claims and counterclaims we can turn to another critic of psychobiography, Joshua Wolf Shenk (2005), the author of *Lincoln's Melancholy.* Although he disparages the entire field of psychobiography in the opening and closing sections of his book, Shenk has arguably produced a psychobiography. He retrieves important evidence of Lincoln's lifelong struggle with clinical depression, utilizing the mood disorders criteria delineated in the *Diagnostic and Statistical Manual of Mental Disorders* (DSM). He argues that Lincoln's successful struggle against despair and suicidality during his young and middle adult years cultivated the capacities for ironic self-observation, psychological resilience, and the sheer physical endurance that served him so effectively as president and commander in chief during the Civil War. In the introduction to this biography, Shenk insists that he is not writing a psychobiography, because he believes that would require him to embrace a particular psychological theory and then fit the life into that theory, an endeavor he has no interest in pursuing. He then proceeds to draw upon contemporary biological and descriptive psychiatry to establish Lincoln's biogenetic vulnerability to depression, his first-degree relatives' documented history of depressive illness—including his mother's sadness, his father's distant moodiness, and a female cousin's adjudication as insane—all victims of what one family member called "the Lincoln horrors."

Lukacs and Shenk equate psychobiography with the application of psychoanalytic *meta-psychological* theory. And indeed, Freud has been traditionally considered to have fathered psychobiography with the 1910 publication of *Leonardo da Vinci and a Memory of His Childhood.* Unfortunately, while Freud carefully catalogued the scientific prescriptions to be followed (for example, avoid arguments built on a single clue, avoid pathologizing and idealizing the subject, avoid drawing strong clues from weak evidence), he proceeded to ignore them. His erroneous use of a bad translation of Leonardo's childhood dream helped advance his theory of artistic sublimation but also demonstrated theorizing at its worst—the overgeneralization of findings based on inferential error (Stannard, 1980). Erik Erikson (1975) called this type of error the "sin of originology"—the exclusive reliance on childhood events to fully explain adult personality. Robert Coles (1975) puts it slightly differently when he warns us that whenever we come across the words, *the one key factor,* when reading a biographical study, we can be sure we will be discovering more about the biographer's theory than about the life under scrutiny. As historiographer and methodologist Alan Megill has argued, "evidence is a frail reed, liable to be bent by subjectivity and undermined by carelessness and an uncritical attitude.... [it] can be trampled underfoot by acknowledged or unacknowledged desire" (Megill, 2007, p. 75).

If the critics are correct in their claims that psychobiography is the manipulation of a life study to validate the author's cherished theory, then it arguably cannot be classified as serious history, biography, psychology, or scholarship of any kind (Fischer, 1970; Manuel, 1972; Stannard, 1980). Yet it is fallacious to hold up poorly executed psychobiographies as exemplars, and then to use this as evidence to reject the field entirely (Elms, 1994; Gay, 1985; Runyan, 1988). There is no logical reason to claim that "bad" psychoanalysis is the only theoretical approach to psychobiography. Responsible psychobiographers are committed to addressing validity problems, and are therefore obligated to embrace a critical attitude when analyzing and theorizing about historical events (Clark, 1967), while utilizing a critical pluralism when selecting and applying theories (Runyan, 1988).

NARRATIVE AND ITS PROBLEMS

The proposed use of life stories to organize complex data about persons is no surprise to cognitive therapists and cognitive scientists. There is a robust research tradition, which flowered during the "cognitive revolution" so ably described by the "early" Jerome Bruner and was then redirected by the rise of narrative psychology and social constructivist perspectives equally ably described by the "later" Jerome Bruner and his colleagues (Bruner, 1990). We know that narrative organizes and integrates disparate, overwhelming and confusing data and allows it to be remembered, analyzed, and sometimes understood and tolerated (Simon, 1983). Indeed, narrative is how the human mind turns the passage of days into "human time" (Ricoeur, 1984, p. 4). Narrative requires four constituents to even be considered as narrative: agentivity, linearity (sequential order), sensitivity to canon and context, and a specific perspective or set of perspectives (Bruner, 1990).

However, as powerful as McAdams and Pals's (2006, p. 204) argument for inclusion of "self-defining life narratives, complexly and differentially situated," as a component of the science of personality psychology, narrative brings significant validity problems.

David Hackett Fisher (1970) closely examined the types of error typical of biographical and historical work in *Historians' Fallacies: Toward a Logic of Historical Thought.* He delineated the dangers of fallacious reasoning into the categories of question framing, factual verification, factual significance, generalization, narration, causation, motivation, composition, analogy, semantic distortion, and substantive distraction. These all apply to biographical exploration as well.

Megill (2007) has analyzed the specific and complex relationship of history and narrative in *Historical Knowledge, Historical Error,* forcefully arguing that history is often equated with remembered life narratives and is sometimes appropriated to commemorate communal experiences (like the Holocaust), to edify and guide contemporary social policy making, and to shore up cultural traditions. Megill argues that these are misuses (and sometimes abuses) of history, which should be a discipline that approaches all sources and traces of the past with skepticism. Narrative is well suited for organizing and rendering autobiographical memories, commemorations, edifications, and the making or shoring up of important traditions. However, it also exerts immense emotional power and seductiveness, opening up communities and disciplines to a host of potential errors, especially confirmatory and retrospective biases—the other naturally occurring processes human minds use to understand and make decisions. Instead, the integrity of historical understanding also demands a commitment to objectivity, or rather, commitments to multiple "divergent but interconnected objectivities," including a "disciplinary objectivity," which is actually a "consensus of a subgroup of historians;" a "dialectical objectivity" involving a sensitivity to the peculiarity of historical objects, persons, and events they study, describe, analyze and interpret; a "procedural objectivity" to be found in historians' methodologies; and "above all the unrealizable ideal of absolute objectivity"—in other words, the God's eye view, the grand narrative of history that was once thought to be attainable and was then shattered by the Babel of modernity. The tension created by this impossibility makes the practice of history possible; omniscient beings have no need for the discipline of history (2007, p. 114).

More effectively than anyone else working in the contemporary social sciences, Runyan (1982, 1988) has argued for the crucial importance of life histories and psychobiographies, while simultaneously facing down their inherent epistemological limitations and sources of error. In his classic book on the topic, Runyan (1982, p. 14) identified two major themes of concern: (1) "appropriately rigorous criteria and procedures for evaluating . . . life histories"; and (2) "the interplay of rational and intellectual considerations with social and political factors in the process of generating and critically evaluating explanatory accounts of lives, whether in clinical case formulations or psychobiographical formulations." His most famous and effective demonstration is the examination of alternative explanations of life events through the case of the painter Vincent Van Gogh's self-amputation of his ear. He argues that such alternative explanations should be weighed using the following criteria: logical soundness; comprehensiveness in accounting for events-within-an-event; robustness in the face of falsification; consistency when all available evidence is considered; how the explanation fits into other general knowledge about the person, event, or human behavior; and credibility when stacked up against competing hypotheses or explanations. The "social and political interests" of the inquirers must also be considered when evaluating an explanation as the product of "least developed inquiry," a "comprehensive explanatory inquiry," or the ideal, "fully rational explanatory inquiry" (1982, pp. 47–50).

The foregoing methodological issues are presented here to show that while narrative has the power to mislead, seduce, and overpower, there are rigorous approaches to holding these validity dangers in check. Indeed, as Bromley (1977) has shown, "ordinary language" approaches to understanding human and social phenomena as found in historical and biographical work will be superior *in certain clinical and research situations* to the deductive-nomological approaches and hypothetical-statistical tests that are considered as the gold standard of science (also see Heimer, 2001; Weinstein, 1995).

CASE STUDIES

How can the foregoing discussion of the power and limitations of historical and biographical knowledge assist social work theorizing in clinical settings? I present three cases in which I have applied the theoretical and methodological thinking described here to my clinical work and which attempt to demonstrate its significance and utility.

CASE ONE

Ronnie was a twenty-seven-year-old white male from rural Kentucky, now living in a subdivision in a metropolitan area. He was referred by the court for evaluation and treatment after his arrest for terroristic threatening by brandishing his hunting rifle as a postal worker entered his yard. Working in a community practice setting, I elicited the usual biopsychosocial history and found that his significant use of marijuana and caffeine contributed to his everyday and clinical presentations of an extremely angry, nervous, "jumpy," and impulsive person. He reported being in an unhappy marriage, and he attributed his current relationship problems to being a lifelong "fuck-up." When I asked about this self-definition, he revealed that this term had been used regularly by his now deceased parents. Ronnie had been a defiant kid and now had seemingly become an antisocial adult. He had enough insight to mordantly observe that this might have led to his threatening the mailman, "who walked up onto my yard even though I told him before to use the driveway," and his ongoing arguments with his wife about his daily pot-smoking.

He reported that he had one sister who lived in another state, with whom he rarely communicated because she "hated" him. His only satisfying moments were spent on the job as a repair technician in the back of a computer shop, where he worked alone and in silence, peacefully consuming an average of two pots of coffee during the morning and ten cans of highly caffeinated soft drinks over the course of the afternoon. His evening use of marijuana had become important for "calming down" after a stressful day at work. As we worked on his legal and substance use problems over the next five sessions, I also asked him to elaborate on his life story. He found this difficult to do, as he was more accustomed to thinking in terms of "lists" of complaints about himself, his wife, and the authority figures in his life. He seemed to see himself as a person who deservedly faced consistent bouts of bad luck. In *DSM-IV* terms, he was recurrently depressed and substance-dependent, with antisocial, schizoid, obsessive-compulsive, and paranoid personality traits.

His responses to my therapeutic suggestions were a mixture of overcompliance ("I quit caffeine cold turkey yesterday and I went crazy again!") and truculent resistance ("I'd never even talk with a goddam shrink unless the judge wasn't making me"). As we explored his difficulties with treatment, I asked him if there was something in his life history that made him so angry about our work together, especially considering that it was producing positive legal outcomes and some symptom relief. He then shared a previously unreported story of his experiences of working with a child psychotherapist at age ten. "Therapists are liars. I liked the guy and I thought he liked me. But then he dropped me like a hot rock." When I asked how this had happened, he said that after a few months of treatment, the therapist asked for a private meeting with his parents. Driving home after Ronnie's individual session, his father told him he would not be going back because the psychologist had told his parents that Ronnie was "untreatable." Ronnie remembered, "It was the worst day of my life, even worse than when I buried my parents. I liked going a lot. It was the one place I felt like someone liked me. And when he got to know me even *he* figured out that I was a total fuck-up."

I suggested to Ronnie that this was indeed one possible explanation but that it did not "fit" with the usual way clinical work was conducted. Ronnie appeared surprised, but then soon fell back into his gloomy self-appraisal. "I've seen other shrinks, and they all seem to agree with my first one. Besides, my parents are dead, so that's that!" I thought about the session a great deal, recognizing his problematic self-schemas, and the negative working model that was influencing Ronnie's sessions with me. There was an increasing probability that he would end treatment prematurely. During the next session, I suggested that Ronnie write a note to his child therapist asking about what had happened. When he refused, I offered to call the therapist to find out more about this defining, biographical event, and he agreed. I called the next day and found that Dr. Johnson had died several months before. I reported this at our next session Ronnie smiled grimly and continued to resist my hypothesis that this situation was probably more complicated than he had remembered. I then suggested that we write to Dr. Johnson's estate to see if we could obtain Ronnie's file, and he grudgingly filled out the release of information. I knew this was a long shot, but was pleased when the file arrived several weeks later.

As I reviewed Dr. Johnson's meticulous notes, I found that he had seen Ronnie as an emotionally abused child living with wealthy and socially powerful parents who disparaged him constantly. The clinician noted that after a few sessions of "testing" the therapist, Ronnie had "warmed up" and was delightful to work with. Convinced that Ronnie would never move beyond his chronic depression unless his parents' approaches changed, he made the appointment with them. His notes about that brief session recounted that he confronted Ronnie's parents about their harsh criticisms and punishments. They became argumentative, accusing him of being incompetent because he was blaming parents for the obvious psychopathology of a child. "He's never coming back here!" was their final response, despite his plea to continue his work with Ronnie even if they were uninterested in doing couple or family work. They even refused his request for a termination session with Ronnie.

I found reading this file to be very moving, as I understood that it contradicted Ronnie's powerful memories about his therapist. I knew it could prove a significant challenge to his self-schemas and his working model of psychotherapy. Worried that this also could be psychologically disorganizing, I called Ronnie and told him that I had received the file and that it probably contained what had actually happened. He agreed to come an hour early, read the file, and then have our session. Ronnie was overwhelmed by the contents of the file, and spent the session reading parts of it aloud as we tried to reconstruct what had happened. While he knew his parents' capacity for cruelty, he was amazed that they had ended his therapy so abruptly. He appeared deeply gratified that the termination had not been Dr. Johnson's decision, and reread passages describing his therapist's observations about Ronnie's positive qualities, vulnerabilities, and potentials. Over the next four sessions, Ronnie returned with the file, and we discussed his interpretations of the session notes. This also opened up dialogue about his experiences as a child, which now became more accessible to him. He appeared to now alternate between wooden, schizoid self-presentations and more affectively open expressiveness during our session. I began to like him more and, of course, he knew this was a change in my attitude, too.

At one point he found himself unable to remember a specific childhood event recounted in the file, and I suggested that he call his older sister in Ohio to see if she could fill in the "blank spaces." As usual Ronnie refused, claiming that she hated him. However, at the next session he reported that he had called her and had told her the story of the file. This led to her recounting her perspectives of what family life had been like for her, and she shared her distress about how badly their parents had treated Ronnie. She also told Ronnie that she carried a lot of guilt about abandoning him and escaping their abuse when she left for boarding school and then college. They made plans for a visit a few weeks later, which went very well. Ronnie gradually began to see himself differently, and while he remained very entrenched in habits developed over a lifetime, he began to realize that because he did not yet grasp his personal history, there were things that he did not know or understand about himself, his family, and other people. This confusion also suggested hope, and created possibilities for clinical work over the next year.

DISCUSSION OF CASE ONE

Many colleagues have remarked at how unusual it was for me to have pursued Dr. Johnson's file, and then to have shared it with my client. As I have recently applied the theoretical and methodological frameworks discussed here, I realized that this case was an example of taking history seriously. Like any serious biographer, I had retrieved archival material to develop evidence for one of the alternative accounts of my subject's life, and this had been important for my understanding of the client (Runyan, 1983). It opened up new frameworks for Ronnie to begin to recognize and face the complexities of his childhood and adolescence. Charles Taylor makes a philosophical observation that has clinical applications for this case: "To repudiate my childhood as unredeemable in this sense is to accept a kind of mutilation as a person; it is to fail to meet the full challenge involved in making sense of my life. This is the sense in which it is *not* up for arbitrary determination what the temporal limits of my personhood are" (1989, p. 51). While Ronnie could not articulate this profound sense of "mutilation," his suffering reflected what Taylor has metaphorically identified.

The development of strong archival evidence (Dr. Johnson's file) was crucial in a case where the client would have most likely continued to reject any therapeutic attempts to challenge his deep schemas about himself, his sister, and authority figures. As opposed to a treatment approach that mutually constructed an alternative narrative as a treatment goal, the file served as indisputable evidence that Ronnie needed to reexamine his long-held beliefs—something my persuasive powers alone would have been unlikely to accomplish. Additionally, this biographical approach led to Ronnie's recognition of other "gaps" and motivated him to connect with his older sister. This was very beneficial for Ronnie, who was able to further expand his autobiographical narrative and self-understanding through discussions with his sister ,who was indeed an "eyewitness" to his early development. Ronnie also benefited from her sympathetic understanding of his suffering, which led to Ronnie developing more insight about the impact of his early experiences on the way he related to people as an adult. These events allowed Ronnie to move from precontemplative to preparation stages (Prochaska, DiClemente & Norcross, 1992) as we confronted the forensic aspects of his treatment.

My account of this case, while framed in a "study of lives" approach, also utilized standard *DSM-IV* diagnostic practices; psychodynamic object relations and relational approaches (Borden, 2000, 2009); a Bowenian intervention (Walsh, 2003); and elements of motivational interviewing (Miller & Rollnick, 2002). In sum, biographical theory enhanced and guided the use of other intervention theories during the course of this case, as therapist and client developed an evidentiary database for building an alternative account of the client's life (Runyan, 1983).

CASE TWO

Hank was a forty-year-old, African American construction worker from rural Kentucky referred for his substance abuse and family problems. In the first session I learned that ten months earlier, Hank and his construction crew had been working out of town, when in the early hours of the morning a fire broke out in their hotel. Hank awakened his crew members, and they all were able to escape within minutes. Haunted by the screams he was hearing from those still trapped, he reentered the engulfed structure to try to rescue them, as firefighters had not yet arrived. Hank described plunging deep into the hotel and running to the rooms where he thought he could hear screams, but he soon was overcome by carbon monoxide and scorching temperatures. In tears, he recounted banging on doors, hoping he could extract people and lead them to safety. But he soon realized that the persons whose voices he had heard were almost certainly dead. He recalled running at full speed through the hallway. "Suddenly, it felt like someone had taken a crowbar and nailed me in the stomach. I went down. The breath was knocked out of me. But I crawled because of the pain and because I knew I would die if I didn't." Unknown to him, he was only yards from the lobby, and firefighters found him and dragged him to safety before the entire structure collapsed. Four people were killed in the fire, and fifteen were seriously injured. As he was transported by ambulance to the local emergency room, Hank remembered hearing the EMT workers describing the burned bodies of a mother and father who were found in a bathtub. They had desperately run the shower to counter the flames and smoke. A week later, the hotel owner was arrested for arson when it was discovered that he had purposely set the fire to collect insurance money.

Hank was hospitalized for about a week and returned home. His family doctor referred him for psychotherapy because of his alcohol bingeing, nightmares, intrusive thoughts, and flashbacks. Because he refused to take out-of-town jobs, he was assigned to rehab an office building that had suffered fire damage. As he tore down scorched beams, the water-damaged walls buckled, and the sight and smell of the charred wreckage triggered hundreds of flashbacks over the course of a day's work. He was drinking on the job to "medicate" his internal experiences and bingeing at night so he would not dream. He spoke about the deep shame that he felt when he reflected on being unable to rescue anyone. Although he could not be certain, he believed that the screams he usually heard were those of the mother and father found in the tub.

After initial sessions established that therapy was a "safe place" and Hank mastered deescalation and relaxation skills, we utilized an exposure-based treatment for post-traumatic stress syndrome. As he developed his trauma narrative, Hank relived running through the hotel fire. He would always become "stuck" at the moment he was struck in the stomach. Neither of us could explain why he could not move past this moment, and my experience-distant conjectures were not helpful. Even worse, Hank somehow connected his being struck and falling as perhaps his way of finding an excuse to become incapacitated and rescued. "Maybe I am a coward. Maybe I fooled myself into believing a guy hit me. And we both know that nobody could've been in that hallway to do that to me."

We were really stuck. Out of growing frustration, I drew on my previous forensic experiences of analyzing crime scene photographs and drawings, and suggested to Hank that we obtain the blueprints for the hotel to see if we could precisely reconstruct the locations of his traumatic experiences. Together, we wrote to the prosecutors explaining Hank's need to see the drawings. After we wrote an additional letter to the judge hearing the criminal trial, the blue-prints arrived at my office. When Hank arrived, we unpacked the drawings from the cylinder and unrolled them on the floor. I relied on his expertise as a construction foreman, and Hank began analyzing and explaining the structure and layout of the hotel. I handed him a red pencil and he marked the location of his room, the lobby, and the hallways. He then traced a line that tracked his reentry into the hotel, the possible rooms he tried to enter, and then his final run down the hall. At that point the pencil tip crossed a symbol I did not understand. Hank exhaled as if an enormous burden was being lifted and turned to me. "That line there means there was a little ramp and steel railing for a middle exit door. I didn't remember seeing that before the fire. I'd been staying on the other side of the hotel." He smiled sadly and shook his head. This experience seemed to be extremely helpful to Hank, and we were able to continue our work. Unfortunately, Hank had a complex set of biopsychoso-cial problems that predated his traumatic experiences. He subsequently went through a bitter divorce, temporarily losing custody of his daughter. He had to testify in the criminal trial, which was very painful. Additionally, he lost his foreman job because of his refusal to travel and his incapacity to rehab dam-aged structures. He did not stop drinking. After several years of dropping out and returning to therapy, Hank was arrested for driving while intoxicated. Now court-ordered into mandated treatment, he embarked on a sustained course of combined substance abuse treatment, self-help and treatment groups, and cognitive-behavioral therapy. Ten years after the fire, Hank owns his own busi-ness and has custody of his child.

DISCUSSION OF CASE TWO

Hank and I reached an impasse when he could not remember what had struck and incapacitated him in the fire. More problematic, he had some-how convinced himself that he had fabricated the involuntary fall because he was a coward. No amount of persuasion or logic was helpful. ("You didn't have to reenter the building at all, Hank. You aren't a firefighter.") Hank was irrevocably frozen in this crucial moment, which for him was a test of his personal integrity and self-definition as a man. I did not understand how he was linking this specific event to his self-schema because I did not have any universal, theoretical template in which such a formulation was easily explained. This clinical situation brings to mind the words of Kluckhohn and Murray presented earlier: "Although the personalities of [persons] who have experienced a trauma of the same type will often resemble each other in certain respects, the differences between them may be even more apparent, partly because the traumatic situation in each case had certain unique features, and partly because at the time of the trauma the personality of each [person], being already unique, responded in a unique manner" (1948, p. 37; I have replaced the word *child* with *person* in this passage).

Elicited, hazy memories about the fire were not adequate for Hank. After applying a biographical approach, which required the development of a database of varied and convergent types of evidence, Hank was able to make sense of his autobiographical somatic memories and to develop a coherent narrative of his behavior under fire. While this was insufficient to address his many complex needs, it allowed him to develop a therapeutic alliance with the clinician that weathered many years of partially successful work and eventually a course of court-mandated treatment (Clark, in press).

I believe it is reasonable to claim that Hank would have always rejected any attempted narrative construction that was preferred by the therapist—he demanded solid historical evidence. What Thomas Kohut has written about the uses of history-in-psychology and psychology-in-history seems to apply here: "Finally, [we] may even choose to use theory to structure his account, to organize his thinking and presentation. No matter how theory is presented, however, the past must stand on its own, must be comprehended and made comprehensible on its own terms. Contemporary evidence cannot substitute for historical evidence. Understanding and explanation must remain thoroughly historical, that is, they must derive from the past itself" (2001, p. 349). This is not to refute that long-term memories are indeed constructed and reconstructed rather than "flash bulb" and veridical (Berlin, 2002; Schacter, 2002), but it acknowledges that, in this case, therapeutic remembering simply could not be constructed by a client and clinician with flimsy evidence (Spence, 1982).

Hank needed validation that his experiences were "real" for him and that his failure to continue his rescue efforts was involuntary. No theoretically derived interpretation would have worked for him. His testimony at the homicide trial allowed him to hear the biographical narratives of fellow victims, especially how they had coped since the fire. Throughout treatment, I used Hank's courage and resilience as a way to encourage him to pursue his decade-long recovery process. Even at his most shameful moments of arrest and court referral, we were able to call upon the biographical narrative of his selfless actions during the fire to envision a future, possible self (Markus & Nurius, 1986) who could also be heroic in the mundane tasks of staying sober, going to work, and raising his child. This last point is illustrative of how biographical narratives can open up the clinician's consideration of the person's characteristic adaptations (McAdams, 2006; McAdams &

Pals, 2006), especially those emphasizing agency and purposive behavior (Cantor & Zirkel, 1990).

CASE THREE

This last case describes the development of a multidisciplinary assessment project that has been operational since 1999, called the University of Kentucky Comprehensive Assessment and Treatment Services Project (CATS). Supported by the Kentucky Cabinet for Heath and Family Services, this joint project of the College of Social Work and the College of Medicine has assessed over 2,000 children and their caregivers referred by the Cabinet and the family court system. We began the project with a commitment to develop rich, longitudinal biographical descriptions of children and families to serve as an important dimension of the database for developing conclusions and recommendations for placement, health, and behavioral health treatment and sometimes recommendations regarding termination of parental rights:

> The early decision was to create a program that did not adhere to standard mental health consultation models (i.e., creating evaluations of child psychopathology with only secondary attention to contributing family pathology). The CATS conceptual model would have to meet the following requirements: (a) The model would have to be open to a number of domain-specific theories that were germane to the problems of child maltreatment; (b) the model would need to include interactions among individual, dyadic, family, and systemic phenomena (including professional and welfare institutions; i.e., biopsychosocial dynamics); (c) the model would have to incorporate both adaptive and maladaptive responses to maltreatment; and (d) the model needed to be readily operationalizable and testable over time. . . . Our review of the scientific and clinical literatures, interviews with key informants, and our own clinical knowledge base, garnered from collective decades of experience with children and families, directed us to careful consideration of four theoretical areas of investigation: coping theory, trauma theory, attachment theory, and a transactional model of developmental psychopathology. (Sprang, Clark, Kaak & Brenzel 2004, p. 327)

Utilizing decision and judgment theory, we decided to use multiple types of data when performing the child and caregiver assessments (Berlin & Marsh, 1993). These included psychometric screening; structured observations of caregiver-child relational interactions; structured biopsychosocial and specialized interviews; and analysis of the social services, behavioral health, health, social services, criminal justice, and pediatric/adult medical records. This last domain has been especially important in developing a narrative history of the child, the caregiver, and their relationship—a goal rarely accomplished in other settings because of the time and effort it takes to find and collect the historical record. When all the data are assembled, information from each domain is compared, and convergence and divergence is determined.

For example, a female caregiver reports in her psychosocial interview that she was sexually abused from age ten through fourteen, at which time she began to abuse alcohol and cocaine; she also reports that she has been in intensive outpatient treatment for six months since the removal of her children after neglect was substantiated by the Cabinet and family court. These biographical data can be validated with psychometric screening (e.g., the *Substance Abuse Subtle Screening Inventory*) and content analysis of her criminal justice, social services, and behavioral health records from childhood (to construct and review her own victimization, substance abuse, and foster care history) and from adulthood (to construct and review contemporary, critical life events). The CATS process attempts to do this with all critical life events that concern the overall safety and health of the children in care, and whenever possible, their adult caregivers.

Such intensive biographical and historical review also allows the team to discover gaps and divergences in the life narrative. For example, one mother was referred for assessment with her four children who had been removed after physical abuse was substantiated. She reported that her oldest son had died in a fire ten years ago and her daughter had been placed for adoption. However, there was no trace of this event in the Cabinet record, and the child protective workers had no knowledge of the "accident." A CATS clinician searched the local newspaper archives for the probable time period involved and found a series of newspaper articles that reported the fire and the death of the five-year-old boy who had been left home alone in 1989. As part of the evaluation, CATS clinicians visited the current home and found scores of lit candles placed throughout the cluttered, ramshackle home. This convergence of historical and contemporary data proved extremely important in developing an estimation of risk for future child maltreatment.

In a different case of suspected Munchausen's-by-proxy, my clinical interviews with a thirty-year-old mother of the removed two-year-old child revealed a calm, reasonable, and positive maternal figure who loved her child. However, the review of the mother's and child's medical records by the CATS team pediatrician revealed thirty-five emergency room visits across ten hospitals over an eighteen-month period, providing divergent data and a few alternative accounts to the one produced by my clinical interview.

DISCUSSION OF CASE THREE

The foregoing discussion of narrative and historical validity emphasized several strategies to enhance validity and confidence in the interpretation of data. The CATS assessment utilizes several of these approaches to accomplish this, including a pluralistic theoretical framework to avoid narrow approaches to biopsychosocial theorizing about the cases; the collection of multiple types of data using an interdisciplinary team and various collection techniques; and intensive content analysis of the historical records (see Sprang, Clark, Kaak & Brenzel [2004] for a complete and detailed description of the clinical protocol; see Sprang, Clark & Bass [2005] for an example of the research protocol using these approaches).

This multidimensional, historical approach is especially important because the rulings made by the Cabinet and those by the courts involve grave and often final decisions about the permanent custody, safety, and well-being of children. Consistent with the work of John Monahan and Henry Steadman (1994), we see such requirements for valid assessments and reasonable predictions as demanding that historical factors should be weighed along with contemporary clinical factors; situational and contextual factors; and dispositional and personality factors. After the conclusions and recommendations—grounded in the collected data—are thoroughly studied by the multidisciplinary team, conclusions and recommendations are made. These are stated in probabilistic terms with attention to the specific data convergences and divergences we have noted. Additionally, data gaps and those conclusions held with only limited confidence are explicitly noted.

I have often testified in court (usually when under cross-examination) that there are probably errors in the forty- to eighty-page CATS report, but that the clinicians try to identify and limit most errors through the assessment and report-writing process. Readers familiar with Irving Alexander's (1990) personological approach to clinical assessment will find parallels here, especially in his emphasis on, first, systematically sorting and deliberating about the data; second, avoiding decision foreclosure by asking broad questions of the data; and third, using multidimensional-multimethod approaches to uncovering data convergence and divergence.

Finally, this assessment project has led to our recent development of a conceptual framework for therapeutic jurisprudence in child welfare (Clark & Sprang, 2008); our use of historical and archival data to research the relationship between substance abuse and child trauma exposure (Sprang, Tindall & Clark, 2008); and the use of narrative and quantitative data to explore the relationships between caregiver working models and maltreatment risk (Sprang, Clark & Bass, 2005).

FINAL DISCUSSION AND CONCLUSIONS

The purpose of this chapter is to discuss the importance of biography, the study of lives, and other historical data for theorizing in clinical social work. I have argued that such approaches compel us to theorize about persons, their specific situations, and their historical "actualities" (see Erikson, 1975). I have attempted to provide an overview of the importance of thinking historically when theorizing about clinical social work problems. I began with the observation that theory has had an enormous impact on historical decisions made in the twentieth century, and I claimed that all theorizing must centralize the person, while recognizing this as a philosophical and moral choice, not a scientific requirement. I then turned to a discussion of the contemporary problems of studying persons and some of the philosophical and methodological issues of concern. In the third section I discussed attempts by personality theorists to justify a theoretical interest in the study of lives, followed by a review of contemporary issues in psychobiography and the study of lives. Next, I reviewed some of the challenges to the validity of biographical and historical narrative, and important responses and remedies. Finally, I presented three cases—two treatment cases and a description of a multidisciplinary assessment program utilizing historical and biographical data.

I have tried to demonstrate that biographical and historical frameworks assist the clinical theorist as he or she approaches specific cases or develops important protocols for assessment and management. Historical approaches introduce complexity and longitudinal views that preclude simplistic conceptualization. Biographical perspectives push us to see the client as a person-in-history, and provide crucial counter-perspectives to the "view from nowhere" (Nagel,1986) . Again, I turn to Taylor, who has put this more clearly than anyone:

> My underlying thesis is that there is a close connection between the different conditions of identity, or of one's life making sense. . . . One could put it this way: because we cannot but orient ourselves to the good, and thus determine our place relative to it and hence determine the direction of our lives, we must inescapably understand our lives in narrative form, as a "quest." But one could perhaps start from another point: because we have to determine our place in

relation to the good, therefore we cannot be without an orientation to it, and hence must see our life in story. From whichever direction, I see these conditions as connected facets of the same reality, inescapable structural requirements of human agency. (1989, p. 52)

Taylor's thesis squares with Paul Ricoeur's powerful claim that narrative *creates* human time. Additionally, narrative is required for persons to exercise human agency and to understand the actions and purposes of other people. Unlike Walter Benjamin's helpless "angel of history," a being who exercises omniscient, historical vision but has no possibility to act, mortals have limited, narrative, historical understanding, but can and do exercise agency—making personal and social change possible (McAdams, Josselon & Lieblich, 2001, 2006).

With human agency come blind spots and error. Narrative theorists argue that even in the greatest, classic texts, certain passages are "under-read" while others are "over-read" (Abbot, 2002). So it goes in the study of lives: certain facets of a life are centralized (often based on the observer's theoretical perspective), while others are never attended to (again, because of perspective). Many dimensions of a life—especially the role of other people in the subject's life—can be "flattened" or manipulated into the background. This helps the observer to better focus on the favored dimensions of the biographical narrative—often to highlight the subject (Malcolm, 2007). Theorists, clinicians, documentarians, and biographers all have to deal with this foreground/background problem (Coles, 1997). Their chosen approaches have enormous implications for the inclusion and exclusion of crucial data that, framed a different way, might lead to dramatically different interpretations and conclusions. Thus, as Megill (2007) argues, there is never "history"; there are always "histories."

I have further argued that lives should not simply be "constructed" in psychotherapy, but that clinicians and theorists should turn to historical and biographical evidence to engage in the mutual search for evidence-based versions of the past. This commitment moves historical narrative from the fictive to the probable, and responds to the empirical realities of the client-in-situation-over-time. While this kind of knowledge cannot usually meet the narrowest requirements of Carl Hempel's (1966) definition of scientific thinking as deductive-nomological explanation, it is an essential type of knowledge that must be an equal partner with science-based understanding (also see Cohler 1982, 1994; Gordon & Shontz, 1990). Patterns across cases and universals are the raw material of science, argue Kluckhohn and Murray (1953), but the methods of natural science are only one kind of epistemological approach that clients, clinicians, and theorists need in order to understand human lives.

Biography does not centralize external validity and representativeness but instead searches for what we might learn from specific lives (Runyan, 1982) with the hope that what we learn from specific lives rigorously studied can contribute to theory (White, 1952). A well-examined life not only might help us understand a psychological construct such as personality, but might also contribute to our theories of social problems, social movements, and social change (Mills, 1956; Salvatore, 2004). Finally, while biography, history and narrative all present with significant validity and reliability challenges, I hope I have made it clear that there are viable strategies for identifying and managing error that require critical and pluralistic perspectives.

We enjoy moral and epistemological privileges when we serve as clinicians, theorists, and researchers who meet and get to know persons and communities. Getting to know people means listening to and trying to understand the life stories of persons and communities. Human knowledge is personal and participant; "the kind of understanding which is . . . required of the historian inevitably involves a kind of sympathetic *participation* in the person or persons, in the lives and in the minds, in which he is interested, and which he will attempt to describe" (Lukacs, 1997, p. 355). The type of thinking that enhances historical understanding requires an honest search for evidence in the quest for validity, vigorous clarification, careful interpretation, and—at best—consensus between client and clinician, and on a larger scale, among communities, professionals, and scholars (Denzin, 1989).

At the close of his magisterial study of lives, *Children of Crisis,* Robert Coles turned to James Agee's ultimate statement of personal and biographical uniqueness, possibility, vulnerability, and dignity. "To have been presented with [this statement] is to be privileged" (Coles, 2003, p. 692), because it provides a vital phenomenology of the persons the profession attempts to serve:

> All that each person is, and experiences, and shall never experience, in body and in mind, all these things are differing expressions of himself and of one root, and are identical: and not one of these things nor one of these persons is ever quite to be duplicated, nor replaced, nor has it ever quite had precedent: but each is a new and incommunicably tender life, wounded in every breath, and almost as hardly killed as easily wounded: sustaining, for a while, without defense, the enormous assaults of the universe. (Agee, 1941, p. 56)

The disciplined pursuit of history, psychobiography, and the study of lives creates and enhances cultural, social, psychological, and interpersonal theories, which, when drawn upon by the profession, will productively reshape and reinvigorate social work's theorizing, research, and clinical work.

NOTE

The author would like to thank William Borden, Mac Runyan, and Bob Walker for their excellent conversation about the problems raised in this chapter, as well as their editorial suggestions.

REFERENCES

Abbott, H. P. (2002). *The Cambridge introduction to narrative*. New York: Cambridge University Press.

Agee, J., & Evans, W. (1941). *Let us now praise famous men* . Boston: Houghton Mifflin.

Alexander, I. E. (1990). *Personology: Method and content in personality assessment and psychobiography*. Durham, N.C.: Duke University Press.

Athens, L. (2005). Violent encounters: Violent engagements, skirmishes and tiffs. *J o u r - nal of Contemporary Anthropology*, 34, 631–678.

Benjamin, W. (1968). *Illuminations: Essays and reflections*. New York: Schocken Books.

Berlin, S. B. (1990). Dichotomous and complex thinking. *Social Service Review*, 64 (1), 46–59.

Berlin, S. B. (2002*). Clinical social work practice: A cognitive-integrative perspective*. New York: Oxford University Press.

Berlin, S. B., & Marsh, J. C. (1993). *Informing practice decisions*. New York: Macmillan.

Boden, M. A. (2006). *Mind as machine: A history of cognitive science*. Vol. 2. Oxford, U.K.: Clarendon Press.

Borden, W. (2000). The relational paradigm in contemporary psychoanalysis: Toward a psychodynamically-informed social work perspective. *Social Service Review*, 74 (3), 352–379.

Borden, W. (2009). *Contemporary psychodynamic theory and practice*. Chicago: Lyceum Books.

Boundas, C. V. (2007). *Columbia companion to twentieth-century philosophies*. New York: Columbia University Press.

Breazeale, D. (2006). Textual interpretation as performance art: With an excursus on the existential urgency of systematic philosophy. University of Kentucky Distinguished Professor of Arts and Sciences Lecture. Unpublished manuscript.

Breuer, J., & Freud, S. (1895/1957). *Studies on hysteria*. Trans. and ed. James and Alix Strachey. New York: Basic Books.

Broderson, M. (1996). *Walter Benjamin: A biography*. New York: Verso.

Bromley, D. B. (1977). *Personality description in ordinary language*. New York: Wiley.

Bromley, D. B. (1986). *The case study method in psychology and related disciplines*. New York: Wiley.

Bronowski, J. (1973). *The ascent of man.* Boston: Little, Brown.

Bruner, Jerome. (1990). *Acts of meaning.* Cambridge, Mass.: Harvard University Press.

Cantor, N., & Zirkel, S. (1990). Personality, cognition, & purposive behavior. In L. A. Pervin (Ed.), *Handbook of personality theory* (pp. 135–164). New York: Guilford.

Clark, J. (2007). Review of *Handbook of Psychobiography,* William Todd Schultz, ed. (2005). *Social Service Review,* 81 (3), 557–564.

Clark, J. J. (2008). Complex thinking for wicked problems: An application of Sharon Berlin's analysis of dichotomous thinking. In *Special Issue: Honoring the Scholarship of Sharon B. Berlin. Social Work Now,* 39, 38–48.

Clark, J. (In press). Contemporary psychotherapy research: Implications for substance misuse treatment and research. *Substance Use and Misuse.*

Clark, J., & Sprang, G. (2008). Infant mental health, child maltreatment, and the law: A jurisprudent therapy analysis. *Infant Mental Health Journal,* 29 (1), 21–35.

Clark, K. (1967). *The critical historian.* New York: Basic Books.

Cohler, B. J. (1982). Personal narrative and life course. *Life-Span Development and Behavior,* 4, 205–241.

Cohler, B. J. (1994). The human sciences, the life story, and clinical research. In E. Sherman and W. J. Reid (Eds.), *Qualitative Research in Social Work* (pp. 163–174). New York: Columbia University Press.

Coles, R. (1975). *The mind's fate: A psychiatrist looks at his profession.* Boston: Little, Brown.

Coles, R. (1997). *Doing documentary work.* New York: Oxford University Press.

Coles, R. (2003). *Children of crisis.* Boston: Back Bay Books.

Denzin, N. K. (1989). *Interpretive biography.* Newbury Park, Calif.: Sage.

Dollard, J. (1934). *Criteria for the life history.* New Haven, Conn.: Yale University Press.

Ecland, H., & Jennings, M. W. (2003). *Walter Benjamin: Selected writings.* Vol. 4. Cambridge, Mass.: Belknap Press.

Elms, A. (1994). *Uncovering lives: The uneasy alliance of biography and psychology.* New York: Oxford University Press.

Erikson, E. H. (1958). *Young man Luther.* New York: Norton.

Erikson, E. H. (1969). *Gandhi's truth.* New York: Norton.

Erikson, E. H. (1975). *Life history and the historical moment.* New York: Norton.

Ferguson, N. (2007). *The war of the world.* New York: Penguin.

Fiorenza, E. S., & Tracy, D. (1984). *The Holocaust as interruption.* New York: T & T Clark.

Fischer, D. H. (1970). *Historian's fallacies: Toward a logic of historical thought.* New York: Harper.

Freud, S. (1910/1957). Leonardo da Vinci and a memory of his childhood. In J. Strachey (Ed.), *Five lectures on Psycho-Analysis, Leonardo Da Vinci, and other works,* vol. 11 of *Standard Edition of the Complete Psychological Works of Sigmund Freud,* (63–137). London: Hogarth.

Gay, P. (1985). *Freud for historians.* New York: Oxford University Press.

Gellately, R. (2007). *Lenin, Hitler and Stalin: The age of social catastrophe.* New   York: Knopf.

Gordon, J., & Shontz, F. (1990). Representative case research: A way of knowing. *Journal of Counseling and Development,* 69, 62–66.

Heimer, C. A. (2001). Cases and biographies: An essay on routinization and the nature of comparison. *Annual Review of Sociology,* 27, 47–76.

Horwitz, A. V., & Wakefield, J. C. (2007). *The loss of sadness: How psychiatry is transforming normal sorrow into depressive disorder.* New York: Oxford University Press.

Kandel, E. R. (1998). A new intellectual framework for psychiatry. *American Journal of Psychiatry,* 155, 457–469.

Kershaw, I. (2007). *Fateful choices: Ten decisions that changed the world, 1940-1941.* New York: Penguin Press.

Kandel, E. R. (2006). *In search of memory: The emergence of a new science of mind.* New York: Norton.

Kluckhohn, C., & Murray, H. A. (1948). *Personality in nature, society, and culture.* New York: Knopf.

Kohut, Thomas A. (1986). Psychohistory as history. *American Historical Review,* 91, 336–354.

Lukacs, J. (1997). *Historical consciousness: The remembered past.* New Brunswick, N.J.: Transaction.

Lukacs, J. (1998). *The Hitler of history.* New York: Knopf.

Malcolm, J. (2007). *Two lives: Gertrude and Alice.* New Haven, Conn.: Yale University Press.

Malia, M. (2008). *History's locomotives: Revolutions and the making of the modern world.* New Haven, Conn.: Yale University Press.

Manuel, F. E. (1972). The use and abuse of psychology in history. In F. Gilbert & S. E. Graubard (Eds.), *Historical studies today* (pp. 211–237). New York: Norton.

Markus, H., & Nurius, P. (1986). Possible selves. *American Psychologist,* 41 (9), 954–969.

Mazlish, B. (1975). The past and future of psychohistory. *Annual of Psychoanalysis,* 31, 225–236.

McAdams, D. P. (2007). *The person: A new introduction to personality psychology.* New York: Wiley.

McAdams, D. P., Josselson, R., & Lieblich, A. (2001). *Turns in the road: Narrative studies of lives in transition.*Washington, D.C.: American Psychological Association.

McAdams, D. P., Josselson, R., & Lieblich, A. (2006). *Identity and story: Creating self in narrative.* Washington, D.C.: American Psychological Association.

McAdams, D. P., & Pals, J. (2006). A new big five: Fundamental principles for an integrative science of personality. *American Psychologist,* 61 (3), 204–217.

Megill, A. (2007). *Historical knowledge, historical error: A contemporary guide to practice.* Chicago: University of Chicago Press.

Miller, R .B. 2004. *Facing human suffering: Psychology and psychotherapy as moral engagement.* Washington, D.C.: American Psychological Association.

Miller, W. R., & Rollnick, S. (2002). *Motivational interviewing: Preparing people to change.* New York: Guilford.

Mills, C. W. 1956/2000. *The sociological imagination.* New York: Oxford University Press.

Monahan, J., & Steadman, H. J. (1994). *Violence and mental disorder.* Chicago: University of Chicago Press.

Murray, H. A., & Kluckhohn, C. (1953). *Personality in nature, society and culture.* New York: Knopf.

Nassar, S. (1998). *A beautiful mind.* New York: Simon & Schuster.

Nicholson, I. (2005). From the Book of Mormon to the operational definition: The existential project of S.S. Stevens. In W.T. Schultz (Ed.), *Handbook of psychobiography,* (285–298). New York: Oxford University Press.

Pietikainen, P & Ihanus, J. (2003). On the origins of psychoanalytic psychohistory. *History of Psychology 6* (2),171–94

Pippin, R. B. (1999). *Modernism as a philosophical problem.* 2d ed. Malden, Mass.: Blackwell.

Pomper, P. (1985). *The structure of mind in history.* New York: Columbia University Press.

Popper, K. (1982). *Unended quest: An intellectual autobiography.* La Salle, Ill.: Open Court.

Prochaska, J. O., DiClemente, C. C., & Norcross, J. C. (1992). In search of how people change: Applications to addictive behaviors. *American Psychologist, 47* (9), 1102–1114.

Putnam, H. (1981). *Reason, truth and history.* Cambridge, U.K.: Cambridge University Press.

Putnam, H. (1999). *The threefold cord: Mind, body and world.* New York: Columbia University Press.

Nagel T. (1986). *The view from nowhere.* New York: Oxford University Press.

Reamer, F. G. (2002). *Criminal lessons.* New York: Columbia University Press.

Reamer, F. G. (2005). *Heinous crime: Cases, causes & consequences.* New York: Columbia University Press.

Ricoeur, P. (1984). *Time and narrative.* Trans. Kathleen McLaughlin and David Pellauer. Chicago: University of Chicago Press.

Runyan, W. M. (1982). *Life histories and psychobiography: Explorations in theory and method.* New York: Oxford University Press.

Runyan, W. M. (1988). *Psychology and historical interpretation.* New York: Oxford University Press.

Runyan, W. M. (1997). Studying lives: Psychobiography and the conceptual structure of personality psychology. In R. Hogan (Ed.), *Handbook of personality* (pp. 41–69). New York: Academic.

Runyan, W. M. (2006). Psychobiography and the psychology of science: Understanding relations between the life and work of individual psychologists. *Review of General Psychology, 10,* 147–162.

Sacks, O. (1973). *Awakenings.* New York: Doubleday.

Sacks, O. (1996). *Anthropologist on Mars: Seven paradoxical tales.* New York: Knopf.

Salvatore, N. (2004). Biography and social history: An intimate relationship. *Labour History, 87,* 187–192.

Schacter, D. (2002). *The seven sins of memory.* Boston: Houghton Mifflin.

Schultz, W. T. (2005). *Handbook of psychobiography.* New York: Oxford University Press.

Shenk, J. W. (2005). *Lincoln's melancholy: How depression challenged a president and fueled his greatness.* Boston: Houghton Mifflin.

Simon, H. (1983). *Reason in human affairs.* Stanford, Calif.: Stanford University Press.

Slife, B. D. (2004). Theoretical challenges to therapy, practice and research: The constraint of naturalism. In M. J. Lambert (Ed.), *Bergin and Garfield's handbook of psychotherapy and behavior change* (pp. 44–83). New York: Wiley.

Solzhenitsyn, A. I. (1967). *The Nobel lecture on literature.* New York: Harper & Row.

Spence, D. P. (1982). *Narrative truth and historical truth: Meaning and interpretation in psychoanalysis.* New York: Norton.

Sprang, G., Clark, J. J., & Bass, S. (2005). Predicting the severity of child maltreatment using multidimensional assessment and measurement approaches. *Child Abuse and Neglect: An International Journal, 29,* 335–350.

Sprang, G., Clark, J. J., Kaak, O., & Brenzel, A. (2004). Developing and tailoring mental health technologies for child welfare: The Comprehensive Assessment and Training Services (CATS) project. *American Journal of Orthopsychiatry,* 74 (3), 325–336.

Sprang, G., Tindall, M. S., & Clark, J. J. (2008). Trauma exposure and the drug endangered child. *Journal of Trauma Studies,* 21 (3), 333–339.

Stannard, D. E. (1980). *Shrinking history: On Freud and the failure of psychohistory.* New York: Oxford University Press.

Stolorow, R. D., & Atwood, G. E. (1979). *Faces in a cloud: Subjectivity in personality theory.* New York: Aronson.

Strauss, J. S. (2008). Prognosis in schizophrenia and the role of subjectivity. *Schizophrenia Bulletin,* 34 (2), 201–203.

Taylor, C. (1989). *Sources of the self: The making of the modern identity.* Cambridge, Mass.: Harvard University Press.

Wakefield, J. C. (1995). When an irresistible epistemology meets an immovable ontology. *Social Work Research,* 19 (1), 9–17.

Wakefield, J. C., & Baer, J. (2008). Levels of meaning and the case for theoretical integration. In *Special Issue: Honoring the Scholarship of Sharon B. Berlin. Social Work Now,* 39 (1), 21–28.

Walsh, F. (2003). *Normal family processes: Growing diversity and complexity.* 3d ed. New York: Guilford.

Wasserstein, B. (2007). *Barbarism and civilization: A History of Europe in our time.* New York: Oxford University Press.

Weinstein, F. (1995). Psychohistory and the crisis of the social sciences. *History and Theory,* 34, 299–319.

White, R. W. (1952). *Lives in progress.* New York: Holt, Rinehart and Winston.

White, R. W. (Ed.) (1963). The study of lives: Essays on personality in honor of Henry A. Murray. New York: Atherton.

5 PLACE MATTERS

Toward a Rejuvenated Theory of Environment
for Direct Social Work Practice

SUSAN P. KEMP

NO ONE LIVES IN THE WORLD IN GENERAL.

—CLIFFORD GEERTZ (1996)

WHAT DOES *ENVIRONMENT* mean in direct social work practice? Now more than ever, this is a question that the profession and its scholars must engage. From global warming and related threats of massive environmental change, to the cascading impacts of global capitalism on local neighborhoods and communities, environmental issues are increasingly pressing. The burdens of these environmental challenges fall inequitably on poor communities, on communities of color, and on the countries of the global South—on those communities, in other words, to whom social workers are particularly accountable.

It is tempting to view environmental issues as primarily the concern of policy makers, planners, and community practitioners. Indeed, social workers in direct practice tend to circumvent the environment, save in its most proximal forms, to focus on person-centered, and specifically psychological, theories, practice models, and services. In people's lives, however, "big" environmental changes are experienced not globally but locally, as the impacts of climate change, development, gentrification, disinvestment, displacement, and degradation are felt in homes and neighborhoods (Fullilove, 2004; Mabogunje, 2002). Everyday places sustain or undermine access to resources and opportunities, connections to others, emotional and physical health, spirituality, identities, and memories. A growing body of research evidence links environmental and place-based stressors to poor health and mental health outcomes (see, for example, Belle, 1982; Evans, 2004; Evans & Marcynyszyn, 2004; Fried, 1982, 2000; Macintyre et al., 2002; Makowsky, 1982; Taylor & Repetti, 1997); in turn, environmental resources contribute to improved health and well-being (see, for example, Kuo, 2001; Taylor et al., 1998; Wilson, 2003).

Just as, collectively, the world's citizens can no longer ignore global evidence of environmental damage and depletion, so, too, must we in direct practice engage the deep complicity of environmental factors, for better or worse, in all aspects of human life. Once again, therefore, this chapter addresses the vexing question of the relative neglect of the environment in direct social work practice. Efforts to bring the environment more fully into practice are fraught with difficulties, both conceptual and practical. I therefore propose a focus on place, which in various forms of the everyday and the here and now is woven through most of the issues that bring people and social workers together, as a way out of this dilemma.

In itself, of course, an interest in place is not a new idea: social work's earliest practice, in the settlement houses and charity organization societies, was place-based. Nor am I alone in refocusing on place as an important focus for contemporary social work practice (see, for example, Saleeby, 2004). My goal, however, is not simply to encourage the reintegration of place into practice, but to more closely examine the underlying, predicate question of what "place" is, as the basis for more deeply considering the potential in place as a site where social work can in practice (as well as in theory) bring person and environment together. This attempt to take place "seriously" (Rodman, 2003, p. 218) serves, in turn, as the basis for some preliminary considerations of the possibilities for rejuvenating "place-sensitive" (Gieryn, 2000) social work practice.

THE PERSON-ENVIRONMENT CONUNDRUM

Although social workers claim a distinctive professional jurisdiction framed by a dual commitment to person-in-environment, for the better part of a century, and certainly since the 1920s, this commitment has been honored at best unevenly. The environment has been largely a "side operation" (Perlman, 1972) of the profession's clinical mainstream, creating a potentially disabling split between the profession's espoused purposes and its practice on the ground.

This tilt to the person—the profession's "historical gnat," as Carol Meyer (1989) termed it—is maintained in contemporary practice by complex, interlocking factors: the funding, structure, and delivery of services (billable hours, market-driven services, agency-based rather than community-centered services); theoretical paradigms that cluster around person-changing interventions; the continuing vibrancy of private practice, which closely resembles psychotherapy (and the attractions of which are completely understandable given social work salaries); and the growing centrality of evidence-based practice, with attendant dilemmas around the lack of an evidentiary base for contextual and environmentally oriented interventions.

The practical status of environmental knowledge and practice within the profession further complicates the issue. On one hand, environmental interventions are perceived as largely commonsensical: they suffer, in Mary Richmond's (1922) words, from the "handicap of the familiar" (p. 103). At the same time, social workers have tended to view the social science knowledge that is essential to understanding environmental issues as inherently complex, global, abstract, and inhospitable, and therefore as unlikely to be applicable in practice (Germain, 1979). Given these various challenges, complexities, and misperceptions, it is perhaps not surprising that the profession's evidentiary base, at least as this is conventionally defined, is increasingly well developed in the area of person-centered models and interventions, but notably slight in relation to environment-centered strategies.

Furthermore, many practice formulations conflate environmental factors with individual and collective values, attitudes, and behaviors. Those of us familiar with public child welfare, for example, know well the regularity with which "dirty houses" feature in child neglect assessments. When it comes to case planning, however, this information is more likely to serve as a proxy for inadequacies in parental attitudes and behaviors than as a prompt for meaningful attention to environmental and structural factors. Similarly, assessments of poor neighborhoods as disorganized, dangerous, toxic, or pathological tend to flow down and attach to residents, who by extension are perceived as sharing the negative attributes of their communities. At the same time, many supposedly structural measures of poverty environments are in reality composites of behavioral data (rates of teen pregnancy, for example, or crime, or school dropout), aggregated upward and presented as markers of community conditions (O'Connor, 2002).

Formulations such as these bring us back, once again, to character (and culture) rather than structure, resulting in the foregrounding of person-changing interventions and, concomitantly, in relatively truncated environmental interventions, typically in one of two forms: concrete services directed to the remediation of particular environmental deficits, or services provided within clients' home environments, such as home visitation or intensive family preservation services. Since in either case person-centered interventions constitute the primary focus of intervention, the fundamentally humanistic structure of the profession's organizing assumptions remains undisturbed.

Finding theoretical and practical ways into the person-environment conundrum at the level of direct practice is thus a challenging task. The ecological systems paradigm (Meyer, 1983) provides an essential heuristic for identifying factors at multiple ecological levels, but it is not, as Jerome Wakefield (1996) has pointed out, a domain-specific practice theory (nor, indeed, did Carol Meyer regard it as such). One cannot "do" ecological systems theory. Yet relatively little work has been done to translate emerging knowledge on the mechanisms and effects of person-environment transactions into practice theories and models.

Particularly elusive—and herein lies the thorniest element of the profession's historical dilemma—are theories (and related models and methods) that hold person and environment together, engaging the intimate, dialectical interplay between person and environment without falling back on old, inherently unhelpful binaries.[1] Absent such theories, the tendency will persist in direct practice to put the person in the foreground and—despite its evident power in shaping life opportunities, experiences, and the perspectives not only of clients but of the larger society—to treat the environment as simply a backdrop to the varied drama of human life.

Increasingly, I am interested in place as a site for addressing this dilemma. Place is both intensely relevant in people's lives, and readily available, directly and indirectly, to intervention. In place, furthermore, person and environment interpenetrate, functioning not simply interactively (a conceptual frame that in fact maintains their essential separateness), but rather as mutually constituting entities. People make places; places also make people. A focus on place thus allows us to hold person/environment (or agency/structure) together not only practically, but conceptually.

In the spirit of Sharon Berlin's (1990) incisive and elegantly framed arguments for complexity and nuance in professional knowledge and practice, I draw on a wide range of interdisciplinary scholarship to argue for a more dimensional view of place than that which typically prevails in the social work literature. Viewed thus, place is a complex, dynamic entity, containing within it not only the array of everyday human experience and activity, but also the working out on the ground of larger structures of power and privilege. Produced through the interactions of people with and within (and across) physical settings, place is indisputably linked to human experience, identity, and meaning. Human processes of naming, claiming, living, caring, and destroying create place: in places, through the day and over time, people build lives and identities, and struggle to meet their needs and goals. At the same time, as the site where larger social and political processes take everyday forms, place is itself "an agentic player in the game" (Gieryn, 2000, p. 466).

RE/THINKING PLACE

Place is the local, lived articulation of sense, body, identity, environment, and culture: A person is always in and of place. Place is captured in the intersubjective sharing of experience and social practice. Place in this sense is not opposite to space, but connected to and produced by spatial practices and logics.

—S. E. KELLY (2003, P. 2280)

Place is an inherently slippery idea, challenging to define in large part because it is so familiar (Cresswell, 2004). Indeed, urban historian Dolores Hayden (1995) describes place as "one of the trickiest words in the English language, a suitcase so overfilled one can never shut the lid" (p. 15). In this section I attempt both to embrace and to contain this complexity, with the goal of presenting an understanding of place that is at once multidimensional and accessible, and thus of practical relevance to direct social work practice.

PEOPLE/PLACE RELATIONSHIPS

Although conceptualizing place has become even trickier in a world increasingly connected in cyberspace, most people still think of it in more immediate, material terms. Viewed thus, three defining, mutually interconnected features emerge from the voluminous interdisciplinary literature on the subject (for excellent summaries, see Agnew, 1987; Gieryn, 2000). First, place is "somewhere": a tangible, geographic *location*, albeit one of variable size and flexible boundaries. Location is not place, however, until and unless it involves human interaction. Second, therefore, place is *locale*, a physical and material environment that has some relationship to human endeavor. More than land, trees, buildings, streetscapes, or the physical territory of a neighborhood, place is a "meaningful location" (Cresswell, 2004, p. 7), animated by human occupancy and engagement. Although typically associated with people's direct experience, place is also imaginative, symbolic, and metaphoric (Cresswell, 1997). As people live in places, change them, name them, imagine them, leave and return to them, imbue them with meaning and value, and hold them in memory, they develop, third, a *sense of place*. For humanist geographer Yi-Fu Tuan (1977), sense of place captures the deeply experiential process between person and setting; a personal and collective orientation to place (not always positive) that connects to identity and well-being. *Who* we are relates to *where* we are: "As people fashion places, so, too, do they fashion themselves" (Feld & Basso, 1996, p. 11; see also Proshansky, 1978).

For indigenous peoples, place and self are one; when a Hawaiian educational leader says, "I am shaped by my geography" (Meyer, 2001, p. 128), she is referring to more than simply the surface imprint of place on personhood. Indigenous cosmologies of place deeply interweave place, spirituality, self (in its collective sense), symbolism, and identity. For Aboriginal Australians, identity is rooted in the "dreamtime"—physical landscapes layered with ancestral meanings and stories. For New Zealand Maori, the point of reference for genealogy and thus identity is the tribal place of one's ancestors. Capturing this same interpenetration of self and place in Native American cosmologies, Keith Basso (1996) titled his beautiful ethnography of the Western Apache, *Wisdom Sits in Places*. In indigenous cultures, to care for place is to nurture the collective self; living in balance and harmony with the earth is the foundation of spiritual, physical, emotional, and mental well-being (Salmon, 2000; Wilson, 2003; Zapf, 2005). This connection with the land is spiritual, symbolic, and physical; "I'm not in the place but the place is in me" (Suopjarvi, cited in Zapf, 2005, p. 637).

Although a deep awareness of people/place interrelationships is common to many non-Western cultures, Western philosophical paradigms tend to separate place and self, relegating place to the physical world and defining self as consciousness. Nevertheless, an increasingly influential body of work in cultural anthropology, cultural geography, and environmental psychology, much of it informed by phenomenology (see, for example, Heidegger, 1962; Husserl, 1973; Merleau-Ponty, 1962; Casey, 1997, 2001), points to the centrality of place in all human experience. For phenomenologists, "there is *no self without place, and no place without self*" (Casey, 2001, p. 684 [emphasis in original]). In this view, people/place relationships are not just reciprocal (as, for example, in ecological models), but mutually constitutive.

From a phenomenological perspective, place is the "most fundamental form of bodily experience" (Feld & Basso, 1996, p. 9), a visceral sensibility that is preconscious and nonmentalistic, unmediated by thought or reason (Casey, 1997). We know place sensuously, through sight, smell, sound, touch, and taste: "the cues from place dive under conscious thought and awaken our sinews and bones, where days of our lives have been recorded" (Fullilove, 2004, p. 10). The body goes out into and experiences place; in turn, place experiences "take up residence" (Casey, 2001, p. 688) in the body, becoming part of the deep structure of meaning and identity. Impressions of place lie dormant in the body, "ready to be revived when the appropriate impressions or sensation arises" (Casey, 2001, p. 688). When we are away from beloved places, a familiar smell or sound can suddenly take us there. Returning, our bodies greet the familiar; we respond to the particularity of light, the shape of hills or buildings, the feel of land or pavement beneath our feet. Place, in this sense, is primordial, a fundamental ontological building block of human subjectivity and well-being (Tuan, 1977; Casey, 1996).

As places get under our skins, they become repositories of individual and collective meaning (Altman & Low, 1992; Hidalgo & Hernández, 2001). Whether place meanings accrue gradually, over long experience, or suddenly, through an intense or defining encounter, whether experiences in place are positive, negative, or mixed (Manzo, 2005), they leave people "forever marked." People inevitably revise and rework their place attachments in new settings, but prior attachments nonetheless interact, often in complex ways, with present experiences and functioning. For the respondents in Carol Stack's (1996) ethnographic study of the reverse migration of African Americans to their childhood homeplaces in the rural South—places that in retrospect were both a "hard fact" and a "lost sanctuary" (p. 18)—the "call to home" was nonetheless irresistible.

Counter-intuitively, "displacement is no less the source of powerful attachments than are experiences of profound rootedness" (Feld & Basso, 1996, p. 11). In contemporary life, as historically, displacement comes in many forms, from the transnational flows of immigrants and refugees to the smaller but equally profound changes experienced by children who live in multiple foster homes, or families relocated from public housing projects, or residents pushed out of historically ethnic enclaves by development, gentrification, and unaffordable housing. Indeed, people on the move are typical of the "growing rupture of people and places" in contemporary society (Feldman, 1990, p. 184). In terms of impacts and outcomes, it matters a great deal whether or not the move is voluntary and/or planful. As Mindy Fullilove (2004) concluded from her research on the displacement of hundreds of inner-city African American communities by urban renewal projects, separation from place is "an operation that is best done with care" (p. 11).

When people are forced to move, the loss of beloved and familiar places can have devastating consequences (Fried, 1963; Fullilove, 1996). In early research on migrant children, for example, Robert Coles (1967) concluded that constant changes of place function in these children's lives as a "chronic disaster," disrupting healthy development and psychosocial functioning. The "root shock" (Fullilove, 2004) of involuntary displacement causes grief and trauma, not just through the loss of social ties but also through the "traumatic separation of the self from a community landscape of meaning" (Hummon, 1992, p. 260). At the personal level, displacement "undermines trust, increases anxiety about letting loved ones out of one's sight, destabilizes relationships, destroys social, emotional, and financial resources, and increases the risk for every kind of stress-related disease, from depression to heart attack (Fullilove, 2004, p. 14). At the community level, displacement ruptures emotional and physical ecosystems, fracturing "the elegance of the neighborhood" (Fullilove, 2004, p. 14).

In contemporary life, as in the past, displacement often occurs in the name of progress, its problematic human implications veiled by the improvements that apparently come with urban redevelopment, gentrification, or public works such as highways and urban rail systems. Yet, as we know from the generational experiences of Holocaust survivors, African Americans (Johnson, 1998), diasporic immigrant communities (Uehara et al., 2001), or Native Americans (Evans-Campbell, 2008), the implications of traumatic displacement ripple across the life course and into future generations. In these communities, the historical trauma of displacement, genocide, and place-based oppression reverberates into the present, influencing personal and collective experience and well-being in contemporary places.

Grasping the complex porosity of person and place—the "fateful complicity of body and place," as Casey (1997, p. 242) termed it—is essential to a more detailed understanding of the meaning and salience of place in human life. Yet the humanist perspectives presented thus far are not in themselves sufficient for the reinvigorated understanding of place I have in mind. As anthropologist Margaret Rodman (2003) cautioned her own discipline, "Places are not inert containers. They are politicized, culturally relative, historically specific, local, and multiple constructions" (p. 205). Social workers likewise need to think in complex ways about the deep interconnections between "the way that experience is lived and acted out in place and how this relates to, and is embedded in, political and economic practices that are operative over broader spatial scales" (Merrifield, 1993, p. 517). To do so, we must add at least two further dimensions to our conceptualization of place: first, an understanding of place as dynamic, multiscalar, and relational; and second, a critical understanding of place as socially constructed, and thus a site of power. Rather than separating lives lived in places from the larger spatial and sociopolitical structures that produce those settings (the impact of global political and economic patterns on urban planning or local housing markets, for example), we must instead understand that in everyday lives, space and place "melt into each other" (Merrifield, 1993, p. 520).

"STRETCHING" PLACE: STRUCTURE AND POWER

Place is local, but it is not only so. Within place, lives are linked dynamically to other lives in other places; place is itself linked outward to places and spaces beyond itself (think about the globally produced array of goods in your local supermarket). The local is global, the global local. Recent theoretical and empirical work seeks to more accurately capture this dynamic fluidity and multidimensionality. From these perspectives, place is a process, unfolding dynamically over time through changes within and beyond itself. The development of suburbs, for example, had profoundly negative implications for many urban communities (for example, Pulido et al., 1996); now that these communities are once again gentrifying, pulling in the affluent and pushing out low-income families, these processes are in turn affecting the suburbs (Leinberger, 2008). As geographer Doreen Massey (1994) points out, place is not simply "here" but is "progressive," existing at multiple, simultaneous, and overlapping scales. This "stretchy" view of place—a "sense of place which is extroverted, which includes a consciousness of its links to a wider world" (Massey, 1994, p. 155)—helps us to understand places not as bounded but as nodes in networks of other places and spatial entities (Cummins et al., 2007).

Viewing place relationally shifts our often flat, static understandings of local environments to a more nuanced view of place as always on the move. People flow in and out, the physical and built environment changes constantly, the tides of the global economy relentlessly shape local job markets, local resources, and local cultures. When we understand place as dynamic and fluid, rather than fixed, we can better see both the multidimensionality of place (Rodman, 2003) and the multiplicity of people's experiences of and relationships to any one particular place. Just as there is no singular "place," neither is there a single sense of place (Massey, 1994). Indeed people's experiences in place vary widely, and on multiple dimensions (Popay, Thomas et al., 2003; Popay, Williams et al., 2003).

Place is also and always a site of power. In place, broader social systems come to ground and are manifested in everyday life. Far from being just a neutral setting for human experience, place is itself a "social relation that is involved in the production and reproduction of social structures, social action, and relations of power and resistance" (Gotham, 2003, p. 724). Tim

Cresswell (2004) describes place as "space invested with meaning in the context of power" (p. 12). Dolores Hayden (1995) notes that "[place] carries the resonance of homestead, location, and open space . . . as well as a position in a social hierarchy" (p. 15). Processes of inclusion and exclusion, privilege and inequality, dominance and oppression, subjugation and collective action take place not in but *through* place (Gieryn, 2000; Sibley, 1995). Place-based processes contribute, for example, to the social marginality of persons with disabilities (Dear et al., 1997), those with chronic mental illness (Parr, 2000), or people without housing. These include representations of people as "in place or out of place" (Cresswell, 1996, 1997); the physical structuring of the built environment, such that some people are denied full access to "public" spaces (Davis, 1999); and a web of social policies and practices, from urban planning to community policing, that define and maintain patterns of spatial demarcation and segregation.

By no means neutral, places are "landscapes of power" (Zukin, 1991) that produce and reinforce larger patterns of privilege and oppression: a "living archaeology through which we can extract the priorities and beliefs of the decision-makers in our society" (Weisman, 2000, p. 1). Dangerous and physically segregated public housing projects perpetuate and compound the social difficulties of poor families. Conversely, privileged residential neighborhoods, created and sustained at the expense of less advantaged communities (Pulido et al., 1996), are rich in resources and opportunities. One community's ability to resist the siting of a waste transfer station or to effectively protest the routing of air traffic over its residential neighborhoods, for example, is directly and reciprocally related to the likelihood that another, less powerful community will have to accommodate these environmental burdens. Increasingly, these patterns of privilege and disadvantage include the "secession of the successful" (Reich, 1991) to gated enclaves, socially and spatially separated from the wider society, replacing diversity and interdependence with homogeneity and isolation, and further cementing race and class divisions. As Setha Low (2003) points out, "adding gates, walls, and guards produces a landscape that encodes class relations and residential (race/class/gender) segregation more permanently in the built environment" (p. 387).

Viewed through the lens of power, place identity becomes more complex, affirming and nourishing but potentially also oppressive. Place is deeply implicated in the construction and maintenance of social identities based in race, class, ethnicity, gender, sexuality, age, or ability (Kobayashi & Peake, 2000). Spatial practices, such as urban planning and architecture, create places in conformity with dominant (typically Eurocentric) cultural and aesthetic ideals; places (and the people who live in them) that diverge from these ideals are constructed as different (Duncan & Duncan, 2001). Stereotypical representations of places by outside groups, such as the pervasive and pathologizing trope of the "black ghetto" (Gregory, 1998), differentiate and classify both places and people, reproducing in the process larger social patterns of inclusion and exclusion.

The intersection of place and racialization is particularly complex (Kobayashi & Peake, 2000). Delaney (1998) asserts that "'race' is *what it is and what it does* precisely because of *how* it is given spatial expression" (p. 18). This claim takes tangible form in the place histories of racial and ethnic minorities, which have been fundamentally shaped by historical processes of segregation, exclusion, and marginality (McKittrick & Woods, 2007). Institutional structures, policies, and norms create and maintain place-based differentials in opportunities, resources, and risks (for example, Pulido et al., 1996). Stigmatized assumptions link communities of color and the locales they inhabit. Racist behaviors actively produce and maintain spatial segregation (Sugrue, 1996). And, accordingly, individuals and groups internalize stereotypes that conflate negative ideas about places and ideas about people.

In a study of youths' work identities in two Latino neighborhoods in San Antonio, Texas, for example, Bauder (2001) found a troubling convergence between external perceptions of these neighborhoods, the internal representations of local youth, and the approaches of local youth-serving institutions. The first neighborhood, the site of a large public housing project, was highly stigmatized. As one resident said, "When people say 'west side' they automatically think you're poor, you belong to gangs and you're on welfare" (Bauder, 2001, p. 473). These place-based stereotypes were internalized by local youth and reinforced by community institutions, which channeled youth into less desirable, second-tier jobs. The second neighborhood, home to a more acculturated community and with no public housing, was viewed externally as "poor but honest." Youth in this community had more mainstream employment expectations, and community organizations routinely connected young people to adults and resources beyond the neighborhood.

This study brings home the complex role of place in the social reproduction of inequality. In one neighborhood, the stigma of poverty and public housing is reproduced and reinforced in social practices that deflect Latino youth from mainstream opportunities; in the other community, equally poor but less stigmatized, a more positive place identity is reflected in optimistic, pro-active approaches to youth development.

From a very different perspective, Kay Anderson's (1991) compelling historical study of "Chinatown" in Vancouver, Canada, shows how the historical association of Chinatown with vice, danger, dirt, and immorality not only justified exclusionary practices toward Chinese people and property but supported and intensified the assumed cultural superiority of white residents (by defining "us" in contrast to "them"). In Anderson's analysis, Chinatown is as much a Eurocentric construction as it is an ethnic enclave that expresses Chinese cultural norms and aspirations.

Place-based inequities are real, and growing: acknowledging and responding to these inequities is essential. Yet we must be very careful to ensure that in the process we do not unwittingly replicate dominant and pathologizing stereotypes, which render invisible the reality that "marginalized places" are "networks and relations of power, resistance, histories, and the everyday, rather than locations that are simply subjugated, perpetually ghettoized, and ungeographic" (McKittrick & Woods, 2007, p. 7).

Structural inequities come to ground in place, but in place they are also made vulnerable to refusal and resistance. Social workers, who by definition stand at the interface of people, their everyday environments, and larger social institutions, have both the opportunity and the responsibility to make visible "different geographic stories" (McKittrick, 2007, p. x). Doing so challenges reductionist, stereotypical views of marginalized communities and opens up new possibilities for place-based agency and intervention.

THE DIALECTICS OF PLACE

To summarize: conceptualizing place for contemporary social work practice necessarily involves a series of both/and moves. In this dialectical view, place is:

- Both material, visceral, meaningful experience *and* socially and historically constructed
- Both local *and* global (a progressive sense of place)
- Here and now, but also fluid, dynamic, and in process
- A site of shared but also widely diverse experience
- A site of power inequities *and* also a site of agency and resistance

TOWARD A PRAXIS OF PLACE

Given all this, what does it mean to "take place seriously" (Casey, 1997) in direct practice? Two interconnected, perhaps self-evident, practice implications flow from a dialectical approach to place: first, a call for deeper engagement with the experiential and material dimensions of place in clients' lives; and second, support for renewed investment in place making, by which I mean practices that transform both places and people.

I am interested in place-based interventions that are more deeply responsive to the meaning and reality of place in people's lives; that incorporate a critical perspective on the shaping of local places by larger economic, political, and social factors; and that support and facilitate people's everyday agency and well-being in place. I therefore emphasize the following: a dual focus on structural and personal factors; practice grounded in local knowledge but attentive also to larger spatial issues; and participatory, dialogic approaches to place-based knowledge and change. The writings of Paolo Freire (1970, 1973) provide an essential foundation for this approach, as does recent work on critical pedagogies of place (Brandt, 2004; Gruenewald, 2003).

In the following section, I look briefly at some strategies for eliciting place-based knowledge in direct practice, ideally in the context of participatory, empowering interventions. Used collaboratively, these strategies are not just preparatory to place-based interventions (in the way that conventional assessments tend to precede intervention). Rather, the process of gathering and interpreting sociospatial data itself builds capacities and skills (Nicotera, 2007). As Gotham (2003) learned in his research with public housing residents: "the ways in which the urban poor understand their own relationship to space *make a difference* to their actions and identities" (p. 732; original emphasis).

KNOWING PLACE

DEVELOPING AN ETHNOGRAPHIC IMAGINATION

We must try to understand place mindfully.

—M. T. FULLILOVE (2004, P. 235)

Place-sensitive practice begins with social workers learning more about the places at the center of their clients' everyday lives. More detailed place knowledge in turn shapes practice. When rotting garbage piled up in their urban neighborhood, Jane Addams and the women of Hull House not only documented the problem but did something about it, from "a systematic investigation of the city system of garbage collection" (Addams, 1910, p. 202) to getting themselves appointed as garbage inspectors. Hull House's famous maps, with their fine-grained view of the impacts of race and class on neighborhood structure, likewise provided new perspectives on issues the settlement women saw at first hand every day (Residents of Hull House, 1895).

The early caseworkers were equally knowledgeable about the homes and neighborhoods of poor families. In contemporary direct practice, however, social workers are much less likely to spend time in the places where their clients live, work, raise their families, celebrate community, or struggle to build a new life after displacement from somewhere else. Nonetheless, most agencies serve clients drawn from relatively well-defined geographic areas. Even if social work services are primarily office-based, deep curiosity about the implications of neighborhood environments in clients' lives is essential to fully contextualized practice, and thus to professional competence.

The best way to learn about place is to engage it firsthand. Where possible, social workers should spend informal time in the neighborhoods and communities in which their clients live, walking, observing, and absorbing the texture of daily life in place. What is the built environment like? Is there open space? What is the mix of people? How do they make use of the neighborhood? How safe is it? Do people keep to their homes or are they out in the community? What kinds of resources are available, and for whom? What is the cultural environment? Are there green spaces and parks? How adequate and accessible is public transportation? What about shops and other services?

Beyond these observations, social workers must also learn about neighborhoods from the people who live there. Without these perspectives, we risk making assessments that reflect (and reproduce) dominant stereotypes. What do neighborhood leaders and cultural guides have to say about their neighborhood? How do other residents describe the neighborhood? What is its history? How has it changed? What has this meant for the people who live there? What are the good things about the community? What is difficult for people living here?

SPATIAL DATA

Aggregate spatial data, available at scales from local to national, add important dimensions to ethnographic impressions gathered on the ground. These data help us to see the larger patterns of risk and opportunity that shape clients' lives in place, often in profound ways. To take just one example, a partial list of place-based environmental factors linked, for better or worse, to children's developmental outcomes (Evans, 2004) includes the following: physical hazards; environmental pollutants and toxins; access to open space;

adequacy of municipal services, such as schools, libraries, health services, and transportation; access to retail and other services, including access to healthy food; housing quality; and availability of developmental resources, such as playgrounds, libraries, and computers. Structural factors such as these profoundly shape child and family experiences and outcomes, and should thus routinely be factored into social work decision-making processes.

GEOGRAPHIC INFORMATION SYSTEMS

Geographic information systems (GIS) allow professionals and communities to understand person/place relationships in different ways. Geographer Mei-Po Kwan (Kwan, 2002; Kwan & Lee, 2003), for example, used GIS to illuminate the daily travel patterns of African American and Asian women in Portland, Oregon. The three-dimensional space/time "aquariums" generated by Kwan's study graphically reveal the differential "life-ways" of these groups of women, opening new perspectives on women's experiences in and across places. Incorporated into practice, graphical displays such as these could be used as the basis for critically reflective dialogue on the lives of women from different ethnic and racial groups in place.

Combined with ethnographic, visual, and narrative methods to create multidimensional understandings of people's place experiences, GIS data become even more relevant for social work practice. In a recent interdisciplinary collaboration, for example, Matthews and his colleagues (2005) integrated GIS and ethnographic methods to create layered pictures of the experiences of low-income women and children in the context of welfare reform, and of families of children with disabilities.

In social work settings, GIS is being used primarily for administrative and planning purposes. In Washington state, for example, child welfare administrators use GIS plots of the spatial distribution of foster placements to identify promising locations for foster parent recruitment (Stone, 2008): "When people see these maps ... they want to know what they can do" (p. 1). In California, researchers collect GIS data on the spatial distribution of foster placements in relation to children's home neighborhoods, showing patterns of dispersion and displacement, and enabling administrators and policy makers to evaluate efforts to strengthen neighborhood-based foster care (Stone, 2008).

Experiences in other fields, such as participatory urban planning, suggest that clients and workers may find it equally helpful to "see the map." Many social work clients have lives that are spatially complex; not infrequently, as figure 5.1 suggests, these become even more complicated with social services

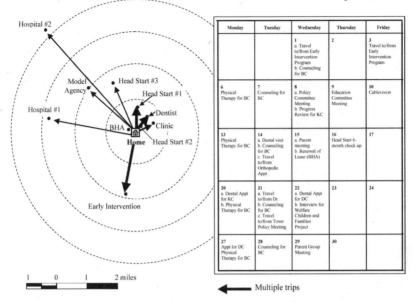

Calendar of events - one sample month

Monday	Tuesday	Wednesday	Thursday	Friday
		1 a. Travel to/from Early Intervention Program b. Counseling for BC	**2**	**3** Travel to/from Early Intervention Program
6 Physical Therapy for BC	**7** Counseling for BC	**8** a. Policy Committee Meeting b. Progress Review for KC	**9** Education Committee Meeting	**10** Cablevision
13 Physical Therapy for BC	**14** a. Dental visit b. Counseling for BC c. Travel to/from Orthopedic Appt.	**15** a. Parent meeting b. Renewal of Lease (BHA)	**16** Head Start 6-month check up	**17**
20 a. Dental Appt for KC b. Physical Therapy for BC	**21** a. Travel to/from Dr. b. Counseling for BC c. Travel to/from Town Policy Meeting	**22** a. Dental Appt for DC b. Interview for Welfare Children and Families Project	**23**	**24**
27 Appt for DC Physical Therapy for BC	**28** Counseling for BC	**29** Parent Group Meeting	**30**	

Hospital #2

Model Agency
Head Start #3
Head Start #1
Hospital #1
Dentist
BHA
Clinic
Home Head Start #2

Early Intervention

1   0   1   2 miles

◄─── Multiple trips

FIGURE 5.1 A map and calendar representation of trips made and meetings attended during one month by a primary caregiver in a disability family.

SOURCE: MATTHEWS, DETWILER, & BURTON (2005)

involvement. Making these spatial realities visible is essential to resisting the centrifugal force of person-centered explanatory frameworks and building multidimensional understandings of clients' daily lives.

The mother of a child in foster care, for example, faces an array of geographic challenges linked to her involvement with child welfare services. Her child is in one setting; the child welfare office where weekly visitation typically occurs is in another; she likely is mandated to undertake services such as substance abuse treatment and parenting classes in yet other settings; she is either working or involved with job-related services; and not infrequently, she is unstably housed. And, by the way, she rides the bus, or rather multiple buses, since there's no direct route to her current neighborhood. What might be gained from a more deliberately spatial analysis of her everyday experience?

The GIS data illuminating larger spatial patterns in child welfare services could also be used by social workers—for example, as reflective tools in collaborative decision-making processes. In direct social work practice, evaluative processes necessarily involve some calibration of the particular against the general (that is, we interpret the experiences of "this" client system by placing them in the context of what we know about such clients in general). Clients' spatial experiences can likewise be contextualized by reference to larger spatial patterns. Consider the implications in case planning of the following questions. What, in general, is the spatial pattern of child and family experiences in this foster care system? What does *this* family's spatial map look like? Looking across these two levels of data, what should be prioritized in this family's case planning? What tradeoffs might have to be made to reach these goals (to balance placement near birth parents against placement with extended family, for example, or to reduce time spent accessing services)? And, more pointedly, if place matters, how will that commitment be reflected in the decisions being made?

LEARNING FROM CLIENTS

Local Knowledge   Place comes to life in people's everyday experiences. To fully understand the meaning of place for individuals and groups, social workers need to access the situated, place-based, and culturally specific knowledge that people acquire in the course of their daily lives. This knowledge has multiple dimensions, including factual knowledge, practical knowledge derived from navigating life in place, experiential knowledge, and the holistic orientation one gets from immersion in a particular context (Antweiler, 1998). It is not, however, uniformly shared. Furthermore, it is "comprehensive, systematic, methodical, but not very conscious, verbalised, [or] susceptible to verbalisation" (Antweiler, 1998, p. 16). Local knowledge is therefore best accessed through multiple methods, including listening and talking to people, observation, documentation (mapping, photography, video, film), and participatory processes, such as guided community walks.

Since everyday knowledge forms the basis for local capacity and competence (Antweiler, 1998), surfacing, validating, and responding to it is an essential element of contextual and empowering practice. As Brandt (2004) notes, "the systematic study of local knowledge provides spaces of resistance and hope" (p. 97). At the same time, situated knowledge has its own limitations. Antweiler (1998) cautions that local knowledge is not necessarily either democratic or critical, that solutions based on it are not by definition socially just, and that it is not always shared by most or even all members of a group. Therefore, as with our understandings of place itself, practice should both respect local understandings *and* attempt to broaden people's perspectives through opportunities for critical dialogue and access to other sources of spatial information.

Place Narratives   Humans use narratives and stories to make sense of, internalize, reorder, and act on their place-based experience. Indeed, vernacular, lay, and indigenous place knowledge is typically presented in story form (Popay, Thomas et al., 2003; Popay, Williams et al., 2003). Place narratives allow for deeper engagement with clients' spatial experience, particularly in practice settings where social workers have little or no physical access to clients' neighborhoods and communities. Inviting and engaging with clients' place narratives not only validates people's place experiences (Burton et al., 2004; Saari, 2002), but also provides the opportunity for "moral proximity," a different kind of knowing about what place means in clients' lives. As people share the geographies of their everyday lives, some of the inevitable distance (social and spatial) between clients and workers is bridged. Methods for eliciting place narratives can be written or oral, including storytelling, diary writing, interviews, and narrative writing.

Visual Methods   Visual methods, such as photography, video, film, mapping, sketches, and art are increasingly popular as mechanisms for accessing and reflecting on local experiences in and perspectives on place. As the citizen-generated maps of three ethnically and economically differentiated Los Angeles communities make clear (Figures 2, 3, and 4), visual forms open up powerful perspectives on people's experiences in place, both positive and negative. The images generated by residents of higher income Westwood show a much greater spatial range and sense of the city as a whole than those from lower income Avalon-Carter and Boyle Heights—vividly highlighting the interactions among income, social and physical mobility, and access to the city and its resources.

Many visual methods translate quite readily into practice. Clients can photograph the important places in their lives, make maps and drawings such as those in Figures 2, 3, and 4, or collaborate with workers to construct visual time/space diaries, as in Figure 1. What, for example, does a day in the life of a child welfare client look like, if she juggles child care, work, public transportation, mandated services, and a child or children in foster care? Where does she go over the day? How does she get there? How much time does it take? Where are the key places in her life?

Simple tools such as these give visual expression to people's experiences in place, bringing these realities to life for clients and workers. Visual media also provide a tangible medium for critical conversations about local issues

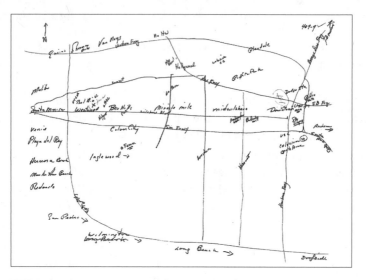

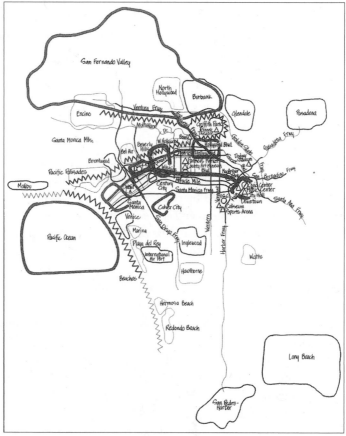

FIGURE 5.2 *Top:* Actual Citizen's Map—Westwood; *bottom:* Composite Citizen Image—Westwood

SOURCE: DEPARTMENT OF CITY PLANNING, LOS ANGELES, CALIF. (N.D.)

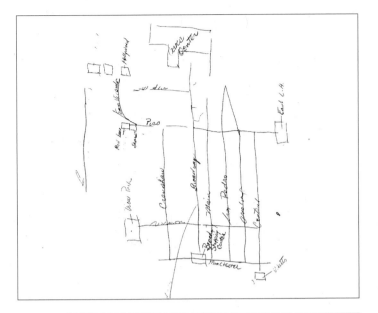

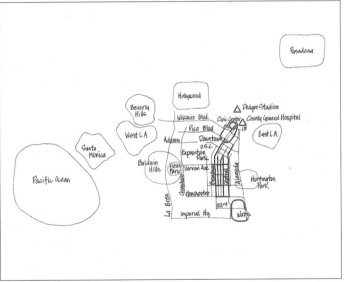

FIGURE 5.3 *Top:* Actual Citizen's Map—Avalon; *bottom:* Composite Citizen Image—Avalon

SOURCE: DEPARTMENT OF CITY PLANNING, LOS ANGELES, CALIF. (N.D.)

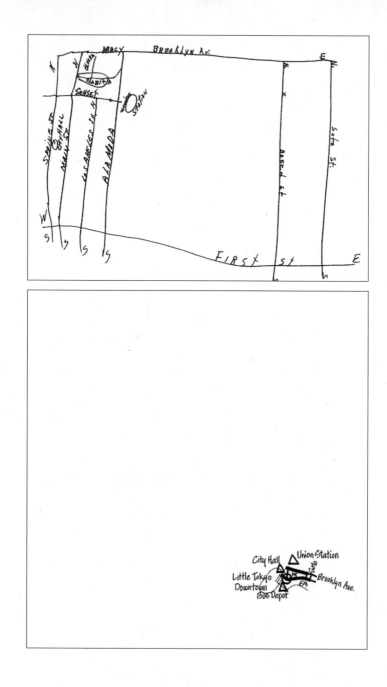

FIGURE 5.4 *Top:* Actual Citizen's Map—Boyle Heights; *bottom:* Composite Citizen Image—Boyle Heights

SOURCE: DEPARTMENT OF CITY PLANNING, LOS ANGELES, CALIF. (N.D.)

and conditions, setting the stage for deeper exploration of the ways in which individual and collective experiences in place are shaped by larger social, political, and economic forces. As people collectively share their visual perspectives, finding differences as well as commonalities in their views on the places they share (Castleden et al., 2008), the "multivocality" (Rodman, 2003) of people in place can begin to emerge.

AN INTEGRATIVE CASE EXAMPLE: YOUTH AS PLACEMAKERS

Increasingly, collaborative community planning efforts and community-based participatory research projects use a range of spatial methods to engage local residents in place-based evaluation, planning, and change. Dennis (2006) documents a project designed to involve youth from a local after-school youth program in a community planning process. With facilitation by university students in urban planning and design, young people used photography, narratives, drawing, and community visioning to assess their neighborhood. The project involved several phases:

1. An initial workshop was held, during which youth produced collages of their "ideal" neighborhood, discussed them, and from the discussion generated a list of youth concerns and ideals.

2. For two weeks youth maintained journals, recording their perceptions and appraisals of the neighborhood, positive and negative, using text and drawings.

3. A second workshop was held, during which youth discussed their journals and produced a master list of youth concerns.

4. Photography "homework" was assigned, in which youth documented the places they like in the neighborhood, and the places they want to change.

5. A third workshop was held, during which youth worked in groups to discuss their photos, focusing on preferred and problematic neighborhood spaces.

6. A final workshop concluded the project, in which youth worked with the design students to plan the transformation of vacant lots into green space for the after-school program. As part of this process, the students' maps and qualitative data were linked to quantitative data, providing a larger picture of patterns of use and movement through the neighborhood and linking neighborhood conditions to larger social and economic issues.

This project, which was located in a typical social service agency, positioned urban youth as knowledgeable, capable participants in community change efforts, deliberately shifting the focus of intervention from youth as service recipients to youth as active place makers. As young people contributed positively to their neighborhood, they in turn gained important developmental benefits from participating in community change efforts.

PLACE MAKING

Placemaking is the ongoing work of transforming the places we find ourselves into places in which we can truly dwell as individuals and communities of people. The practice of making our places changes and maintains the physical world and our ideas about it while it also creates communities of people who share concerns, interests, hopes, desires, and fears.

—SCHNEEKLOTH & SHIBLEY, 2005

Place making, a concept borrowed from architecture, anthropology, and urban planning (Schneekloth & Shibley, 1995, 2005), brings to life the possibilities in a rejuvenated role for place in social work practice. Through collaborative engagement in "the ongoing work of transforming the places we find ourselves to places we can truly dwell," place becomes an active, bidirectional vehicle for change: as people change their places, they also change themselves. Examples of place making include collaborative community-building projects, urban farms and gardens, community-ownership buildings (Leavitt & Saegert, 1990), tenant activism, farmers' markets, and many forms of youth activism in place (Sutton et al, 2006). Place, in this sense, "provides the conditions of possibility for creative social practice" (Cresswell, 2004, p. 39).

As intentional practice, place making rests on three major assumptions (Schneekloth & Shibley, 2005). First, it assumes that people care deeply about place: "The foundational belief of placemaking is that people desire to live in *beloved places*. People care about their places; they want places they can love, places that are healthy for working, building community, and raising families" (Schneekloth & Sibley, 1995, p. 5; see also Burton et al., 2004). This perspective goes against the grain of notions that in contemporary life people are increasingly alienated or disconnected from place. It also challenges the pernicious but enduring assumption—embedded, for example, within culture of poverty analyses—that marginalized people somehow lack the resources and moral energy to invest in the places where they live (Feldman & Stall, 1994). By asserting people's commitment to place even in the face of adversity, place making refocuses attention on spatial agency—the deeply intentional, often difficult, frequently struggled over, yet essentially human process of creating place in the world, at scales ranging from the home and neighborhood to the transnational community.

Second, a focus on place making assumes both that people will work on making their places and that they are competent to do so. Consistent with social work's philosophical belief in the strengths that inhere in people and communities, place making focuses not only on people's willingness but also on their capacity to invest in everyday, constructive action within place. Anthropologist Devon Peña (2006) documents, for example, the richly varied place making of transnational diasporic Latino/a and Chicano/a communities in the "interstitial spaces" of cities like Los Angeles and San Antonio (p. 5). These communities remake existing urban patterns into culturally relevant forms: dense urban environments that afford opportunities for celebration and conviviality, for urban gardens, for extended family life, for engagement with water and with nature, and for culturally appropriate blurring and overlap of common and private spaces.

Third, the relevant unit of analysis in place making is people-in-place—not just people, or just place: "This is a practice concerned with relationships—of people to place and to each other" (Schneekloth & Shibley, 2005). A focus on place making thus extends social work's core interest in interpersonal relationships to encompass and engage people's place attachments.

Place making is important in all human experience. However, it is particularly vital for populations and communities that have experienced displacement and marginality. In these communities, place making provides a means to contest stigma, develop coping strategies, establish and strengthen social ties with others, build social networks, and resist social and spatial demarcations. For African Americans, homeplace is a site of comfort, connection, and solidarity: "a safe place where black people could affirm one another and by so doing heal many of the wounds inflicted by racist domination" (hooks, 1990, p. 42; see also Burton et al., 2004; Feldman & Stall, 1994). At the same time, as hooks (1990) makes clear, homeplace is a "site of resistance and liberation struggle" (p. 45). As Feldman and Stall (1994) demonstrate in their ethnographic study of the place-making activities of low-income women in Chicago public housing, the women's struggle to establish a preschool program, to open a laundromat, and to resist the encroachment of a baseball stadium both protected and nurtured their beloved (though problematic) place, and empowered them as women and as citizens.

The resilient, culturally grounded place-making practices of marginalized communities also have the potential to serve as models for transformative change in society at large. The emphasis in place making on mutuality, interdependence, and communal responsibility disrupts and calls into question dominant practices in place, providing the opportunity to "see place as the location of cooperation, stewardship, and social justice, rather than just sites to be dominated, enclosed, commodified, exploited, and segregated" (McKittrick & Woods, 2007, p. 6).

Most place-making projects emerge organically from felt community needs. Peña (2006) notes that the place-making practices he documents are bottom-up (not top-down) and place-based (not externally driven): "In this manner people exert agency to reinvent themselves by remaking places, though surely never under circumstances of their choosing" (p. 12). Place making honors and is grounded in local leadership and involvement. Yet many place-making projects necessarily involve strategic partnerships with allied professionals, typically from the design professions and spatial disciplines (Schneekloth & Shibley, 1995). Social workers can likewise focus more intentionally on place, both validating and amplifying the importance of homeplace and place making in people's lives (Burton et al., 2004), and lending skills and resources to local, community-based efforts.

PLACE MATTERS

This chapter makes the case for renewed attention to place in direct social work practice, informed by more robust conceptual frameworks than those typically available in the social work literature. The dialectical approach to place presented here allows for contextually "thick" understandings of person/environment relationships: multidimensional, multilevel, rich in awareness of the specificities and heterogeneities inherent in person/place relationships, close to human experience in its most visceral sense, but also providing access to the role of social, structural, and material factors in everyday contexts. Indeed, to borrow language from geographer David Seamon (1987), a dialectical view of place captures the "psycho-social-environmental whole" that social workers have long claimed as an organizing focus.

Although in this chapter I have emphasized theory, and given only limited attention to the methodological and interventive work on place currently proliferating across multiple disciplines, systematic attention to building strong methodological, empirical, and evidentiary foundations for

Casey, E. S. (1996). How to get from space to place in a fairly short stretch of time: Phenomenological prolegomena. In S. Feld & K. H. Basso (Eds.), *Senses of Place* (pp. 13–52). Santa Fe, N.M.. School of American Research.

Casey, E. S. (1997). *The fate of place: A philosophical history.* Berkeley: University of California Press.

Casey, E. S. (2001). Between geography and philosophy: What does it mean to be in the place-world? *Annals of the Association of American Geographers, 91* (4), 683–693.

Castleden, H., Garvin, T., & First Nation, H. (2008). Modifying Photovoice for community-based participatory indigenous research. *Social Science and Medicine, 66,* 1393–1405.

Coles, R. (1967). *Migrants, sharecroppers, and mountaineers.* Boston: Little, Brown.

Cresswell, T. (1996). *In place/out of place: Geography, ideology, and transgression.* London: UCI Press.

Cresswell, T. (1997). Weeds, plagues, and bodily secretions: A geographical interpretation of metaphors of displacement. *Annals of the Association of American Geographers, 87* (2), 330–345.

Cresswell, T. (2004). *Place: A short introduction.* Malden, Mass.: Blackwell.

Cummins, S., Curtis, S., Diez-Roux, A., & Macintyre, S. (2007). Understanding and representing "place" in health research: A relational approach. *Social Science and Medicine, 65* (9), 1825–1838.

Cummins, S., Macintyre, S., Davidson, S., & Ellaway, A. (2005). Measuring neighbourhood social and material context: Generation and interpretation of ecological data from routine and non-routine sources. *Health and Place, 11* (3), 249–260.

Davis, M. (1999). *Suburbs of fear.* New York: Vintage Books.

Dear, M., Wilton, R., Gaber, S. L., & Takahashi, L. (1997). Seeing people differently: The sociospatial construction of disability. *Environment and Planning D: Society and Space, 15* (4), 455–480.

Delaney, D. (2002). The space that race makes. *The Professional Geographer, 54* (1), 6–14.

Dennis, S. F. (2006). Prospects for qualitative GIS at the intersection of youth development and participatory urban planning. *Environment and Planning A, 38* (11), 2039–2054.

Department of City Planning, Los Angeles, Calif. (n.d.). *The visual environment of Los Angeles.* LACA (Los Angeles City Archives), Box C-065.

Duncan, J. S., & Duncan, N. G. (2001). The aestheticization of the politics of landscape preservation. *Annals of the Association of American Geographers, 91* (2), 387–409.

Evans, G. W. (2004). The environment of child poverty. *American Psychologist, 59* (2), 77–92.

Evans, G. W., & Marcynyszyn, L. A. (2004). Environmental justice, cumulative environmental risk, and health among low- and middle-income children in upstate New York. *American Journal of Public Health, 94* (11), 1942–1953.

Evans-Campbell, T. (2008). Historical trauma in American Indian/Native Alaska communities. *Journal of Interpersonal Violence, 23* (3), 316–338.

Feld, S., & Basso, K. H. (1996). Introduction. In S. Feld & K. H. Basso (Eds.), *Senses of place* (pp. 2–11). Santa Fe, N.M.: School of American Research.

Feldman, R. M. (1990). Settlement-identity: Psychological bonds with home places in a mobile society. *Environment and Behavior, 22* (2), 183–229.

Feldman, R. M., & Stall, S. (1994). The politics of space appropriation: A case study of women's struggles for homeplace in Chicago public housing. In I. Altman & A. Churchman (Eds.), *Women and the environment* (pp. 167–199). New York: Plenum.

Freire, P. (1970). *Pedagogy of the oppressed.* New York: Seabury.

Freire, P. (1973). *Education for critical consciousness.* New York: Seabury.

Fried, M. (1963). Grieving for a lost home. In L. Dahl (Ed.), *The urban condition* (pp. 151–171). New York: Basic Books.

Fried, M. (1982). Endemic stress: The psychology of resignation and the politics of scarcity. *American Journal of Orthopsychiatry,* 52 (1), 4–19.

Fried, M. (2000). Continuities and discontinuities of place. *Journal of Environmental Psychology,* 20 (3), 193–205.

Fullilove, M. T. (1996). Psychiatric implications of displacement: Contributions from the psychology of place. *American Journal of Psychiatry,* 153 (12), 1516–1523.

Fullilove, M. T. (2004). *Root shock: How tearing up city neighborhoods hurts America and what we can do about it.* New York: Ballantine.

Geertz, C. (1996). Afterword. In S. Feld & K. H. Basso (Eds.), *Sense of place* (pp. 259–262). Santa Fe, N.M.: School of American Research.

Germain, C. B. (1979). Introduction: Ecology and social work. In C. B. Germain (Ed.), *Social work practice: People and environments* (pp. 3–22). New York: Columbia University Press.

Gieryn, T. (2000). A space for place in sociology. *Annual Review of Sociology,* 26, 463–493.

Goodchild, M. F., & Janelle, D. G. (2004). *Spatially integrated social science.* New York: Oxford University Press.

Gotham, K. F. (2003). Toward an understanding of the spatiality of urban poverty: The urban poor as spatial actors. *International Journal of Urban and Regional Research,* 27 (3), 723–737.

Gregory, S. (1998). *Black Corona: Race and the politics of place in an urban community.* Princeton, N.J.: Princeton University Press.

Gruenewald, D. A. (2003). The best of both worlds: A critical pedagogy of place. *Educational Researcher,* 32 (4), 3–12.

Hayden, D. (1995). *The power of place: Urban landscapes as public history.* Cambridge, Mass.: MIT Press.

Heidegger, M. (1962). *Being and time.* New York: Harper & Row.

Hidalgo, M., & Hernández, B. (2001). Place attachment: Conceptual and empirical questions. *Journal of Environmental Psychology,* 21 (3), 273–281.

hooks, b. (1990). Homeplace. In b. hooks, *Yearning: Race, gender, and cultural politics* (pp. 41–49). Boston: South End Press.

Hummon, D. M. (1992). Community attachment: Local sentiment and sense of place. In I. Altman & S. M. Low (Eds), *Place attachment* (pp. 253–277). New York: Plenum.

Husserl, E. (1973). *Experience and judgment.* Evanston, Ill.: Northwestern University Press.

Johnson, C. Y. (1998). A consideration of collective memory in African American attachment to wildland recreational places. *Human Ecology Review,* 5 (1), 5–15.

Kelly, S. E. (2003). Bioethics and rural health: Theorizing place, space, and subjects. *Social Science and Medicine,* 56 (11), 2277–2288.

Kobayashi, A., & Peake, L. (2000). Racism out of place: Thoughts on whiteness and an antiracist geography in the new millennium. *Annals of the Association of American Geographers,* 90 (2), 392–403.

Kuo, F. E. (2001). Coping with poverty: Impacts of environment and attention in the inner city. *Environment and Behavior,* 33 (1), 5–34.

Kwan, M.-P. (2002). Feminist visualization: Re-envisioning GIS as a method in feminist geographic research. *Annals of the Association of American Geographers, 92* (4), 645–661.

Kwan, M.-P., & Lee, J. (2004). Geovisualization of human activity patterns using 3D GIS: A time-geographic approach. In M. F. Goodchild & D. G. Janelle (Eds.), *Spatially integrated social science* (pp. 48–66). New York: Oxford University Press.

Leavitt, J., & Saegert, S. (1990). *From abandonment to hope: Community-households in Harlem.* New York: Columbia University Press.

Leinberger, C. B. (2008, March). The next slum? *Atlantic Monthly, 301* (2), 70–75.

Low, S. M. (2003). The edge and the center: Gated communities and the discourse of urban fear. In S. M. Low & D. Lawrence-Zúñiga (Eds.), *The anthropology of space and place: Locating culture* (pp. 387–407). Malden, Mass.: Blackwell.

Mabogunje, A. L. (2002). Poverty and environmental degradation: Challenges within the global economy. *Environment, 44* (1), 8–18.

Macintyre, S., Ellaway, A., & Cummins, S. (2002). Place effects on health: How can we conceptualise, operationalise and measure them? *Social Science and Medicine, 55,* 125–139.

Makowsky, V. P. (1982). Sources of stress: Events or conditions? In D. Belle (Ed), *Lives in stress: Women and depression* (pp. 35–53). Berkeley: Sage.

Manzo, L. C. (2005). For better or worse: Exploring multiple dimensions of place meaning. *Journal of Environmental Psychology, 25,* 67–86.

Massey, D. (1994). A global sense of place. In D. Massey. *Space, place, and gender* (pp. 146–156). Minneapolis: University of Minnesota Press.

Matthews, S. A., Detwiler, J. E., & Burton, L. M. (2005). Geo-ethnography: Coupling geographic information analysis techniques with ethnographic methods in urban research. *Cartographica, 40* (4), 75–90.

McKittrick, K., (2007). *Demonic grounds: Black women and the cartographies of struggle.* Minneapolis: University of Minnesota Press.

McKittrick, K., & Woods, C. (2007). Preface: "No one knows the mysteries at the bottom of the ocean." In K. McKittrick & C. Woods (Eds.), *Black geographies and the politics of place* (pp. 1–13). Cambridge, Mass.: South End Press.

Merleau-Ponty, M. (1962). *Phenomenology of perception.* New York: Humanities Press.

Merrifield, A. (1993). Place and space: A Lefebvrian reconciliation. *Transactions of the Institute of British Geographers, 18* (4), 516–531.

Meyer, C. H. (Ed.) (1983). *Clinical social work in the ecosystems perspective.* New York: Columbia University Press.

Meyer, C. H. (1989). Keynote address: Third oral history day. *Newsletter of the Alumni Association of the Columbia University School of Social Work* (Winter-Spring), 25–27.

Meyer, M. A. (2001). Our own liberation: Reflections on Hawaiian epistemology. *Contemporary Pacific, 13* (1), 124–148.

Nicotera, N. (2007). Measuring neighborhood: A conundrum for human services researchers and practitioners. *American Journal of Community Psychology, 40,* 26–51.

O'Connor, A. (2002). *Poverty knowledge: Social science, social policy, and the poor in U.S. history.* Princeton, N.J.: Princeton University Press.

Parr, H. (2000). Interpreting the hidden social geographies of mental health: Ethnographies of inclusion and exclusion in semi-institutional places. *Health and Race, 6* (3), 225–237.

Peña, D. G. (2003). Endangered landscapes and disappearing peoples? In J. Adamson, M. M. Evans, & R. Stein (Eds.). *The environmental justice reader* (pp. 58–81). Tucson, Ariz.: University of Arizona Press.

Peña, D. G. (2006). Toward a critical political ecology of Latina/o urbanism. http://www
.acequiainstitute.org/images/Toward_a_political_ecology_of_Chicana-o_sustainable_
urbanism_Draft_of_June_2006_.pdf. Accessed 6 February 2008.

Perlman, H. H. (1972). Once more with feeling. In E. J. Mullen, J. R Dumpson & Associates
(Eds.), *Evaluation of social intervention* (pp. 191–209). San Francisco: Jossey-Bass.

Popay, J., Thomas, C., Williams, G., Bennett, S., Gatrell, A., & Bostock, L. (2003). A proper
place to live: Health inequalities, agency and the normative dimensions of space. *Social
Science and Medicine, 57* (1), 55–60.

Popay. J., Williams, G., Thomas, C., & Gatrell, A. (2003). Theorizing inequalities in
health: The place of lay knowledge. In R. Hofrichter (Ed.), *Health and social justice:
Politics, ideology, and inequity in the distribution of disease* (pp. 385–409). New York:
Jossey-Bass.

Proshansky, H. M. (1978). The city and self-identity. *Environment and Behavior, 10* (2),
147–169.

Pulido, L., Salawi, S., & Vos, R. O. (1996). An archaeology of environmental racism in Los
Angeles. *Urban Geography, 17* (5), 419–439.

Reich, R. (1991). Secession of the successful. *New York Times Magazine,* 20 January 1991.

Residents of Hull House. (1995). *Hull-House maps and papers: A presentation of nationali-
ties and wages in a congested district in Chicago, together with comments and essays on
problems growing out of social conditions.* New York: Thomas Y. Crowell.

Reynolds, B. C. (1934). *Between client and community: A study in responsibility in social
casework.* Northampton, Mass.: Smith College for Social Work.

Richmond, M. E. (1922). *What is social casework?* New York: Russell Sage Foundation.

Rodman, M. C. (2003). Empowering place: Multilocality and multivocality. In S. M. Low &
D. Lawrence-Zúñiga (Eds.). *The anthropology of space and place: Locating culture* (pp.
204–223). Malden, Mass.: Blackwell.

Saari, C. (2002). *The environment: Its role in psychosocial functioning and psychotherapy.*
New York: Columbia University Press.

Saleeby, D. (2004). "The power of place": Another look at the environment. *Families in
Society, 85* (1), 7–16.

Salmon, E. (2000). Kincentric ecology: Indigenous perceptions of the human-nature relationship. *Ecological Applications, 10* (5), 1327–1332.

Schneekloth, L. H., & Shibley, R. G. (1995). *Placemaking: The art and practice of building
communities.* New York: Wiley.

Schneekloth, L. H., & Shibley, R. G. (2005). Placemaking: A democratic project. *Reconstruction: Studies in Contemporary Culture, 5* (3), 18 pp. http://reconstruction.eserver.
org/053/schneekloth.shtml Accessed 17 January 2008.

Seamon, D. (1987). Phenomenology and environment-behavior research. In E. H. Zube
& G. T. Moore (Eds.), *Advances in environment and behavior design.* Vol. 1. New York:
Plenum.

Sibley, D. (1995). *Geographies of exclusion: Society and difference in the West.* London:
Routledge.

Stack, C. (1996). *Call to home: African Americans reclaim the South.* New York: Basic
Books.

Stone, A. (2008). Mapping software helps Washington State find foster parents. *Government Technology: Solutions for Government in the Information Age.* http://www.gov-
tech.com/gt/241680. Accessed 19 February 2008.

Sugrue, T. (1996). *The origins of the urban crisis: Race and inequality in postwar Detroit.* Princeton, N.J.: Princeton University Press.

Sutton, S. E., Kemp, S. P., Gutierrez, L., & Saegert, S. (2006). *Urban youth programs in America: A study of youth, community, and social justice conducted for the Ford Foundation.* Seattle: University of Washington Press.

Taylor, F. E., Wiley, A., Kuo, F. E., Sullivan, W. C. (1998). Growing up in the inner city: Green spaces as places to grow. *Environment and Behavior,* 30 (1), 3–27.

Taylor, S. E., & Repetti, R. L. (1997). Health psychology: What is an unhealthy environment and how does it get under the skin? *Annual Review of Psychology,* 48, 411–47.

Tuan, Y.-F. (1977). *Space and place: The perspective of experience.* Minneapolis: University of Minnesota Press.

Uehara, E. S., Farris, M., Morelli, P., & Ishisaka, A. (2001). "Eloquent chaos" in the oral discourse of killing fields survivors: An exploration of atrocity and narrativization. *Culture, Medicine, and Psychiatry,* 25, 29–61.

Wakefield, J. C. (1996). Does social work need the eco-systems perspective? Part I: Is the perspective clinically useful? *Social Service Review,* 70 (1), 183–203.

Wilson, K. (2003). Therapeutic landscapes and First Nations peoples: An exploration of culture, health, and place. *Health and Place,* 9 (2), 83–93.

Zapf, M. K. (2005). The spiritual dimension of person and environment: Perspectives from social work and traditional knowledge. *International Social Work,* 48 (5), 633–642.

Zukin, E. (1991). *Landscapes of power: From Detroit to Disneyland.* Berkeley: University of California Press.

6 A FAMILY RESILIENCE FRAMEWORK FOR CLINICAL PRACTICE

Integrating Developmental Theory and Systemic Perspectives

FROMA WALSH

THEORY, RESEARCH, AND practice in the field of mental health are inescapably intertwined. Each can inform and enrich the others. As a clinical scholar, educator, and practitioner over the past three decades, I have endeavored to integrate the three in the development of a family resilience framework to guide intervention and prevention efforts with families facing serious life challenges. I have also found it essential to bridge theory and research on "normal" human development in the social sciences with preoccupations in the field of mental health on individual psychopathology and family deficits.

From the mid- to late twentieth century, the field of mental health was so heavily skewed toward pathology that it might more aptly have been called the field of mental illness. My clinical training taught me how to diagnose psychopathology, but gave no attention to healthy functioning or how practitioners might recognize and promote it. I was drawn to the field of family therapy, which was just flowering in the late 1960s. It was refreshing to cast off deterministic theories of early childhood, maternal causality for individual problems. The systemic paradigm expanded focus from the mother-child dyad to the multiple influences in functioning through ongoing transactional processes in the broad network of relationships. Yet the family field, as well, initially overfocused on family deficits. Clinical theory, supported by impressionistic studies of clinical cases, shifted focus from the "schizo-phrenogenic mother" to the "schizophrenogenic family" at the root of an individual's disorder. This deficit skew reflected prevailing assumptions in the mental health field and the broader culture that most families were more or less dysfunctional.

As coordinator of the family studies in a National Institute of Mental Health–sponsored schizophrenia research program (1971–1977), I sought to include a normal control group; my colleagues chided me that I wouldn't find any normal families and they certainly wouldn't recommend their own. I noted that perhaps the definition of a normal family was one that had not yet been clinically assessed. Undaunted, I did find well-functioning families and was impressed by their vitality and diversity. Yet I found that families themselves worried about their adequacy. One mother even asked if her family could receive a "certificate of normality"! In our preoccupation with family deficits, clinicians, researchers, and families themselves were blinded to family strengths.

That experience led me to pursue doctoral studies in human develop-ment to expand my knowledge about family and social processes that foster healthy functioning, well-being, and positive growth. My scholarly work, clinical teaching, and practice became increasingly strengths-oriented, shift-ing focus from how families have failed to how they can succeed.

Two myths about normal families have clouded our understanding (Walsh, 2003b, 2003c). First, the erroneous assumption that healthy fami-lies are problem-free can lead researchers and clinicians to overpathologize ordinary families struggling with stressful life challenges or traumatic expe-riences. Second, the assumption that a single, universal model of the healthy family is essential, fitting an idealized image of families of the 1950s, has led to faulty presumptions that varying family structures and gender roles are inherently dysfunctional and harmful for children. In the 1950s Har-vard sociologist Talcott Parsons observed a small sample of white, intact, middle-class suburban families with traditional gender roles: father as full-time breadwinner and head of the family, and mother in a socio-emotional supportive role, with full-time responsibilities of homemaking, child rear-ing, and elder care (Parsons & Bales, 1955). Unfortunately, the researchers made a leap from this descriptive study of a small, particular sample at a particular time in society, to declare this a prescriptive universal model of the healthy family, one that has been widely influential. Prominent psy-chiatrists took this model further, contending that families deviating from this norm would inevitably damage their children. Postmodern theory has raised our awareness that scholars and clinicians bring their own assumptive maps into every evaluation and intervention, embedded in cultural norms, professional orientations, and personal experiences (Walsh, 2003c). The media have been saturated with images of dysfunctional families—unstable, failing, falling apart, damaging their children, and causing social and moral decay. We need to keep mindful that views of normality, health, and dysfunction are socially constructed, permeating all research and clinical transactions, assessments, and aims. Moreover, with social and economic transformations of recent decades, theory, research, and practice must be relevant to the growing cultural diversity and multiplicity of family kinship arrangements.

There is abundant research evidence that no single model fits all—or even most—families today (Walsh, 2003b. The very definition of *family* must be broad, to encompass varied family forms, including dual-earner families, single-parent households, stepfamilies, foster and adoptive families, and families headed by gay and lesbian parents, as well as extended formal and informal kin networks. Research finds that families can thrive and children can be raised well in a variety of kin arrangements: What matters most are effective family processes.

Over the past two decades, family therapy theory and practice have shifted toward a collaborative, strengths-based orientation. Systems-oriented family process research has provided empirical grounding for the assessment of healthy family functioning (see Walsh, 2003d). Yet family typologies tend to be static and acontextual: most offer a snapshot of interaction patterns within the family but lack a developmental perspective and a contextual view of family challenges, resources, and sociocultural influences. Most studies select "normal," "nonclinical" samples not in crisis. Since families most often come for help in periods of crisis, we must be cautious not to reflexively label their distress or differences from research norms as family pathology.

In my own research, I was particularly impressed by families in the normal control group in which parents had experienced childhood trauma and suffering, yet had emerged hardier, built strong families, and raised their children well. And as I became more open to searching for strengths, I also found them in clinical families, even those with seriously troubled members.

I was drawn to the concept of resilience since, by definition, it focuses on strengths under stress, in crisis, and in response to adversity (Walsh, 2003a). It is a flexible construct, since different strengths might be needed in varied adverse situations and would also depend on resources and constraints. I set out to develop a family resilience framework that would be useful in guiding clinical research and practice. The following theory and research informed the development of this framework:

- Resilience conceptualization & research
- Family systems theory & research
- Family developmental/life cycle theory
- Family stress theory: coping, adaptation
- Trauma studies: PTSD, posttraumatic growth
- Concepts of compassion fatigue & vicarious resilience

THE CONCEPT OF RESILIENCE

Resilience can be defined as the ability to withstand and rebound from disruptive life challenges, strengthened and more resourceful. Resilience involves dynamic processes that foster positive adaptation in the context of significant adversity (Luthar, Cicchetti & Becker, 2000). It is a common misconception that resilience means invulnerability; vulnerability is part of the human condition. Nor is resilience simply the ability to bounce back unscathed. Rather resilience involves struggling well, effectively working through and learning from adversity, and integrating the experience into the fabric of individual and shared life passage.

Resilience has become an important concept in mental health theory and research over the past two decades as studies challenged the prevailing deterministic assumption that traumatic experiences and prolonged adversity, especially in childhood, are inevitably damaging. Pioneering research by Rutter (1987), Werner (1993), and others found that many children who experienced multiple risk factors for serious dysfunction, such as parental mental illness, traumatic loss, or conditions of poverty, defied expectations and did remarkably well in life. Although many lives were shattered by adversity, others overcame similar high-risk conditions, able to lead loving and productive lives and to raise their children well. Studies found, for instance, that most abused children did not become abusive parents (Kaufman & Ziegler, 1987).

Clinicians often work with individuals and families who suffer from trauma, who are overwhelmed by daunting challenges, and whose lives have been blocked from growth by multi-stress conditions. What makes the difference for those who rise above adversity?

INDIVIDUAL RESILIENCE
IN MULTISYSTEMIC PERSPECTIVE

To account for these differences, early studies by child development scholars focused on personality traits for resilience, or hardiness, reflecting the dominant cultural ethos of the "rugged individual" (Walsh, 1996). Influenced by psychoanalytic theory, resilience was assumed to be due to innate traits, or character armor, that made some children impervious to the damage of parental pathology. "The invulnerable child" was likened to a "steel doll" that would not break under stress (Anthony & Cohler, 1987). Most studies focused on individuals who thrived despite a parent's mental illness or maltreatment. Theory limited the view of the family narrowly to the mother-child dyad. The contributing—or counterbalancing—influence of the father or other family members was generally not assessed. In cases where there was a disturbed parent, scholars and practitioners dismissed the family as hopelessly dysfunctional and sought positive extrafamilial resources to counter the negative impact. Thus, families were seen to contribute to risk, but not to resilience.

The work of Sir Michael Rutter (1987) led researchers toward a systemic perspective, recognizing the complex interaction between nature and nurture in the emergence of resilience over time. As studies were extended to a wide range of adverse conditions—such as growing up in impoverished circumstances, dealing with chronic medical illness, or recovering from catastrophic life events, trauma, and loss—resilience came to be viewed in terms of an interplay of multiple risk and protective processes over time, involving individual, family, and larger sociocultural influences. Individual vulnerability or the impact of stressful conditions could be outweighed by positive mediating influences.

In a remarkable longitudinal study of resilience, Werner (1993; Werner & Smith, 1992) followed the lives of nearly 700 multicultural children of plantation workers living in poverty on the Hawaiian island of Kauai. By age eighteen about two-thirds of the at-risk children had done poorly as predicted, with early pregnancy, needs for mental health services, or trouble in school or with the law. However, one-third of those at risk had developed into competent, caring, and confident young adults, with the capacity "to work well, play well, and love well," as rated on a variety of measures. In later follow-up studies through middle adulthood, almost all were still living successful lives, with stable relationships and employment. When hurricane Iniki devastated the island, fewer were traumatized compared to the general population, showing that overcoming early life adversity made them hardier, not more vulnerable, in the face of later life challenges.

Of note, several individuals who had been poorly functioning in adolescence turned their lives around in adulthood, most often crediting supportive relationships and religious involvement. Such findings counter deterministic assumptions that negative effects of early life trauma are irreversible. Rather, a developmental perspective is required, recognizing the potential, despite a troubled childhood or adolescence, for human resilience to emerge across the life course. There are important clinical implications. We must be cautious not to frame resilience as a static set of traits or typology—some have it and others do not—or to label and dismiss as "not resilient" those who are struggling at a particular time This research affirms the potential, throughout life, for those who have suffered to gain resilience and to turn their lives around.

RELATIONAL "LIFELINES" FOR INDIVIDUAL RESILIENCE

IN MY SURVEY of over two decades of resilience research with varied populations and methodologies, the crucial influence of significant relationships stood out across studies. Individual resilience of individuals was nurtured by bonds with kin, intimate partners, and mentors, such as coaches and teachers, who supported their efforts, believed in their potential, and encouraged them to make the most of their lives.

In the field of mental health, the prevailing theoretical lens has blinded many to the family resources that can foster resilience, even where a parent's functioning is seriously impaired. A family resilience perspective recognizes parental strengths and potential alongside limitations. Furthermore, grounded in a systemic orientation, it looks beyond the parent-child dyad to consider broader influences in the kin network, from sibling bonds to couple relationships and extended family ties. This approach fundamentally alters the deficit-based lens from viewing troubled parents and families as *damaged* and beyond repair to seeing them as *challenged* by life's adversities with potential for fostering healing and growth in all members.

In the field of traumatology, researchers are increasingly shifting attention from posttraumatic stress disorder to better understand the resilience and posttraumatic growth experienced by many individuals in the aftermath of trauma events (Calhoun & Tedeschi, 2006; Tedeschi & Calhoun, 1996). Van der Kolk and colleagues have advanced a bio-psycho-social understanding of trauma, its treatment, and its prevention, including attention to variables that influence vulnerability, resilience, and the course of posttraumatic reactions (van der Kolk, McFarlane & Weisaeth, 1996). The effects of trauma depend greatly on whether those wounded can seek comfort, reassurance, and safety with others. Strong connections, with trust that others will be there for them when needed, counteract feelings of insecurity, helplessness, and meaninglessness. Despite the groundbreaking work of Figley on the impact of catastrophic events on the family (Figley & McCubbin, 1983), only recently are approaches being developed to strengthen family and community resilience in response to major trauma (Walsh, 2007).

A family resilience orientation to practice seeks out and builds relational lifelines for resilience of the family unit and all members. It recognizes strengths and potential alongside vulnerabilities. A multisystemic view expands focus to tap extended kin, community, and spiritual resources.

THE CONCEPT OF FAMILY RESILIENCE

The concept of family resilience extends beyond seeing individual family members as potential resources for individual resilience. It focuses on risk and resilience in the family as a functional unit (Walsh, 1996, 2003). A basic premise in this systemic view is that serious crises and persistent adversity have an impact on the whole family. In turn, key family processes mediate the recovery—or maladaptation—of all members *and* the family unit. The family response is crucial. Major stresses can derail the functioning of a family system, with ripple effects for all members and their relationships. Key processes in resilience enable the family system to rally in times of crisis, to buffer stress, reduce the risk of dysfunction, and support optimal adaptation.

FAMILY STRESS, COPING, AND ADAPTATION

The concept of family resilience extends theory and research on family stress, coping, and adaptation (Hill, 1958; McCubbin & Patterson, 1983; McCubbin, H., McCubbin, M., McCubbin, A., & Futrell, 1998; McCubbin, H., McCubbin, M., Thompson & Fromer, 1998, 2002). It entails more than managing stressful conditions, maintaining competence, shouldering a burden, or surviving an ordeal. It involves the potential for personal and relational transformation and growth that can be forged out of adversity.

Tapping into key processes for resilience, families that have been struggling can emerge stronger and more resourceful in meeting future challenges. Members may develop new insights and abilities. A crisis can be a wake-up call, heightening attention to important matters. It can become an opportunity for reappraisal of life priorities and pursuits, stimulating greater investment in meaningful relationships. In studies of strong families, many report that through weathering a crisis together their relationships were enriched and became more loving than they might otherwise have been.

UTILITY OF A FAMILY RESILIENCE FRAMEWORK FOR CLINICAL PRACTICE

As Werner has affirmed, resilience theory and research offer a promising knowledge base for practice; the findings of resilience research have many potential applications; and the building of bridges between clinicians, researchers, and policymakers is of utmost importance (Werner & Johnson, 1999).

My efforts over more than a decade have focused on the development of a family resilience framework for clinical and community-based intervention and prevention. The practice applications have been developed, refined, and reformulated over many years of clinical teaching, supervision, and direct practice grounded in a developmental systems orientation.

This resilience-oriented approach builds on developments in the field of family therapy that have refocused attention from family deficits to family strengths (Walsh, 2003a). The therapeutic relationship is collaborative and empowering of client potential, with recognition that successful interventions depend on tapping into family. Our language and discourse are strengths-oriented and empowering. This approach is less centered on therapist techniques; what matters more is the therapist's relationship with families: with compassion for their struggle and conviction in their potential. Assessment and intervention are redirected from how problems were caused to how they can be solved, identifying and amplifying existing and potential competencies. Therapist and clients work together to find new possibilities in a problem-saturated situation and overcome impasses to change. This positive, future-oriented stance refocuses from how families have failed to how they can succeed.

A family resilience framework is distinguished from a more general family strengths perspective by its focus on strengths *in the context of adversity* (Walsh, 1998). It links symptoms of distress with stressful events and conditions in the family and wider environment. Families most often come for help in crisis, but often they don't initially connect presenting problems with relevant stressors. A basic premise guiding this approach is that crises and persistent challenges affect the whole family, and in turn, key family processes mediate the adaptation of all members and relationships.

This family resilience framework can serve as a valuable conceptual map to guide intervention efforts to target and strengthen key processes as presenting problems are addressed. As families become more resourceful, risk and vulnerability are reduced, and they are better able to meet future challenges. Thus, building resilience is also a preventive measure.

This conceptual approach alters the mental health field's prevalent deficit-based lens, from regarding parents and families as *damaged* and beyond repair to seeing them as *challenged* by life's adversities with potential to foster healing and growth in all members. Rather than rescuing so-called "survivors" from "dysfunctional families" this practice approach engages distressed families with respect and compassion for their struggles, affirms their reparative potential, and seeks to bring out their best qualities. Efforts to foster family resilience aim both to avert or reduce dysfunction and to enhance family functioning and individual well-being (Luthar et al., 2000). Such efforts have the potential to benefit all family members as they fortify relational bonds and strengthen the family unit.

PUTTING ECOLOGICAL AND DEVELOPMENTAL PERSPECTIVES INTO PRACTICE

This family resilience framework combines ecological and developmental perspectives to understand and strengthen family functioning in relation to its broader sociocultural context and multigenerational life-cycle passage.

From a *bio-psycho-social systems orientation*, risk and resilience are viewed in light of multiple, recursive influences involving individuals, families, and larger social systems. Problems can result from an interaction of individual, family, or community vulnerability in the impact of stressful life experiences. Symptoms may be primarily biologically based, as in serious illness, or largely influenced by sociocultural variables, such as barriers of poverty and discrimination that render some families or communities more at risk. Family distress may *result* from unsuccessful attempts to cope with an overwhelming situation. Symptoms may be generated by a crisis, such as traumatic loss in the family or by the wider impact of a large-scale disaster. The family, peer group, community resources, school or work settings, and other social systems can be seen as nested contexts for nurturing and reinforcing resilience. A multidimensional, holistic assessment includes the varied contexts, seeking to identify common elements in a crisis and in family responses, while also taking into account each family's unique perspectives, resources, and challenges.

A *developmental perspective* is also essential to understand and foster family resilience. Families navigate varied pathways in resilience with emerging challenges over time. A pile-up of multiple stressors can overwhelm family resources. The impact of a crisis may also vary in relation to its timing in individual and family life-cycle passage. Past experiences and stories of adversity and family response can generate catastrophic expectations or can serve as models in overcoming difficulties.

VARIED ADAPTATIONAL PATHWAYS IN RESILIENCE

Most major stressors are not simply a short-term single event, but rather, a complex set of changing conditions with a past history and a future course (Rutter, 1987). Family resilience involves varied adaptational pathways over time, from the approach to a threatening event on the horizon, through disruptive transitions, subsequent shockwaves in the immediate aftermath, and long-term reorganization. For instance, how a family approaches an impending death, facilitates emotional sharing and meaning making, effectively reorganizes, and fosters reinvestment in life pursuits will influence the immediate and long-term adaptation to loss for all members and their relationships (Walsh & McGoldrick, 2004). Likewise, the experience of divorce proceeds from an escalation of predivorce tensions through disruption and reorganization of households and parent-child relationships; most will experience transitional upheaval again with remarriage and stepfamily integration (Hetherington & Kelly, 2002). Given such complexity, no single coping response is invariably most successful; different strategies may prove useful in meeting new challenges. Some approaches that are functional in the short term may rigidify and become dysfunctional over time. For instance, with a sudden illness, a family must mobilize resources and pull together to meet the crisis, but later must shift gears with chronic disability and attend to other members' needs over the long haul (Rolland, 1994). Practitioners work with families at various steps or transitions along their journey, helping them to integrate what has happened and to meet immediate and future challenges.

PILE-UP OF STRESSORS

Some families may do well with a short-term crisis but buckle under the strains of persistent or recurrent challenges, as with prolonged joblessness or chronic illness. A pile-up of internal and external stressors can overwhelm the family, heightening vulnerability and risk for subsequent problems. One couple's escalating conflict and the husband's heavy drinking brought them to therapy. It was essential to situate these symptoms in the context of the family's barrage of strains and losses over two years: in the midst of raising three small children, the husband's brother died suddenly in a car crash and the grief-stricken paternal grandfather suffered a stroke, requiring extensive caregiving; the husband's family business then crumbled, leaving the family without income or health insurance. Reeling from one crisis to the next, they found the cumulative pressures overwhelming, fueling conflict and drinking. Beyond conflict management, resilience-oriented counseling helped the couple to locate kin and community resources, and to support each other in healing from their losses and meeting ongoing challenges.

FAMILY LIFE-CYCLE PERSPECTIVE

Functioning and symptoms of distress are assessed in the context of the multigenerational family system as it moves forward across the life cycle (Carter & McGoldrick, 1999). A family resilience practice approach focuses on family adaptation around nodal events that are stressful and disruptive. These include complications with predictable, normative transitions, such as parenthood and adolescence, and those with unexpected, untimely events, such as disabilities or death of a child.

We pay particular attention to the timing of symptoms: their co-occurrence with recent or impending events that have disrupted or threatened the family (Walsh, 1983). For instance, a son's sudden drop in school grades may be precipitated by his father's recent job loss, although family members may not initially note any connection. Frequently individual symptoms coincide with stressful transitions, such as parental remarriage, that require boundary shifts and redefinition of roles and relationships. It is important to attend to the extended kin network beyond the immediate household. One woman's depression was triggered by the death of her godmother, who had been her mainstay through a difficult childhood. In assessing the impact of stress events, it is essential to explore how they were handled by the family: their approach, immediate response, and long-term "survival" strategies.

LEGACIES OF THE PAST

A multigenerational perspective is also required. Distress is heightened when current stressors reactivate painful memories and emotions from the past, as in posttraumatic stress reactions. The convergence of developmental and multigenerational strains increases the risk for complications (Carter & McGoldrick, 1999). Unresolved past losses often resurface with a current or threatened loss (Walsh & McGoldrick, 2004). Family members may lose perspective, conflate immediate situations with past events, and become overwhelmed by or cut off from painful feelings and contacts. It is important to inquire about family stories of past adversity and how they influence future expectations, from an optimistic outlook to catastrophic fears. Particularly noteworthy are multigenerational anniversary patterns (Walsh, 1983). Many families function well until they reach a point in life-cycle passage that had been traumatic a generation earlier. One wife became terrified of losing her husband in a routine surgery; it was noted on a genogram that he was the same age as her father at his death.

In sum, symptoms of distress are assessed in temporal context as well as family and social contexts. A family timeline and a genogram are essential tools for clinicians to schematize relationship information, track systems patterns, and guide intervention planning (McGoldrick, Gerson, & Petry, 2008). While genograms are most often used to focus on problematic family-of-origin patterns, a resilience-oriented approach also searches for positive influences, past, present, and potential. We inquire about resourceful ways a family or an elder dealt with past adversity and models of resilience in the kin network that might be drawn on to inspire efforts to master current challenges. Key principles of the practice framework are outlined in Tables 6.1 and 6.2.

BROAD RANGE OF PRACTICE APPLICATIONS

The very flexibility of the concept of family resilience lends itself to many varied applications. A family resilience framework can be applied usefully with a wide range of crises and persistent life challenges. Interventions utilize principles and techniques common among many strength-based practice approaches, but attend more centrally to links between symptoms and significant family stressors, identifying and fortifying key processes in coping and adaptation. This approach also affirms the varied pathways that can be forged for resilience over time.

TABLE 6.1 Family Resilience: Conceptual Framework for Practice

RESILIENCE-ORIENTED PRACTICE APPLICATIONS

Facilitate family's ability to rebound from crises and master life challenges, emerging strengthened and more resourceful:

- Recover from crisis, trauma, loss
- Navigate disruptive transitions (job loss, migration, separation/divorce) manage persistent stresses, master overwhelming challenges (multi-stressed low-income families; chronic illness or disability)
- Overcome barriers to success (at-risk youth, school dropout)
- "Bounce forward": adapt to changing conditions, new challenges, become proactive

META-FRAMEWORK FOR CLINICAL AND COMMUNITY-BASED SERVICES

- Relational view of human resilience
- Shift from deficit view of families:
  From damaged to challenged by adversity
  Focus on potential for repair and growth
- Grounded in developmental and systemic theoretical orientations:
  Bio-psycho-social-spiritual influences over the family life cycle and across the generations
- Crisis events impact family system; family response influences adaptation of all members, relationships, and family unit
- Contextual view of crisis, symptoms of distress, and adaptation:
  Family and sociocultural influences
- Temporal influences (timing of symptoms and family crisis events; pile-up of stressors, persistent adversity; varying adaptational challenges over time; individual and family developmental phases; multigenerational patterns)

Therapists, as compassionate witnesses and facilitators, help family members to share their experiences of adversity, often breaking down walls of silence or secrecy around painful or shameful events, to build mutual support and empathy. Respect for family strengths in the midst of suffering readily engages so-called "resistant" families, who are often reluctant to come for mental health services out of a belief (often based on experience) that they will be judged as disturbed or deficient and blamed for their problems. Instead, family members are viewed as intending to do their best for one

TABLE 6.2 Practice Principles to Strengthen Family Resilience

Convey conviction in potential to overcome adversity through collaborative efforts.

Use respectful language, framing to humanize and contextualize distress:

  View as understandable, common in adverse situation (normal response to abnormal or extreme conditions).

  Decrease shame, blame; depathologize.

Provide safe haven for sharing vulnerabilities, fears, challenges.

  Therapist serves as compassionate witness for stories of suffering and struggle.

  Facilitate family communication, empathy, mutual support.

Identify, affirm, and build strengths, competencies alongside vulnerabilities, limitations.

Build relational lifelines to support resilience.

  Tap into kin, community, and spiritual resources to deal with challenges.

  Draw on models, mentors.

  Build collaborative teams, networks.

Help family seize opportunities for learning, positive change, and stronger bonds.

  Shift focus from problems to possibilities.

  Gain mastery, healing, and transformation out of adversity.

  Rekindle or reorient future hopes and aspirations.

Integrate adverse experience and resilient response into fabric of individual and relational life passage.

---

another and struggling with an overwhelming set of challenges. Therapeutic/counseling efforts are directed at mastering those challenges through collaborative work.

This approach also encourages attempts toward reconciliation of past relational wounds (Walsh, 2006). Adult children, finding difficulty in giving care to their dying mother because of lingering anger at her alcohol abuse and neglect during their childhood, are helped to see her in a new light through learning more about her life journey, gaining compassion for her struggles and courage alongside her limitations. Not all family members may be successful in surmounting obstacles, but all are seen to have dignity and worth.

Clinical training, research, and community projects can benefit from being grounded in a family resilience metaframework. A multisystemic assessment may lead to a variety of interventions or a combination of individual, couple, family, and multifamily group modalities, depending on the relevance of different system levels to problem resolution. Putting an ecological view into practice, interventions may involve community agencies, or workplace, school, healthcare, and other larger systems. Resilience-based family interventions can be adapted to a variety of formats, including periodic family consultations or more intensive family therapy. Psycho-educational multifamily groups emphasize the importance of social support and practical information, offering concrete guidelines for crisis management, problem solving, and stress reduction as families navigate through stressful periods and face future challenges. Therapists may identify specific stresses the family is dealing with and then help them develop effective coping strategies, measuring success in small increments, and maintaining family morale. Brief, cost-effective psycho-educational "modules" timed for critical phases of an illness or life challenge encourage families to accept and digest manageable portions of a long-term coping process (Rolland, 1994).

The Chicago Center for Family Health, which I codirect with John Rolland, has developed a range of training, clinical, and community services grounded in this family resilience metaframework. Programs have been designed to address a range of challenges (Walsh, 2002a; 2006):

- serious illness, disability, end-of-life challenges, and loss (Rolland & Walsh, 2005)
- recovery from major disaster and terrorist attacks (Walsh, 2007)
- refugee and migration challenges
- adaptation with divorce, single-parenting, and stepfamily reorganization
- family stresses and resources with job loss, transition, and new employment
- family-school partnerships for the success of at-risk youth
- challenges of stigma for gay and lesbian families

To illustrate the value of a resilience-oriented practice approach, I present here a brief description of our work with Bosnian and Kosovar refugee families. In 1998 our Center was called upon to develop resilience-based multifamily groups for Bosnian refugees in Chicago, and the following year, for ethnic Albanians arriving from Kosovo. As a result of the Serbian genocidal campaign of "ethnic cleansing," families in both regions experienced the devastating destruction of homes and communities; they suffered widespread atrocities, including brutal torture, rape, murder, and the disappearance of loved ones.

Our family resilience approach was sought out because traditional mental health services were viewed in the refugee community as unhelpful, stigmatizing, and pathologizing, particularly in the deficit-based posttraumatic stress disorder diagnosis of a mental disorder and the narrow focus on treating individual symptoms. In contrast, <u>a resilience-oriented approach contextualizes the distress as understandable suffering in an abnormal and traumatizing situation.</u> In my experience, mental health professionals often don't appreciate the sense of shame that people so often feel when they are expected to reveal their vulnerabilities and suffering. This resilience approach locates the trauma not in the individuals, but in the extreme situation they have experienced. Our approach with the refugee families was experienced as respectful, healing, and empowering.

This program, called CAFES for Bosnian and TAFES for Kosovar families (Coffee/Tea And Family Education & Support), utilized a nine-week multifamily group format, which tapped into the strong family-centered values in their culture. It was located in a neighborhood storefront, where residents felt comfortable and could easily gain access to services. It offered a compassionate setting to encourage families to share their stories of suffering and struggle, while drawing out and affirming family resources, such as their courage, endurance, and faith; their strong kinship networks and deep concern for loved ones; and their determination to rise above their tragedies to forge a new life. To foster a spirit of collaboration and to develop resources within their community, Bosnian/Kosovar paraprofessional facilitators were trained to colead groups.

The positive response to these projects led to the development of the Kosovar Family Professional Educational Collaborative (KFPEC), an ongoing partnership between mental health professionals in Kosovo, through the University of Pristina, and teams of American family therapists, through the auspices of the American Family Therapy Academy, the Chicago Center for Family Health, and the University of Illinois. The aim of this project was to provide resilience-based, family-focused education and training in Kosovo to enhance the capacities of mental health professionals and paraprofessionals to address overwhelming service needs in their war-torn region by strengthening family capacities for coping and recovery in the wake of trauma and loss. In describing the value of this approach, Rolland and Weine noted:

> The family, with its strengths, is central to Kosovar life, but health and mental health services are generally not oriented to families. Although "family" is a professed part of the value system of international organizations, most programs do not define, conceptualize, or operationalize a family approach to mental health services in any substantial or meaningful ways. Recognizing that the psychosocial needs of refugees, other trauma survivors, and vulnerable persons in societies in transition far exceed the individual and

psychopathological focus that conventional trauma mental health approaches provide, this project aims to begin a collaborative program of family focused education and training that is resilience-based and emphasizes family strengths. (Rolland and Weine, 2000, p. 35)

Over an initial twelve-month period (2000–2001), five teams of American family therapists conducted weeklong training sessions in Pristina. Bringing varied approaches to family therapy, they all emphasized a resilience-based perspective to address family challenges, encouraging Kosovar professionals to adapt the framework and develop their own practice models to best fit their culture and service needs. Readings found to be valuable were translated into Albanian. Between visits, contact has been sustained through e-mail and collaborative writing.

Interviews with families inquired about their strengths in the midst of their tragedy. The positive influence of belief systems was striking, in particular, the power of religious faith (Islam) and the inspiration of strong models and mentors—mothers who carried on courageously despite the loss of husbands and sons; uncles and aunts who raised orphaned children and kept the spirit of their deceased parents alive. Many attributed their resilience to their cohesiveness and adaptive role flexibility: As one family member related, "Everyone belongs to the family and to our homeland, alive or dead. . . . Everyone matters and everyone is counted and counted upon. . . . When cooking or planting everyone moves together fluidly, each person picking up what the previous person left off." Although the grief with loss is immeasurable, the ability to rise above the tragedy and fill in missing roles was remarkable. (Becker et al., 2000, p. 29)

KEY PROCESSES IN FAMILY RESILIENCE

The Family Resilience Framework in Table 6.3 was developed as a conceptual map for clinicians to identify and target key processes that can strengthen family capacities to rebound from crises and master persistent life challenges (Walsh, 2003a). This framework is informed by three decades of social-scientific and clinical research seeking to understand crucial variables contributing to individual resilience and family systems research on well-functioning families (see Walsh, 2006). I have synthesized and organized findings from the numerous studies to identify key processes for resilience within three domains of family functioning: family belief systems, organization patterns, and communication processes.

TABLE 6.3 Walsh Framework: Key Processes in Family Resilience

BELIEF SYSTEMS

Making Meaning of Adversity

- View resilience as relationally-based
- Normalize, contextualize distress
- Sense of coherence: Crisis as meaningful, comprehensible, manageable challenge
- Appraise adverse situation; options; future expectations, fears

Positive Outlook

- Hope, optimistic bias; confidence in overcoming barriers
- Courage / encouragement; affirm strengths and potential
- Active initiative and perseverance (Can-do spirit)
- Master the possible; accept what can't be changed

Transcendence and Spirituality

- Larger values, purpose
- Spirituality: faith, rituals and practices, congregational support
- Inspiration: new possibilities, dreams; creative expression; social action
- Transformation: learning, change, and growth from adversity

ORGANIZATIONAL PATTERNS

Flexibility

- Rebound, reorganize to adapt to new challenges
- Regain stability: dependability, predictability to counter disruption
- Strong authoritative leadership: nurture, guide, protect
- Varied family forms: cooperative parenting / caregiving teams
- Couple / co-parent relationship: mutual respect; equal partners

Connectedness

- Mutual support, collaboration, and commitment
- Respect individual needs, differences, and boundaries
- Seek reconnection, reconciliation of wounded relationships

Social and Economic Resources

- Mobilize kin, social and community networks; recruit mentors
- Financial security; work / family balance; institutional supports

TABLE 6.3 *(continued)*

COMMUNICATION / PROBLEM SOLVING

Clarity

- Clear, consistent messages (words, deeds)
- Clarify ambiguous information; truth seeking / truth speaking

Open Emotional Expression

- Share range of feelings
- Mutual empathy; tolerate differences
- Responsibility for own feelings, behavior; avoid blaming
- Pleasurable interactions, respite; humor
Collaborative Problem-solving
- Creative brainstorming; resourcefulness
- Shared decision-making; negotiation, fairness, reciprocity
- Focus on goals, concrete steps: build on success; learn from failure
- Proactive stance: prevent crises; prepare for future challenges

FAMILY BELIEF SYSTEMS

Family belief systems, influenced by cultural beliefs, emerge through family and social transactions. They powerfully influence members' experience of adverse events, their suffering, and their options. They organize family approaches to crises, and they can be fundamentally altered by such experiences (Reiss, 1981). Adversity generates a crisis of meaning and potential disruption of integration (Neimeier, 2001. Resilience is fostered by shared beliefs that increase options for effective functioning, problem solving, healing, and growth. Clinicians can foster these facilitative beliefs by helping members make meaning of crises, gain a hopeful, positive outlook, and tap transcendent or spiritual experiences.

MAKING MEANING OF ADVERSITY

High-functioning families value strong affiliations and approach adversity as a *shared* challenge (Beavers & Hampson, 2003). "We Shall Overcome," the rallying song in the 1960s civil rights movement and in social justice movements worldwide, expresses this core belief: in joining together, individuals strengthen their ability to overcome adversity. Clinicians can help distressed families forge this *relational view* of strength, in contrast to the Euro-American cultural ethos of the "rugged individual."

Well-functioning families have an evolutionary sense of time and becoming—a continual process of growth, change, and losses across the life cycle and the generations (Beavers & Hampson, 2003). Clinicians can offer this family life-cycle orientation to help members to see disruptive transitions also as milestones or turning points on their shared life passage. By *normalizing* and *contextualizing* distress, family members can enlarge their perspective to see their reactions and difficulties as understandable in light of a traumatic event, a painful loss, or daunting obstacles they face. The tendency for blame, shame, and pathologizing is reduced by viewing their problems as human dilemmas and their feelings and vulnerability as "normal"—that is, common and expectable among families facing similar predicaments.

Meaning-making is of utmost importance in facing adversity (Frankl, 1984). Families do best when helped to gain a *sense of coherence* (Antonovsky, 1998), by recasting a crisis as a challenge that is comprehensible, manageable, and meaningful to tackle. It involves efforts to clarify the nature of problems and available resources. The meaning of adversity and beliefs about what can be done vary with different cultural norms; some are more fatalistic, while others stress personal responsibility and agency (Walsh, 2006). The subjective appraisal of a crisis and resources influence their coping response and adaptation (Lazarus & Folkman, 1984). Family members attempt to make sense of how things have happened through *causal or explanatory attributions*. When a crisis strikes like a bolt out of the blue, as did the September 11, 2001, terrorist attacks in the United States, ambiguity about the causes and casualties, along with uncertainties about the future, can shatter core assumptions, such as invulnerability, predictability, and security, complicating the challenges of meaning-making and recovery (Kauffman, 2002; Neimeier, 2001; Walsh, 2002b). Efforts to clarify ambiguous losses facilitate the healing process (Boss, 1999).

POSITIVE OUTLOOK

Considerable research documents the strong psychological and physiological effects of a positive outlook in coping with stress, recovering from crisis, and overcoming barriers to success. *Hope* is as essential to the spirit as oxygen is to the lungs: it fuels energy and efforts to rise above adversity. Hope is a future-oriented belief: no matter how bleak the present, a better future can be envisioned. In problem-saturated conditions, it is essential to rekindle hopes and dreams in order to see possibilities, tap into potential resources, and strive to surmount obstacles toward aspirations. Hope for a better life for their children keeps many struggling immigrant families from being defeated by their own daunting challenges.

High-functioning families tend to hold a more optimistic outlook toward life (Beavers & Hampson, 2003). Seligman's (1990) concept of "learned optimism" has particular relevance for fostering resilience. His earlier research on "learned helplessness" showed that with repeated experiences of futility and failure, people stop trying and become passive and pessimistic, generalizing the belief that bad things always happen to them and that nothing they can do will matter. Seligman then reasoned that optimism could be learned, and helplessness and pessimism unlearned, through experiences of successful mastery, building confidence that one's efforts can make a difference. His research led to programs in schools for high-risk youth to build confidence and competence. He cautioned, however, that a positive mindset is not sufficient for success if life conditions are relentlessly harsh, with few opportunities to rise above them. As Aponte (1994) notes, many youth and families who feel trapped in impoverished, blighted communities lose hope, suffering a deprivation of both "bread" and "spirit." This despair robs them of meaning, purpose, and a sense of future possibility. Thus, to rebuild and sustain a positive outlook, interventions need to foster successful experiences *and* a nurturing community context.

Similar to an optimistic bias, epidemiologists have found that "positive illusions" sustain hope in dealing with adversity, such as a life-threatening illness (Taylor, 1989). Unlike denial, there is awareness of a grim reality, such as a poor prognosis, and a choice to believe they can overcome the odds against them. This belief fuels efforts that can reduce risk, enhance the quality of life, and maximize the chances of success.

Affirming family strengths and potential in the midst of difficulties helps families counter a sense of helplessness, failure, and blame, as it reinforces pride, confidence, and a "can do" spirit. Encouragement bolsters courage to take initiative and persevere in efforts to master a harrowing ordeal.

Initiative and perseverance—hallmarks of resilience—are fueled by shared confidence that family members will find a way to surmount an ordeal. This conviction bolsters efforts and makes them active participants in a search for solutions. By showing confidence in one another, families support efforts and build competencies.

Mastering the art of the possible is a vital key for resilience, since some things cannot be changed (Higgins, 1994). Clinicians can help families take stock of their situation—the challenges, constraints, and resources—and then focus energies on making the best of their options. This requires coming to accept that which is beyond their control and can't be changed. Families with an Eastern philosophical or religious orientation tend to have greater ease in accepting things beyond their control or comprehension than do those with a Western mastery orientation, which emphasizes instrumental problem solving, mastery, and control. When families are immobilized, or trapped in a powerless victim position, they can be helped to direct efforts toward current and future possibilities: playing the hand that is dealt as well as possible. Although past events can't be changed, they can be recast in a new light to foster greater comprehension and healing. When immediate conditions are overwhelming or beyond control, family members can be encouraged to carve out aspects they can master. For instance, when they can't control the outcome of a loved one's terminal illness, they can become meaningfully engaged in caregiving and end-of-life preparations, easing suffering, and making the most of the time they have left. Family members often report that by being more fully present with loved ones this most painful time became the most precious in their relationship. In the aftermath of loss, survivors are helped by finding ways to transform the living presence of a loved one into cherished memories, stories, and deeds, which carry on the spirit of the deceased and best aspects of their relationship (Walsh & McGoldrick, 2004).

TRANSCENDENCE AND SPIRITUALITY

Transcendent beliefs and practices provide meaning and purpose beyond each family's immediate plight (Beavers & Hampson, 2003). Most families find strength, comfort, and guidance in adversity through connections with their cultural and religious traditions (Walsh, in press). Rituals and ceremonies facilitate passage through significant transitions and linkage with a larger community and common heritage (Imber-Black, Roberts, and Whiting, 2003). Suffering, and any injustice or senselessness, are ultimately spiritual issues (. Spiritual resources, through deep faith, practices such as prayer and meditation, and religious/congregational affiliation, have all been found to be wellsprings for resilience (see Walsh, 2009). Many find spiritual nourishment outside formal religion, through practices of meditation and deep personal connection with a universal spirit, nature, or expression in music and the arts. Studies of successful African American families find that strong faith and congregational involvement help them to rise above barriers of poverty and racism. In health crises, medical studies suggest that faith, prayer, and spiritual rituals can strengthen healing through the influence of emotions on the immune and cardiovascular systems. While faith can make a difference, we must be cautious not to attribute failures to recover to lapses in spiritual piety or positive beliefs.

The paradox of resilience is that the worst of times can also bring out our best. A crisis can yield learning, transformation, and growth in unforeseen directions. It can be an epiphany, awakening family members to the importance of loved ones or jolting them to repair old wounds or reorder priorities for more meaningful relationships and life pursuits. Many people emerge from shattering crises with a heightened moral compass and sense of purpose in their lives, gaining compassion for the plight of others. The experience of adversity and suffering can inspire creative expression through the arts, as in jazz. It may spark community action on behalf of others, and even a life course committed to helping others or working for social justice. It's most important to help families in problem-saturated situations to envision a better future through their efforts and, when hopes and dreams have been shattered, to imagine new possibilities, seizing opportunities for invention, transformation, and growth.

FAMILY ORGANIZATIONAL PATTERNS

Contemporary families, with diverse structures, must organize in varied ways to meet the challenges they face. Resilience is strengthened by flexible structure, connectedness (cohesion), and social and economic resources.

FLEXIBILITY: BOUNCING FORWARD

Flexibility is a core process in resilience. Often the ability to rebound is thought of as "bouncing back" like a spring, to a preexisting shape or norm. However, after many major transitions and crises, families can't simply return to "normal" life as they knew it. A more apt metaphor for resilience might be "bouncing forward," adapting to meet new challenges (Walsh, 2002b). Families often need help to navigate new terrain and undergo structural reorganization. With parental disability, divorce, or remarriage, families must construct a new sense of normality as they recalibrate relationships and reorganize patterns of interaction to fit new conditions.

At the same time, it is essential to regain stability and continuity in the wake of disruptive changes. For instance, the adaptation of immigrant families is fostered by finding ways to sustain connections with valued customs, kin, and community left behind (Falicov, 2003).

Firm, yet flexible, authoritative leadership is most effective for family functioning through stressful times. Parents and other caretakers need to provide nurturance, protection, and guidance through disruptive and uncertain times. Children and other vulnerable family members especially need reassurance of continuity, security, and predictability. For instance, children's adaptation to divorce is facilitated by strong parental leadership and dependability, as new single-parent household structures, visitation schedules, rules, and routines are set in place. The complex challenges in stepfamily integration contribute additional strains. Families do best if they can forge workable parenting coalitions across household boundaries and can knit together biological and step-relations, including step- and half-siblings and extended family.

CONNECTEDNESS

Connectedness, or cohesion, is essential for effective family functioning (Olson & Gorell, 2003; Beavers & Hampson, 2003). A crisis can shatter family cohesion if members are unable to turn to one another. Resilience is strengthened by mutual support, collaboration, and commitment to weather troubled times together. At the same time, family members need to respect each other's differences and boundaries. They may have quite varied reactions and pacing in response to the same event.

Family therapists can be most helpful in facilitating repair of wounded relationships and reconnection with estranged family members. Intense pressures in times of crisis can spark misunderstandings and cutoffs. A crisis can also be seized as opportunity for reconciliation.

With the death or loss of a parent, children need reassurance that they won't lose other significant relationships. When children are placed in foster care, although it may not be safe for them to live with a parent, it's important to find ways for them to sustain vital connections with their family network through photos, keepsakes, e-mail, letters, structured visits, and links to their cultural and religious heritage.

SOCIAL AND ECONOMIC RESOURCES

Kin and social networks are vital lifelines in times of trouble, offering practical and emotional support. The significance of role models and mentors for resilience of at-risk youth is well documented. Involvement in community groups and faith congregations also strengthens resilience. Families that are more isolated can be helped to access these potential resources.

Community-based coordinated efforts, involving local agencies and residents, are essential to meet the challenges of a major disaster and widespread trauma. Such multisystemic approaches facilitate both family and community resilience (Walsh, 2007). Financial security is crucial for resilience. Loss of a job or breadwinner, or a serious illness can drain a family's economic resources. Financial strain is the most significant risk factor in single-parent families where parents are overwhelmed and children fare poorly.

Most important, the concept of family resilience should not be misused to blame families that are unable to rise above harsh conditions by simply labeling them as "not resilient." Just as individuals need supportive relationships to thrive, family resilience must be supported by social and institutional policies and practices that foster the ability to thrive, such as flexible work schedules for parents and quality, affordable healthcare, child care, and elder care services. It is not enough to help families overcome the odds against them; mental health professionals must also strive to change the odds.

COMMUNICATION/PROBLEM-SOLVING PROCESSES

Communication processes foster resilience by bringing clarity to crisis situations, encouraging open emotional expression, and fostering collaborative problem solving. It must be kept in mind that cultural norms vary considerably in how sensitive information and feelings are shared within families and with professionals.

CLARITY

Clarity and congruence in words and deeds facilitate effective family functioning and the well-being of members. In times of crisis, communication and coordination can easily break down. Ambiguity fuels anxiety and blocks understanding and mastery. By helping families to clarify crucial information about their situation and future expectations, we can facilitate meaning-making and informed decision making. Shared acknowledgment of the reality and circumstances of a painful loss fosters healing, while secrecy, denial, and cover-up, especially in stigmatized situations such as suicide or AIDS, can impede recovery and lead to estrangement (Imber-Black, 1995; Walsh & McGoldrick, 2004).

When discussion of crises is shut down, anxiety may be expressed in a child's symptoms. Commonly, well-intentioned families avoid painful or threatening topics, wishing to protect children or frail elders from worry or waiting until they are certain about a precarious situation, such as an unclear medical prognosis or a divorce. However, anxieties about the unspeakable can generate catastrophic fears. Parents can be helpful by giving assurance that they will keep them informed as the situation develops and that they are open at any time to discuss questions or concerns. Parents may need guidance on age-appropriate ways to share information and can expect that as children mature, they may revisit past events to gain greater comprehension or bring up emerging concerns. For example, family sessions helped parents address their eight-year-old daughter's fears of loss in learning of her mother's breast cancer. As she later approached puberty, they needed to deal with a worry that surfaced that she, too, could develop breast cancer.

EMOTIONAL EXPRESSION

Open communication, supported by a climate of mutual trust, empathy, and tolerance for differences, enables members to share a wide range of feelings aroused by crisis and chronic stress. Family members may be out of sync over time; one may continue to be quite upset as others feel ready to move on. A breadwinner or single parent may suppress their own emotions in order to keep functioning for the family; children may try to help out by stifling their own feelings and needs or trying to cheer up parents. When emotions are intense or family members feel overwhelmed, conflict is likely to erupt and may spiral out of control.

Gender socialization leads to common differences in crises, with men tending more to withdraw or become angry, while women are more likely to express sorrow or anxiety. Masculine stereotypes of strength often constrain men from showing fear, vulnerability, or sadness. When strong emotions can't be shared with loved ones, the risk is increased for substance abuse, depression, self-destructive or violent behavior, relational distancing, and divorce. For relational resilience, couples and families can be encouraged to share their feelings and comfort one another. Helping families find pleasure and moments of humor in the midst of pain can offer respite and lift spirits.

COLLABORATIVE PROBLEM SOLVING

Creative brainstorming and resourcefulness open possibilities for finding solutions and new pathways. Clinicians can facilitate shared decision making and conflict resolution through negotiation of differences with mutual accommodation, fairness, and reciprocity over time. Resilience is fostered by efforts to set clear goals, take concrete steps toward them, build on small successes, and learn from failures.

Finally, families become more resourceful when they are able to shift from a crisis-reactive mode to a proactive stance. A resilience-oriented approach to practice focuses on the future potential, striving for the best while also preparing for the worst, to prevent problems and avert crises. As families strengthen bonds and build competencies, they are better able to meet future life challenges.

CONCLUSION

Influenced by the medical model and psychoanalytic theory, the field of mental health has focused predominantly on individual psychopathology and family deficits, with family strengths and potential unseen and under-valued. A family resilience conceptual orientation fundamentally alters this perspective, enabling researchers and practitioners to recognize, affirm, and build upon family resources.

By definition, resilience involves strengths under stress and forged through crisis or prolonged adversity. A family resilience framework is espe-cially relevant to clinical practice and social service delivery because most clients seek help in times of crisis. This approach shifts emphasis from fam-ily deficits to family challenges, with conviction in the potential for recovery and growth out of adversity.

The family resilience practice approach described here builds on recent advances in strengths-based, collaborative, systemic therapies in the field of family therapy. It is distinct in focus on strengthening family function-ing in the context of adversity. Incorporating a developmental perspective on stress, coping, and adaptation, this approach links presenting symptoms with disruptive stress events, with ripple effects to all members and relation-ships. How the family responds can foster resilience for all members and their relationships. Beyond coping or problem solving, resilience involves positive transformation and growth. In building relational resilience, fami-lies forge stronger bonds and become more resourceful in meeting future challenges. Thus, every intervention has preventive benefits.

The family resilience framework presented here integrates findings from three decades of research on resilience and well-functioning family systems. It is flexible for application with a wide range of stressful challenges: heal-ing from trauma or loss, navigating disruptive transitions, mastering chal-lenges of persistent adversity, and helping at-risk youth overcome barriers to success. It attends to the ongoing interaction of biological, family, and social influences, and guides assessment of family functioning in sociocultural and developmental contexts. Assuming multiple, varied pathways in resilience, practitioners help each family to forge its own adaptive strategies to master their challenges, fitting their cultural orientation, their kinship and community resources, and their life-cycle passage.

This conceptual framework can usefully be integrated with many strengths-based practice models. By targeting interventions to strengthen key processes for resilience, families become more resourceful in dealing with crises, weathering persistent stresses, and meeting future challenges. Resilience-oriented services foster family empowerment as they bring forth shared hope, develop new and renewed competencies, and strengthen family bonds.

The need to strengthen family resilience has never been more urgent, as families today are buffeted by stresses and uncertainties of economic, political, social, and environmental upheaval. With increasing family diversity, no single model of family health fits all. Yet resilience theory and research support clinical convictions that all families—even the most troubled—have the potential for adaptation, repair, and growth. A family resilience orientation provides a positive and pragmatic framework that guides interventions to strengthen family processes for resilience as presenting problems are addressed. Rather than simply providing a set of techniques to treat or change families, this strength-based approach enables therapists, in collaboration with family members, to draw out the abilities and potential in every family, and to encourage the active process of self-righting and growth. For helping professionals, the therapeutic process is enriched as we bring out the best in families and practice the art of the possible.

REFERENCES

Anthony, E. J. (1987). Risk, vulnerability, and resilience: An overview. In E. J. Anthony & B. Cohler (Eds.), *The invulnerable child*. New York: Guilford Press.

Antonovsky, A. (1998). The sense of coherence: An historical and future perspective. In H. McCubbin, E. Thompson, A. Thompson, and J. Fromer (Eds.), *Stress, coping and health in families: Sense of coherence and resilience* (pp. 3–20). Thousand Oaks, Calif.: Sage.

Beavers, W. R., & Hampson, R. B. (2003). Measuring family competence. In F. Walsh (Ed.), *Normal family processes: Growing diversity and complexity*, 3d ed. (pp. 549–580). New York: Guilford.

Becker, C., Sargent, J., & Rolland, J. S. (2000). Kosovar Family Professional Education Collaborative. *American Family Therapy Monograph*, 80 (Fall): 26–30.

Boss, P. (1999). *Ambiguous loss: Learning to live with unresolved grief.* Cambridge, Mass.: Harvard University Press.

Calhoun, L. G., & Tedeschi, R. G. (Eds.) (2006). Handbook of posttraumatic growth: Research and practice. Mahwah, N.J.: Lawrence Erlbaum.

Carter, B., & McGoldrick, M. (1999). The expanded family life cycle: Individual, family, and social perspectives, 3d ed. Needham Hill: Allyn & Bacon.

Epstein, N., Ryan, C., Bishop, D., Miller, I., & Keitner, G. (2003). The McMaster model: A view of healthy family functioning. In F. Walsh (Ed.), *Normal family processes* (3d ed.)(pp. 581–607). New York: Guilford Press.

Falicov, C. (2003). Immigrant family processes. In F. Walsh (Ed.), *Normal family processes*, 3d ed. (pp. 280–300). New York: Guilford Press.

Figley, C. (Ed.) (2002). *Treating compassion fatigue.* New York: Brunner/Rutledge.

Figley, C., & McCubbin, H. (Eds.) (1983). *Stress and the family: Coping with catastrophe.* New York: Brunner-Mazel.

Frankl, V. (1984). *Man's search for meaning.* New York: Simon & Schuster. (Originally published 1946).

Garmezy, N. (1991). Resiliency and vulnerability to adverse developmental outcomes associated with poverty. *American Behavioral Scientist,* 34, 416–430.

Hernandez, P. (2007). Vicarious resilience: A new concept in work with those who survive trauma. *Family Process,* 46.

Hetherington, E. M., & Kelly, J. (2002). *For better or for worse: Divorce reconsidered.* New York: Norton.

Higgins, G. O. (1994). *Resilient adults: Overcoming a cruel past.* San Francisco: Jossey-Bass.

Hill, R. (1949). *Families under stress.* New York: Harper.

Imber-Black, E. (1995). *Secrets in families and family therapy.* New York: Norton.

Imber-Black, E., Roberts, J., & Whiting, R. (2003). *Rituals in families and family therapy,* 2d ed. New York: Norton.

Kauffman, J. (Ed.). (2002). *Loss of the assumptive world: A theory of traumatic loss.* New York: Brunner-Routledge.

Kaufman, J., & Ziegler, E. (1987). Do abused children become abusive parents? *American Journal of Orthopsychiatry,* 57, 186–192.

Lazarus, A., & Folkman, S. (1984). *Stress, appraisal, and coping.* New York: Springer.

Luthar, S. S., Cicchetti, D., & Becker, B. (2000). The construct of resilience: A critical evaluation and guidelines for future work. *Child Development,* 71, 543–562.

McCubbin, H., McCubbin, M., McCubbin, A., & Futrell, J. (Eds.). (1998). *Resiliency in ethnic minority families. Vol. 2. African-American families.* Thousand Oaks, Calif.: Sage.

McCubbin, H., McCubbin, M., Thompson, E., & Fromer, J. (Eds.). (1998). *Resiliency in ethnic minority families. Vol. 1. Native and immigrant families.* Thousand Oaks, Calif.: Sage.

McCubbin, H., & Patterson, J. M. (1983). The family stress process: The Double ABCX model of adjustment and adaptation. *Marriage and Family Review,* 6 (1–2), 7–37.

McGoldrick, M., Gerson, R., & Petry, S. (2008). *Genograms: Assessment and intervention,* 3d ed. New York: Norton.

Neimeyer, R. A. (Ed.). (2001). *Meaning reconstruction and the experience of loss.* Washington, D.C.: American Psychological Association.

Olson, D. H., & Gorell, D. (2003). Circumplex model of marital and family systems. In Walsh, F. (Ed.), Normal family processes, 3d ed. (pp. 514–544). New York: Guilford.

Parsons, T., & Bales, R.F. (1955). *Family, socialization, and interaction processes*. Glencoe, Ill.: Free Press.

Patterson, J. (2002). Integrating family resilience and family stress theory. Journal of Marriage and the Family, 64, 349–373.

Reiss, D. (1981). *The family's construction of reality*. Cambridge, Mass.: Harvard University Press.

Rolland, J. S. (1994). *Families, illness and disability: An integrative treatment model*. New York: Basic.

Rolland, J. S., & Walsh, F. (2005). Systemic training for healthcare professionals: The Chicago Center for Family Health approach. *Family Process* 44 (3) 283–301.

Rolland, J. S., & Weine, S. (2000). Kosovar Family Professional Educational Collaborative. *AFTA Newsletter,* 79 (Spring), 34–35.

Rutter, M. (1987). Psychosocial resilience and protective mechanisms. *American Journal of Orthopsychiatry*, 57, 316–331.

Seligman, M. E. P. (1990). *Learned optimism*. New York: Random House.

Taylor, S. (1989). *Positive illusions: Creative self-deception and the healthy mind*. New York: Basic Books.

Tedeschi, R. G., & Calhoun, L. G. (1996). The Posttraumatic Growth Inventory: Measuring the positive legacy of trauma. *Journal of Traumatic Stress*, 9, 455–471.

Van der Kolk, B. A., McFarlane, A. C., & Weisaeth, L. (Eds.) (1996). *Traumatic stress: The Effects of overwhelming experience on mind, body, and society*. New York: Guilford.

Walsh, F. (1983). The timing of symptoms and critical events in the family life cycle. In H. Liddle (Ed.), *Clinical implications of the family life cycle* (pp. 120–133). Rockville, Md.: Aspen Systems Publications.

Walsh, F. (1996). The concept of family resilience: Crisis and challenge. *Family Process*, 35, 261–281.

Walsh, F. (1999). Families in later life: Challenge and opportunities. In B. Carter & M. McGoldrick (Eds.), *The expanded family life cycle* (pp. 307–326). Needham Heights, Mass.: Allyn & Bacon.

Walsh, F. (2002a). A family resilience framework: Innovative practice applications. *Family Relations*, 51(2), 130–137.

Walsh, F. (2002b). Bouncing forward: Resilience in the aftermath of September 11. *Family Process*, 41 (1), 34–36.

Walsh, F. (2003a). Family resilience: A framework for clinical practice. *Family Process*, 42 (1), 1–18.

Walsh, F. (2003b). Changing families in a changing world: Reconstructing family normality. In F. Walsh (Ed.), *Normal family processes: Growing diversity and complexity*, 3d ed. (pp. 3–26). New York: Guilford.

Walsh, F. (2003c). Clinical views of family normality, health, and dysfunction. In F. Walsh (Ed.), *Normal family processes: Growing diversity and complexity*, 3d ed. (pp. 27–57). New York: Guilford.

Walsh, F. (2003d). Normal family processes: Growing diversity and complexity, 3d ed. New York: Guilford.

Walsh, F. (2006). Strengthening family resilience, 2d ed. New York: Guilford.

Walsh, F. (2007). Traumatic loss and major disaster: Strengthening family and community resilience. *Family Process*, 46, 207–227.

Walsh, F. (Ed.). (2009). *Spiritual resources in family therapy*. 2d ed. New York: Guilford.

Walsh, F., & McGoldrick, M. (Eds.). (2004). *Living beyond loss: Death in the family,* 2d ed. New York: Norton.

Werner, E. E. (1993). Risk, resilience, and recovery: Perspectives from the Kauai longitudinal study. *Development and Psychopathology,* 5, 503–515.

Werner, E. E., & Johnson, J. L. (1999). Can we apply resilience? In M. D. Glantz and J. L. Johnson (Eds.), *Resilience and development: Positive life adaptations* (pp. 259–268). New York: Academic/Plenum.

Werner, E.E., & Smith, R. (1992). *Overcoming the odds.* Ithaca, N.Y.: Cornell University Press.

PART THREE

THEORY, PRACTICE, AND THE SOCIAL WORK TRADITION

Critical Questions, Issues, and Prospects

7 LOVE AND JUSTICE

A Silenced Language of Integrated Practice?

JANET L. FINN

WHAT'S LOVE GOT to do with it? This lyrical question in popular culture is also a central question of social work and social justice. Has a language and practice of love been lost in the (post)modern practice of social work? Have the powers of professionalization silenced a more intimate discourse of human connection and squelched a motive force for social action? Has the postmodern turn further denigrated a connection to our fundamental humanness as a core value base for the practice of social work? Did a loving practice of social work ever exist? Should a language of love inform and inspire social work today? These are key questions I have been pondering in response to the invitation to contribute a chapter to this volume.[1]

In part, this chapter is inspired by Sharon Berlin's examination of the value of acceptance in direct social work practice (Berlin, 2005). In her essay Berlin unpacks the ambiguous concept of "acceptance" and its multiple meanings in the history and contemporary practice of social work. She uses "acceptance" as a trope for a nuanced reflection on the development and professionalization of social work, the values and value tensions that undergird practice, and the politics of knowledge and practice that have shaped the profession over the past one hundred years. In reading Berlin's essay, I found myself returning to my own musings on the meaning and power of love in the practice of social work and the struggle for social justice. My academic training is in both social work and cultural anthropology. My professional identity is largely that of social worker. Over the past decade, I have been exploring ways to bring critical cultural theory to bear in understanding the construction of social problems, policies, programs, and practices. I have also been grappling with the ways in which ethnographic modes of inquiry relate to the social work experiences of engagement, colearning, and action for personal and social transformation. Several years ago, I began to explore the intertwining forces of love and justice in the context of feminist ethnography. In reading Berlin's essay on acceptance, I found myself returning to those earlier reflections. This chapter stems from a dialogical reading of Berlin and the ensuing reflections on love, justice, and their place in the practice of social work that emerged from that dialogue. It represents my modest effort to engage in dialogue with Sharon Berlin, take the risk of pursuing the subjects of love and justice, and offer food for thought in the spirit of social work's ongoing development and transformation.

A SHORT HISTORY OF ACCEPTANCE

Berlin (2005) travels through time to offer readers an understanding of the ways in which "acceptance" has been named and claimed in the history of social work. She points to the ambiguity of this commonly used yet ill-defined term and highlights key themes associated with it: a feeling of relationship; recognition of common humanity; moral obligation to honor the humanity of our fellow beings; an ethic of understanding, respect, and caring; compassion tempered by respect for autonomy; and recognition of another's rights and reality. In sum, Berlin asserts that acceptance can only be understood in dialectical relationship with possibilities of change.

Berlin revisits the emergence of social work in the late nineteenth century and considers acceptance as a central aspect of nascent practice in the context of profound social and economic change and widespread human suffering. Religious conviction and a humanitarian ethic guided early calls to service. For the friendly visitors, "acceptance" took the form of Calvinist-influenced tough love and practical assistance. The settlement house movement drew on an ethic of sharing and inclusion in responding to the personal concerns and social conditions of the urban poor and working classes (Berlin, 2005, p. 489). Berlin writes of the influence of the social gospel in the settlement house movement, and of the "relational acceptance"—a blending of compassion and autonomy—that was exemplified in the work of Jane Addams. For Mary Richmond and other promoters of casework and social diagnosis, acceptance found expression in an ethic of empathy. Specialized knowledge of diagnosis, interpretation, and intervention moved social work beyond the bounds of loving kindness and into the realm of professional expertise.

Berlin highlights the development of the diagnostic and functional traditions of social work in the 1930s and 1940s, and their influence on the concept of acceptance. While the diagnostic school focused on problem etiology and conflicts rooted in history, functionalists embraced human growth and potential, decoupling past problems from future possibility. Both traditions, however, contributed to a unifying vision of social work that recognized the power of the helping relationship in the change process and the centrality of client self-determination therein. By mid-century, social workers were embracing the therapeutic insights of Carl Rogers on the significance of genuineness, warmth, and unconditional positive regard as hallmarks of the helping relationship. As Berlin (p. 494) describes, this turn toward the power of relationship and personal potential also marked a turn away from attention to structural barriers and conditions of inequality that shape and constrain people's everyday lives. In sum, Berlin writes:

> In looking back to these earlier times, the distance that the historical perspective affords lets us see how easy it is to whittle down the concept of acceptance to make it fit practice realities, theoretical perspectives, cultural assumptions, and the demands of a social order that was, and sometimes still is, taken as reality, as an implacable set of structures to which we all must adjust (Kondrat, 2002). At the same time, we should not imagine that all of the previous efforts were thoroughly flawed or that we have just now figured everything out. In fact, other stories illustrate instances in which our predecessors implemented full-bodied acceptance (Abrams and Curran, 2004). (2005, pp. 496–497)

LOCATING LOVE AND JUSTICE IN SOCIAL WORK'S EARLY YEARS

Let us return now to the question of love. Where might we find a language and practice of love in this history? Where does it intersect with that of acceptance? Where is it the basis of claims for justice? As with acceptance, might an inquiry into love help us grasp historical and contemporary value tensions, power relations, and practice possibilities? Berlin, in her overview of the emergence of social work practice in the United States, describes the Calvinist underpinnings of the friendly visitors' "tough love" approach to helping. She argues that "such love could easily lapse into condescension, judgmentalism, and presumptions of moral superiority" (2005, p. 487). Linda Gordon (1988) offers a similar critique in her examination of the class-based judgments made by early caseworkers on the maternal capacities and quality of home life of poor and working-class women. However, Gordon does not suggest that casework interactions were ever loving in nature. In short, the line between loving care and limiting control is readily crossed, especially when power differences separate the parties involved.

Berlin writes of the ethic of sharing and inclusion that guided the work of Jane Addams and the women of Hull House. I suggest that strong, loving bonds both toward community members and among Hull House residents fueled the fires of reform and justice for Addams and her colleagues. Addams describes the social settlement as "an attempt to express the meaning of life in terms of life itself" (Stebner, 1997, p. 33). She shared sociologist William Cole's belief that the common denominator of the settlement house movement is a personal relationship in which service is carried out in the spirit of friendship (Cole, 1908, p. 4, as cited in Stebner, 1997, p. 33). For many participants in the settlement house movement, their commitments to community betterment were part and parcel of their dedication to the social gospel movement. The two movements fostered a new definition of religion as a way of life. "Religion, according to these movements, was more than an intellectual adherence to a theological tradition. It was the underlying motive of all service and participation within society—to love one's neighbor and to love God" (Stebner, 1997, p. 46). Pragmatic, material actions in the world were intimately linked to a larger sense of the sacredness of life and to loving connections among community members. Addams saw the settlement as a place and practice wherein Christian values could be translated into a concrete expression of humanism. According to Addams (1910):

> That Christianity has to be revealed and embodied in the line of social progress is a corollary to the simple proposition that man's action is found in his social relationships in the way in which he connects with his fellows; that his motives for action are the zeal and affection with which he regards his fellows. By this simple process was created a deep enthusiasm for humanity, which regarded man as at once organ and object of revelation; and by this process came about the wonderful fellowship, the true democracy of the early church, that so captivates the imagination. The early Christians were pre-eminently nonresistant. They believed in love as a cosmic force. . . .
>
> I believe that there is a distinct turning among many young men and women toward this simple acceptance of Christ's message. They resent the assumption

that Christianity is a set of ideas which belong to the religious consciousness, whatever that may be. They insist that it cannot be proclaimed and instituted apart from the social life of the community and that it must seek a simple and natural expression in the social organism itself. The Settlement movement is only one manifestation of that wider humanitarian movement throughout Christendom, put pre-eminently in England, is endeavoring to embody itself, not in a sect, but in society itself. (pp. 96–97)

Complementing this spiritual basis for social action were the deep bonds of friendship among the women of Hull House. Stebner (1997, p. 151) argues that friendship was a powerful component in both individual and social transformation and a "grounding for vocational and spiritual identities" among the women of Hull House. Long-term loving friendships sustained the work of many Hull House residents. These relationships "helped them form the meaning of their lives and became central to their vocation at Hull House" (Stebner, 1997, p. 166). According to Stebner, these loving bonds of friendship enlarged each woman's world and provided a location from which to act in the world. Friendships forged critical consciousness of the connection between the personal and the political, and supported women as they expanded their spheres of social and political influence and partici-pation. As the women of Hull House engaged with the community around them and built lasting ties with neighborhood residents, they learned to see and appreciate the world from the perspective of the less powerful. As their perspectives were challenged and changed, so too were both their visions of how the world could be and their everyday practices of community life (Stebner, 1997, p. 143). The bonds of friendship among women of Hull House were forged in a dialectics of love and justice among the women themselves and in their relations to the larger community of which they were a part.[2] As Stebner concludes, "These relationships were based not only on loving, sup-porting, and critiquing one another but also on making the world more just and loving" (p. 186). Drawing on religious tradition and bonds of friendship, they crafted a powerful amalgam of love and justice that was both process and product of personal and social transformation.

Berlin also speaks to the limits of acceptance for Addams and other white women reformers and their failure to engage with and support the work of African American women activists. In these women's stories of spiritual commitment and social action, we also find a language of love. For exam-ple, Berlin describes acceptance in this context as "extending the bounds of one's own family to take care of others who are cut off from family ties; to impose loving demands on those who receive care" (2005, p. 491). Similarly, theologian Rosetta Ross (2003) offers a rich exploration of the lives and faith of African American women leaders in the struggle for civil rights. She examines the interlocking power of religion and activism in the individual and collective efforts of antebellum activist Sojourner Truth, turn-of-the-century leader Nannie Helen Burroughs, early civil rights activists Ella Baker and Septima Poinsette Clark, and grassroots leaders Fannie Lou Hamer and Victoria Way DeLee, among others. In summarizing the power of faith and love as motive forces in their lives, Ross writes:

> The religious language of love may more appropriately express the values enacted in these women's practices. Love may be identified with recognizing, valuing and respecting persons by seeking their flourishing as human beings, including attending to material well-being, affirming human mutuality through increasing opportunities for all to participate, empowering people to fully realize their potential, and affirming as beneficial the gifts that each individual brings to human society. This emphasis on love as a means of attending to human flourishing through practices of organizing, teaching, protesting, advocating, and agitating pervaded these religious Black women's civic participation. . . . These women's persistent practices of organizing, teaching, and agitating bore witness to their understanding of human mutuality and relationship as divine gifts and to their understanding of divine calling to affirm human community. (2003, p. 235)

Septima Clark, for example, is noted for her important work in adult literacy, which evolved into the Citizenship Education Program, a cornerstone of the civil rights movement. She began her teaching career in 1916 on Johns Island, South Carolina. Seeing the "dismal economic, social, and health conditions" of the residents, Clark recognized the need to engage adults as well as children in critical education. Clark devised a popular education approach to adult literacy and encouraged students to use words to understand and change their worlds. Through critical literacy education Clark bridged her faith and social justice activism. She equated the citizenship program with "Jesus' ministry to the least" (Ross, 2003, p. 80). As Clark describes:

> Despite the fact that during virtually my whole adult life I have been fighting the dominant citizenship of my Low Country—though I feel that actually I am fighting for them as well as for the less privileged and the silent—I love them, all of them. I want to see their lots as well as the lots of the less fortunate, improve steadily. (quoted in Ross, 2003, p. 80)

Clark's commitment to loving engagement with the privileged as well as the disenfranchised was also a commitment to social justice, wherein love is translated into concrete practice. She writes:

> Long experience in Christian missions has taught us that this love and concern for others must be made concrete. Our missionaries could not be content preaching the gospel to hungry folk. They also had to teach them new agricultural methods and help them to provide food for themselves and their families. They provided clinics and hospitals to improve the health of the people and established schools for the education of these new converts. (Quoted in Ross, 2003, p. 81)[3]

Let's pause for a moment and think about the synergistic power of love and justice in the work of these early reformers. They variably drew on a love grounded in faith, in human mutuality, and in intimate connections among women and men, they used its power to fuel and sustain justice-oriented action, and they grappled with tensions of power and privilege therein. What was lost to social work as a discourse and practice of professionalization overshadowed a practice guided by ties and commitments of love? Is it true that, as Mary Richmond argued, the scientific practice of social diagnosis, knowledge of the workings of the human mind, and knowledge of social resources result in "a new power in the world added to the older power of just loving one another" (Richmond, 1922, p. 9, as cited in Berlin, 2005, p. 488)? Or did the growing infatuation with diagnoses, tests, and measurements in effect sacrifice the power of loving one another for the "greater good" of professional expertise?

LOVE AND JUSTICE IN SOCIAL WORK AT MID-CENTURY

Let's now locate our inquiry into love and justice in the mid-twentieth-century social work discourse and practice emerging in the wake of the diagnostic/functional tradition debates. As Berlin describes, from the rancor emerged a common respect for the value of human relationships in the practice of social work and the importance of empathic entry into another's subjective world as part of the helping process (Hamilton, 1958; Robinson, 1978). Social workers began to draw on the humanistic psychology of Carl Rogers in promoting relationships based on three qualities: empathy, genuineness, and unconditional positive regard (Rogers, 1951). Rogers and his colleagues held that these core qualities facilitate a climate in which a relationship of dignity and respect can develop and in which challenging work can be tackled (Rogers, Gendlin, Kiesler & Truax, 1967). Helen Harris Perlman (1979) described the relationship that gives social work its uniqueness as one characterized by a special kind of love rooted in warmth, concern, and, most fundamentally, acceptance. According to Perlman, a good relationship is characterized by warmth, love, caring, acceptance, responsiveness, empathy, genuineness, attentiveness, concern, support, and understanding. It was her belief that we grow in humanness through the nurture of the emotional experience of relationship. She saw the social work relationship as one of caring, and she described caring as "love in its giving, protective, nurturing aspects" (1979, p. 59).

Perlman is noted for finding common ground in the diagnostic and functional debates, honoring the power of the worker-client relationship, recognizing human capacity and potential, and articulating social casework as an interactive process of problem solving. What goes largely unacknowledged is her willingness to embrace a language of love, and to speak to relationship as the *heart* of helping (Perlman, 1979). While Perlman did not make the case for structural change, she challenged the pathologizing of human struggles and celebrated instead the humanizing powers of relationships. She identified caring love as a core part of the practice of social work.

Felix Biestek also speaks to relationship as the essence of social work. While Perlman describes relationship as the heart of social work, Biestek claims relationship as its soul (Biestek, 1957, p. 18). In his 1957 book *The Casework Relationship,* Biestek outlines seven characteristics of the helping relationship: individualization, purposeful expression of feeling, controlled emotional environment, acceptance, nonjudgmental attitude, self-determination, and confidentiality. His description of the social work relationship as "the dynamic interaction of attitudes and emotions between the caseworker and the client, with the purpose of helping the client achieve a better adjustment between himself and his environment" is often cited in social work texts. Less noted is Biestek's depiction of the motive force of social work and social workers: "With the motive of love, he strives for skills in the use of wisdom of science to help his brother in need" (1957, p. 137). It is intriguing that here—despite a half-century of professionalization, of staking of claims to a terrain of expertise and specialized knowledge, and of dogged efforts to establish grounds of scientific objectivity by which to assess the processes and outcomes of social work practice—a language of love still filtered through. However, as social workers came together on the meaning and power of relationship, the profession was largely blinded to the structural realities that shaped and maintained practices of oppression and relations of inequality. If the voice of love in social work's heart and soul was but a whisper at mid-century, the voice of justice was largely silenced altogether.[4]

LOCATING LOVE IN STRUGGLES FOR JUSTICE

Sharon Berlin characterizes the period from the 1960s to the end of the twentieth century as a time of shifting realities for social work (2005, p. 497). She describes the challenges to the social work profession from without and within, as diverse social movements raised questions of difference and power, challenged deeply entrenched structural inequalities in the United States, and demanded an end to U.S imperialism abroad. Mainstream social work was promoting problem-solving processes, embracing the language and concepts of systems theory, and furthering a holistic person-in-environment perspective. At the same time, the social change orientation of the 1960s and 1970s—the civil rights movement, women's movement, antiwar movement, the war on poverty—challenged social work's dominant assumptions and the nature and place of professionalism therein. Critics from within pushed for a more relevant profession, one committed to social justice, human rights, inclusion, and respect for difference. However, calls for justice and a new radicalism within social work seldom invoked a discourse of love. In contrast, for many grassroots activists engaged in frontline struggles for the very issues social work purportedly stood for, a language and practice of love was intricately woven into the whole cloth of social and political commitment.

As demands for social justice were made on multiple fronts, the legitimacy of person-changing interventions as the modus operandi of social work was questioned. Critics challenged social work's knowledge claims and demanded attention to the ways in which issues of difference, power, oppression, and inequality shaped not only social experience but also public policies, social research agendas, and the development of social welfare programs and social work practices. They questioned the fundamental relevance of the social work endeavor. For example, radical social workers were confronting the contradictions of social work and questioning the logic of capitalism in which the profession was embedded. Embracing Marxist political ideology, they called for social justice through transformative change in the structure of society (Bailey & Brake, 1975; Galper, 1975). Theirs was not a language of love.

Pressures on the profession to return to a commitment to social justice bore results. For example, in 1973 NASW published an edited volume entitled *Social Work Practice and Social Justice* that grappled with stark examples of racism and inequality as manifest in correctional, health, education, and welfare systems; the complicity of social work and social workers in perpetuating systemic injustices; and the responsibility of the profession to advocate for justice-oriented social change. The contributors critiqued the dominance of individual pathology approaches to theory and practice, which tended to bracket out attention to social structures. They argued that social work had failed to live up to its professed values of human dignity, worth, and self-determination by ignoring social structures, failing to identify basic social problems and participate in their resolutions, and claiming a stance of professional neutrality regarding issues that are fundamentally political. Bess Dana (1973) challenged social workers to advocate for health care as a right. She called for a practice of social justice based on partnership, collaborative action, promotion of rights, pursuit of new knowledge, and advocacy. As Bernard Ross concluded (1973, p. 152), "Social justice is concerned not just with the equitable distribution of goods and services but with the right and power of persons and groups to obtain their fair share. Thus social workers necessarily accept as a goal the redistribution of goods, services, and power." These renewed demands for justice, however, were bound to a language of rights rather than love.

In contrast to the decoupling of love and justice in professional social work circles, some grassroots activists for social justice and social change continued to make the connections of love and justice explicit in their lives and work. For example, connections of love and justice are woven deeply into the history of social welfare practices and rights claims of women of color in the United States. Some women invoke a faith-based love of humanity as an expression of God's love. Others invoke loving bonds of friendship or the maternal love for family and children. For example, sociologist Nancy Naples (1998), in her study of grassroots women activists in the war on poverty, explores the history of women's activism and puts forth the concept of "activist mothering," wherein maternal love serves as an ethical base and motive force for political action. Naples describes activist mothering as interwoven practices of women's nurturing roles to their own and others' children, combined with political activism. It is activism motivated by love and concern for the well-being of their children, families, and communities. Naples explores activist histories of women of color and highlights ways in which loving practices of mothering are tied to a commitment to challenge racism and fight for social justice. Naples writes:

Women of color as activist mothers, especially those living in poor neighborhoods, must fight against discrimination and oppressive institutions that shape their daily lives, and, consequently, as mothers they model strategies of resistance for their children. For example, African American women's struggle against racism infuses their mothering practice inside and outside of their "homeplace." Lessons carved out of the experiences of "everyday racism" contribute to mothering practices that include "handing down the knowledge of racism from generation to generation." Referring to this practice in her discussion of homeplace as a "site of resistance," bell hooks (1990, p. 46) explains: "Working to create a homeplace that affirmed our beings, our blackness, our love for one another was necessary resistance." (p. 114)

Naples builds on Patricia Hill Collins's (1990) concept of "othermothering" to describe the ways in which some women extend the emotional bonds and networks of kinship and their maternal responsibilities therein to building community institutions and advocating for their neighbors' rights and well-being. In sum, this practice of community work brings the emotional force of mothering into "dynamic relationship with particular historic conditions." Through bonds of love and kinship African American women have also passed down "cultural traditions as well as survival and resistance strategies from one generation to another" (Naples, 1998, p. 115).

In sum, Naples found that "a broadened definition of mothering was woven in and through [women's] paid and unpaid community work, which in turn was infused with political activism" (p. 113). Activist mothers carried their commitment to love and nurturing beyond the bounds of family. They redefined "good mothering" as all actions that addressed the needs of their children and communities. Motherly love may be manifest in public protest or in organization of a campaign to improve day care or health care. In the work of many women of color engaged in civil rights and antipoverty activism, a language and practice of love was central to social action and to the social relationships that nurtured them as women and as activists. The power of kin and friendship sustained interpersonal ties and strengthened both resolve and capacity for justice-oriented action.

In a similar vein, the intimate bonds of love and justice were central to the commitment and practice of African American women civil rights activists, as exemplified by Diane Nash. Nash grew up in a strict Catholic home in Chicago. Her political activism was sparked through participation in nonviolent direct action workshops while a student at Fisk University. Nash joined in the student sit-in movement in 1960, and she went on to become a founding member and leader of the Student Nonviolent Coordinating

Committee (SNCC) and coordinator of the Freedom Rides (Ross, 2003). Nash spoke of the oppressive force of racism and segregation to deny human dignity and mutuality. As Ross (2003) describes, "Nash asserted that the protests in which she and others participated sought to awaken in society the mutuality that she understood as constitutive not only of human relationship but also of democracy" (p. 186). For Nash, a "situation that denies mutuality of persons living in social relationship is a circumstance of radical moral evil, or sin" (p. 187). Nash believed that the response to radical evil was the "militant practice of radical love" (p. 187). She argued that the non-violent movement was based on and motivated by love. Nash "saw the non-violent movement as a process of seeking mutual change for mutual benefit by means of love" (p. 188). Nash states, "We used nonviolence as an expression of love and respect of the opposition, while noting that a person is never the enemy. The enemy is always attitudes, such as racism or sexism, political systems that are unjust; economic systems that are unjust—some kind of system or attitude that oppresses" (p. 188).

Women making connections between love and justice in their lives as women through civil rights and antipoverty activism both contributed to and challenged the "second wave" women's movement emerging in the 1970s. They helped set the stage for critical thinking on social work theory and practice in the ensuing years.

LOVE AND JUSTICE IN THE (POST)MODERN ERA?

Citing William Reid (2002), Berlin notes that "one of the most prominent direct practice trends in the last 25 years has been a recalibration of the authority of the worker and the client" (2005, pp. 499–500). The validity of the social worker as expert and the objectivity and neutrality of social work's knowledge base have come under scrutiny. Critical theorists and practitioners have turned their attention to the ways in which forms and relations of power and inequality shape the social work encounter. They have pointed to the partial and perspectival nature of knowing, the inseparability of forms of knowledge and forms of power, and the ways in which master narratives of difference, pathology, and intervention are deeply embedded in social work thought and practice (Adams, Dominelli & Payne, 2005; Allan, Pease & Briskman, 2003; Chambon, Irving & Epstein, 1999; Pease & Fook, 1999; Sakamoto & Pitner, 2005; Saleebey, 1994). Some critics have pointed to a disconnect between the profession's value stance regarding social justice and the realities of contemporary practice. As Berlin (2005) describes, critics have challenged the predominant, problem-focused models and have called for practice grounded in critiques of power, challenges to imbalances of power, and recognition and promotion of strengths. Post-structural critics have questioned master narratives that have guided the social work enterprise, examined the discourses that shape and constrain practice, and called attention to the interrelated social construction of problems, policies, practices, and subjectivities (Margolin, 1997; Chambon, Irving & Epstein, 1999). Some have called for a critical, anti-oppressive practice of social work that enhances social solidarity, deepens social interaction, and reduces inequality (Dominelli, 2002). Advocates of critical social work argue that the central purpose of social work is social change to redress social inequality. They examine class, race, gender, and other forms of social inequality and their impacts on the marginalization and oppression of individuals and groups. They, too, pay particular attention to the structural arrangements of society that contribute to individual pain (Allan, Pease & Briskman, 2003).

Feminist critics have pointed to the social construction of gender, family, and pathology, the gender-blind nature of most practice modalities, and the questions of power and inequality embedded therein (see, for example, Figueira-McDonough, Netting & Nichols-Casebolt, 1998). Feminist perspectives began to significantly shape the field of social work in the 1980s, with calls for a woman-centered practice, attention to the common concerns of women workers and clients, and exploration of the politics of everyday life (Hanmer & Statham, 1989). While solidarity and connection among women was honored, love per se was at times a suspect force. For example, Hanmer and Statham spoke to the power and place of love and friendship as resources in the lives of women. At the same time, they describe love as a double-edged sword, which, once received and given, "confirms a woman's subordinate social position" (1989, p. 151). Thus, from the perspective of some feminists, love carried with it the freight of dependency and inequality.

The theoretical and political work of women at the Stone Center for Developmental Services and Studies at Wellesley College was also shaping feminist thinking regarding interpersonal practice of psychotherapy and social work (see, for example, Jordan, Kaplan, Baker Miller, Stiver & Surrey, 1991). Women were questioning the assumptions of individual autonomy that informed dominant theoretical models of human development and exploring instead the centrality of relationship in human experience. Feminist theorists and practitioners spoke to the power of human connectedness, of self-in-relationship, and of mutuality in the process of human healing, growth, and change. While not invoking a language of love, their work validated the power of mutuality, empathy, and care as the interpersonal correlates to transformation of unjust social arrangements, both necessary parts of the feminist political project.

These critiques and interventions have, as Berlin describes, encouraged a turn to more reflexive and dialogical approaches to practice, grounded in humility and critical curiosity. They have informed thinking about social work as a transformative process in which both social conditions and participants, including the social worker, are changed in the pursuit of a just world. Some within social work have turned to Brazilian educator Paulo Freire for inspiration. Freire is well known for his liberatory approach to education as a grounded, critical, collective process of consciousness raising. Freire frames liberatory change as a systematic process of critical dialogue to unmask relations of power, examine the roots of oppression and inequality, reduce self-blame, and spark critical consciousness to inform the *praxis* of action and reflection (Freire, 1974).[5] Freire reminds us that dialogue "requires an intense faith in man [*sic*], faith in his power to make and remake, to create and recreate, faith in his vocation to be fully human, which is not the privilege of an elite, but the birthright of all people" (1974, p. 79). Freire believed that honest, genuine dialogue is founded on love, humility, and faith. It cannot exist without hope. Nor can it exist without critical thinking and the possibility of transformation. His work is frequently invoked in calls for a critical practice of social work that envisions and strives to realize a just world. Once again, what tends to go without comment is the centrality of a language of love in Freire's vision of liberatory practice. It seems as if social workers committed to transforming the profession have readily embraced Freire's concept of critical consciousness and dialogical practice, while largely bracketing out his grounding of critical dialogue in a discourse of love.

My own theoretical and political work over the past decade has been profoundly influenced by Freire and other critical social and political theorists and activists seeking to transform social work thought and practice. My colleague Maxine Jacobson and I have been grappling with the contradictions we confronted in our own social work practice and probing the possibilities for making the profession's commitment to social justice the centerpiece of social work (Finn & Jacobson, 2003, 2008). We sought to articulate a critical approach to social work that integrates politics and practice; translates the concept of social justice into concrete action; and honors the complex multicultural terrain of the twenty-first century (see Reisch, 2005, pp. 170–171). In so doing, we have drawn on the contributions of systems thinkers, structuralist, poststructuralist, practice, and feminist theorists, and the insights of those advocating strengths- and empowerment-based approaches to practice. We have also drawn inspiration from those living the everyday contradictions of power and inequality, and engaging in grounded struggles for change. As we reflected on these diverse, challenging influences, we began to build a frame for "social justice work" around five key themes: *meaning, context, power, history,* and *possibility.* What were we pulling from these influences that could help us envision social justice work? Could these five themes be the necessary and sufficient elements for a foundation? As we held these five independent themes in relation and explored their interconnection, what new possibilities for thought and practice might emerge? We began to explore those possibilities. Taken together, the five key themes of the Just Practice framework ask us to consider the following questions: How do people give *meaning* to the experiences and conditions that shape their lives? What are the *contexts* in which those experiences and conditions occur? What forms and relations of *power* shape people and processes? How does *history* make people, and how do people make history as they engage in struggles over questions of meaning and power? How might an appreciation of those struggles help us imagine and claim a sense of *possibility* in the practice of social justice work? We see the Just Practice framework as an integrated approach to social work that theoretically and practically links themes of meaning, power, and history to the context and possibilities of justice-oriented practice. We argue that the Just Practice framework offers not "answers" but a model for critical inquiry that enables us to disrupt assumed truths and explore transformative courses of action. The five key themes provide the basis for question-posing. These questions are translated into action through seven core processes that link theory and practice: *engagement, teaching/learning, action, accompaniment, evaluation, critical reflection,* and *celebration.* These processes, we contend, emphasize mutuality, relationship, and participation, as they challenge expert models and top-down approaches to assessment and intervention. Through these processes, the theory, politics, and ethics of social justice work are translated into *praxis* for personal and social transformation (Finn & Jacobson, 2008).

What I find both intriguing and troubling about this long-term dedication to the integration of social justice and social work is the absence of a discourse of love. While we have written at length about the centrality of relationship, called for practice grounded in humility and connection, and exposed the myriad ways in which unequal power relations constrain meaningful participation, we have been silent on the meaning and power of love in the pursuit of social justice and in the practice of social work. How is it that a discourse of love is so readily silenced and erased? What are the implications of the silencing and subjugation of love for the practice of social justice work? This process of question-posing prompted me on a new quest—looking for love.

LOOKING FOR LOVE—SEARCHING FOR A SILENCED DISCOURSE AND PRACTICE

This search for love began in earnest as I was reviewing revisions to the second edition of *Just Practice: A Social Justice Approach to Social Work* (Finn & Jacobson, 2008). We had developed a more in-depth discussion of relationship, drawing on Perlman's notion of relationship as the heart of social work. We had incorporated insights shared and stories told by practitioners and advocates that spoke fundamentally to the centrality of love in the pursuit of social justice. But it seems that we elided rather than honored the place of love. In writing this essay, I have been prompted to revisit some of these insights and stories and the lessons of love therein. For example, Dennis Saleebey (1990, 1994, 2006), who has written extensively on the strengths perspective and its promise for social work, recognizes the explicit connection of love and justice in Freire's work and embraces it in his own as well. Saleebey has drawn on Freire in articulating his beliefs about dialogue and collaboration that inform a strengths perspective in social work Saleebey (2006) states:

Humans can only come into being through a creative and emergent relationship with others. Without such transactions, there can be no discovery and testing of one's power, no knowledge, no heightening of one's awareness and internal strengths. In dialogue, we confirm the importance of other and begin to heal the rift between self, other, and institution.

Dialogue requires empathy, identification with, and the inclusion of other people. Paulo Freire (1973) was convinced, based on his years of work with oppressed peoples, that only humble and loving dialogue can surmount the barrier of mistrust built from years of paternalism and the rampant subjugation of the knowledge and wisdom of the oppressed. "Founding itself upon love, humility, and faith, dialogue becomes a horizontal relationship of which mutual trust between dialoguers is the logical consequence" (pp. 79–80). A caring community is a community that confirms otherness, in part by giving each person and group a ground of their own, and affirming this ground through encounters that are egalitarian and dedicated to healing and empowerment. (pp. 14–15)

Saleebey, in speaking of the philosophy guiding a strengths perspective, directly highlights the language of both love and faith in Freire's work. Freire's pedagogy of the oppressed can be seen as an early version of liberation theology, a Catholic faith-based movement emerging in the 1960s that linked theology and social justice.[6]. As Phillip Berryman describes, liberation theology is "an interpretation of Christian faith through the poor's suffering, their struggle, and hope, and a critique of society and Christianity through the eyes of the poor" (Berryman, 1987). Liberation theology brings both structural analysis and deep empathy to bear in explaining and deploring the suffering of the poor (Boff, 1989; Farmer, 2003, p. 41). Similar to the nonviolent movement in the struggle for civil rights in the United States, a language and practice of radical love were central to people's movements inspired by liberation theology in Latin America during the 1970s and 1980s.[7] Liberation theology shaped the direction of social activism, including the social work profession, throughout Central and South America. The words of Fr. Ferdinand Cardenal, a liberation theologian and director of Nicaragua's literacy campaign in 1980, capture the fusion of love and justice that informed liberatory political struggles throughout the Americas:

> Politics is the science that is concerned about all those people who live in our nation. In biblical language it is the love I have towards all those who live with me in the same society, the love for my neighbor, for my fellow citizens. Politics in its true sense is a science completely opposed and antagonistic to the selfish, egocentric attitudes which give rise to exploitation. People who take advantage of or exploit others only see them as objects to be manipulated, as cheap labor to be used, while the true politician starts from a basic position of love and concern and sees the people as fellow human beings living in the same nations, sharing and working together.

> We believe that politics is the art of assuring that all people in this nation progress, that all of us conquer and win our freedom, our liberty, our independence, the peace and justice necessary so that love can be nourished, grow, and reign over all. This really is politics—the constant loving search and struggle to improve our lives and the lives of others.

> We believe that our education is not only political but it is based on the political sense that emerges from love and the political sense that attempts to build a world of justice and community . . . This love of course is not purely sentimental emotion but is it the kind of love that is concerned with transforming the degrading living conditions to which fellow human beings are subjected. Politics is the love by which people work together to transform inhuman and unjust conditions; it is part of the noble quest and struggle of humanity for dignity and justice. (Cited in Hope & Timmel 1999, p. 94)

For Cardenal, the call for loving and humble dialogue is intimately connected to processes of political transformation to a just world. His recognition of politics as acts of love also resonates with Phyllis Day's (2006, p. 1)
claim that her text on social welfare policy is "a book about love: of people
helping others, of organizations that ease the way for people in trouble, and
of people joining together to work for the benefit of others." This is an easily overlooked but significant claim about silenced discourses and possible
directions in social work practice and policy. As Day calls on the social work
profession to promote just social policies that reflect and support human
dignity and rights, she also cautions that love must be understood in relation to power

The connections of faith, love, and justice also resonate with the stories shared by contributors to *Just Practice* (Finn & Jacobson, 2008) who
reflected on the shaping of their consciousness and practice of social work
through experiences of living and working in poor communities in Central
and South America. For example Scott Nicholson, a social worker engaged
with human rights advocacy, writes of his work in Colombia:

> I'm accompanying leaders of social organizations in the state of Arauca
> in Colombia. These leaders have been threatened with death by the right-
> wing paramilitary groups—which have close relations with the Colombian
> military. They're also at risk of being imprisoned or killed by the govern-
> ment security forces. Our *compañeras* and *compañeros* ("beloved compan-
> ions") have requested this accompaniment because the paramilitaries and
> the military are less likely to take action in the presence of international
> witnesses . . . For me, international accompaniment is a life-transforming
> gift that I'm receiving from our *compañeras* and *compañeros*. They're risk-
> ing their lives to construct peace with social justice. The radiance of their
> example touches the depth of my being and inspires me to be in solidarity
> with them in their struggle. The intensity of the situation forges deep rela-
> tions of love and solidarity that are more difficult to encounter in the U.S.
> and take longer to develop there—but that are equally beautiful. I believe
> that these relationships are the heart of the "just practice" of social work
> and of genuine spiritual experience. (Nicholson cited in Finn & Jacobson,
> 2008, pp. 316–318)

Nicholson's account embodies the spirit of the settlement house movement, in which loving relationships were inseparable from social commitment and political action.

LOVE AND JUSTICE: AN ETHNOGRAPHIC INTERLUDE

Reflection on colleagues' testimonies of love and justice brought me back to my own experiences as a cultural anthropologist and social worker in Chile documenting stories of women's struggles for human rights and everyday survival in the context of military dictatorship and return to democracy (Finn, 1998, 2001). In October 1992, while doing fieldwork in northern Chile, I had gone on a Sunday afternoon to the plaza in the center of Calama, a bedroom community to the Chuquicamata copper mines, located on the edge of the Atacama Desert. I saw a copper monument dedicated to twenty-six men who had been executed on October 19, 1973, under the Pinochet dictatorship. As I was reading the homage to these men, a small group, made up mostly of women, passed through the main street. They were carrying placards with photos of these same men and banners calling for truth and justice. I joined the march and walked with the group to the edge of town, where a bus was waiting. I asked one of the women if I could join them. She took me by the hand and invited me on the bus, telling me that her name was Maria and she was the widow of one of the executed and this was the annual memorial service organized by the *Agrupación de Familiares de los Ejecutados de Calama*. I learned that the men had been executed by an elite military squad authorized by General Augusto Pinochet in a brutal pass through northern Chile known as the Caravan of Death.[8] First, we paid tribute to the men at the municipal cemetery. Then we traveled to a site in the Atacama Desert where bone fragments of some of the men had been found a few years earlier. We stood hand in hand, singing, calling out the names of the dead, and throwing carnations on their makeshift grave markers.

I became acquainted with Maria and other members of the *Agrupación* over the next few months. I found them to be a diverse group of women bound together through violence and their ongoing struggles for truth and justice. I came to know Violeta, who had turned down a marriage proposal from her partner Mario the day before his death. She had laughed and assured him they had plenty of time. That has become a central part of her story of her ongoing search for truth and justice. She describes herself as bound to Mario by love and a shared commitment to a just future.[9].

And there is Bruni, a mother of two and widow of Bernardo, who had been a union leader in the Dupont explosives factory, located near the copper mines. Bruni had come north to Chuquicamata to do domestic work in Yankee homes, the best work available for a *campesina* with a grade-school education in the 1960s. She married Bernardo in 1967 and describes her wedding as the happiest day of her life. Maria, Violeta, and Bruni did not know one another before the violent execution of their loved ones brought them together in 1973. They and other members of the *Agrupación* crafted their own family of sorts as they shared emotional and material support, and built political solidarity in their search for the remains of their loved ones.

I returned to Chile every year between 1992 and 1998, spending anywhere from days to months in the north. With each visit, my conversations with women in the *Agrupación* grew more intimate. Maria had often talked of her love for Fernando. Like other women of the *Agrupación,* she had built a small shrine in memory of Fernando on prominent display in her living room. There was a poster calling for truth and justice, and a tattered black-and-white photo of her handsome young partner, and next to it, another photo, of the two of them, young lovers, dancing close. Maria has remarried and shares her home with her partner and their children, and the memory of Fernando.

In 1990 remains of some of the bodies were found in a mass grave. In 1995 official action was taken to positively identify the remains that had been recovered years earlier. The women waited anxiously throughout the winter and spring of 1995 for word on the identification of their loved ones. I sat side by side with Maria one winter day, sharing confidences and listening as she talked of her trepidation about the possible identification of Fernando's remains. Maria told me that she did not want to think of Fernando being dead. Instead, she wanted to imagine that he had run off with another woman, that he was in Argentina dancing in the embrace of another, that she would rather lose him to the love of another woman than to violence and death. And I thought of the poignancy of her shrine to two lovers dancing.

In September 1995 a forensic pathologist visited the members of the *Agrupación* in Calama and provided positive identification of thirteen of the twenty-six men. Fernando was among those whose remains were positively identified. Maria remembers:

> It was a moment of joy, having found him, and also of deep sadness and pain after having a whole person, who was beautiful, full of life, then to only find a few bones. You are left with a terrible doubt about whether that bone is really your partner. You can't believe it because the person you love, the father of your children, becomes a bone that you examine from every angle. The doctor showed me this long leg bone and part of a skull. Touching that bone—to have that piece for me was terrible. I wanted to have him in my arms and hold him tight. (Quoted in Allen, 1999, p. 86)

For Bruni, it was the desert itself that she saw as the other woman who kept her husband from her. "Sometimes I think of the desert as a woman, the other woman. My husband is with her now, and I cannot get him back. Someday I am going to write a poem and call it 'Jealous of the Desert.'"[10] Bruni recalls going with a group of women to the governor's office to seek surrender of the bodies and being turned away. There were no answers to cloak her grief: "I always wondered about their last moments alive, if they screamed, or complained, or cried" (quoted in Allen, 1999, p. 28).

In the 1980s Bruni had joined with other women seeking out spaces in the shadows of the dictatorship where they could give voice to their fear, outrage, and claims for justice. Both because of and in spite of their fear, they took great risks to position themselves between their disappeared loved ones and the violence of the military state. Bruni told me about her first trip to the desert, to publicly acknowledge the deaths and begin searching for the bodies, an open challenge to the dictatorship: "There was a small group of us that went to the edge of town. Others were too afraid. I was so filled with fear, I could hardly move. I thought, what if they kill me? What if my children lose their mother, too? But I couldn't not go. In spite of our fear, I took my friend's hand and the two of us set out for the desert. We had to act. We had to say, 'we are here and we will be here'" (Finn, 1998, p. 172).

The women returned each day, risking arrest and defying the dictatorship in their search for their loved ones. Bruni lived the contradiction captured in her words. Her children's survival depended on her absence from home, as she worked sixteen to eighteen hours a day trying to earn enough money to feed and clothe them. She tried to protect them with silence, even as she felt her absence left them painfully exposed. Schoolmates, neighbors, and potential employers were wary, fearing that the violence visited on Bruni and her children would take them, too. And still Bruni continued to dig in the desert, because, bound by the forces of love and justice, she "couldn't not go."

The generous friendship of Bruni, Violeta, and Maria has been a profound gift. At its core is not only a loving bond but also a provocative lesson in the power of love. My experience of their presence and action resonates with that depicted by Marguerite Guzman Bouvard in *Revolutionizing Mother-hood* (1994), her account of the mothers of the disappeared in Argentina. She writes of the mothers' depth of generosity and their "great range of being":

> They carry an agony few of us can imagine yet they are able to experience profound joy and in doing so, have explored the full range of human feeling. . . . The mothers have combined in their work an intensity of feelings, an ethical

position, and shrewd political assessments . . . the mothers refer to love as a motivating force in their political work and as an approach to their actions. For them, love is not an abstraction but it is instead embodied in the strength of their ties, the quality of their relations with other groups, the bonds of affection with their *disappeared* children and all the children and dispossessed of Argentina and in their goal of creating a more just society. (pp. 247–248)

Their experiences resonate with the perspective put forth by Sara Ruddick in *Maternal Thinking* (1989). Ruddick speaks directly to love as basis for ethics and action. She writes that "in protective work, feeling, thinking, and action are conceptually linked. Feelings demand reflections which are, in turn, tested by action, which is, in turn, tested by the feelings it provides. Thoughtful feeling, passionate thought, and provocative acts together test and reveal the effectiveness of preservative love" (p. 70).

It is this love that inspires the women of Calama, the mothers of the Plaza de Mayo of Argentina, and the thousands of others worldwide to take bold and courageous action for justice in the face of unspeakable brutality and insurmountable odds. And it is through the loving connections of friendship, solidarity, and accompaniment with these women that I found my footing to stand for social justice. Why, I wonder, have I bracketed this story out of my "professional" reflections on the practice of social justice work, even though I have shared it many times in the intimate space of a classroom? I am reminded of the words of anthropologist Virginia Dominguez, who argues that "feelings of love and genuine affection often do enter the body of an anthropological work, albeit usually unremarked on and often not even consciously" (2000, p. 378). This rings true of social work as well. Dominguez invites us to make love a more important and acknowledged feeling in our work. She writes: "It is because [love] may be the most closeted of our feelings at the same time that it may be the most enabling one. It is about time that we recognize it when it is there, value it rather than denigrate it, and flaunt it because we are proud of the work that love (and those people) enables us to produce" (p. 378).

INTERPERSONAL INTERPLAY OF LOVE AND JUSTICE

Upon closer reflection, I realized that in writing and revising *Just Practice* (Finn & Jacobson, 2008) we had incorporated stories illustrating the linkage of love and justice at the interface of personal pain and broad-based political struggles, in an attempt to convey the integrated practice of social justice work. We had also included stories that show the intimate interplay of love and justice in the interpersonal realm of social work practice. However, we had left the concept of love itself out as a central theme of social justice work. And yet, these intimate connections of faith, love, and justice resonate for many social workers. For example Catherine Faver has recently written on relational spirituality and social caregiving (2004). Faver describes women's caregiving as being sustained by relationships to their clients and social networks in which they found a "sacred source of love and strength" (p. 241). Faver suggests that "love is the source and sustainer of caring and is the spiritual foundation of helping," and that "caring requires love, and that joy, which is a consequence of love, helps sustain caring" (Faver, 2004, p. 248).

The power of relationship, engagement, and, fundamentally, love is also illustrated in the work of Stephen Rose (2000). Rose describes himself as a white, middle-class social worker, who had much to learn from his encounter with Michael, a black teenager who was his client (Rose, 2000). Rose writes:

> Michael told me, in his different, yet precise language, that I could not care about him inside my life alone, that my (professional) life was inside the agency building and its world, and my personal life never intersected his. To care about him or any other client was to enter his life, as he lived it, where he lived it, as he saw it, and as he felt it. Ten years later, I read the same thing in Paolo Freire's writing: People committed to human dignity and social justice could never fear entering into the lives of those in whose behalf they believed they were working. (p. 403)

Rose experienced a personal epiphany when he realized that his social work training had taught him strategies for distancing himself from Michael, drawing on his expertise to interpret the meaning of Michael's anger, and using his professional power to name Michael's experience. Rose recalls:

> I was trained not to share power in constructing or producing what we worked on together, in not perceiving him worthy or capable of partnership with me. . . . In other words, my professional status included the illusion of ownership of meaning of another person's experience through the delegated power to interpret it. Professional knowledge was built into my packaged identity, the medium through which domination reigned. (p. 404)

In effect, Rose's social work training had prepared him to disconnect from Michael's humanity:

Nothing that was said about Michael in any record I had seen or professional literature I had read could have ever imagined the depth of love he felt and expressed, the personal caretaking or household skills he displayed, or the sacrifice he made every day as the sole breadwinner for and caregiver to his family. (p. 407)

As Rose opened himself to listen to and learn from Michael, he found his identity, positionality, and privilege challenged. Rose describes his encounter with Michael as an explosive learning experience where Michael was the teacher who transformed his safe, knowable world into an "active contradiction." "We existed in relation, Michael and me; we were not discrete entities linked in a linear equation, but relationally connected parts of a larger social world whose requirements created both Michael's suffering and rage and my position to respond to it" (pp. 405–406). Rose named love as a central force in Michael's life and was then able to rethink his own humanity in relationship to Michael. As Rose reworked his assumptions, not only was his relationship with Michael transformed, but also his relationship with social work.

Another example of the power and place of love in the practice of social justice work comes from Patricia Deegan, a clinical psychologist and founder of the National Empowerment Center. Deegan has been diagnosed with mental illness and has dedicated herself to "pressing back against the strong tide of oppression" experienced by people labeled with mental illness. Drawing from her expertise and that of others diagnosed with mental illness, Deegan (1996) argues:

It is not our job to pass judgment on who will and will not recover from mental illness and the spirit breaking effects of poverty, dehumanization, degradation and learned helplessness. Rather our job is to participate in a conspiracy of hope. It is our job to form a community of hope which surrounds people with psychiatric disabilities. It is our job to create rehabilitation environments that are charged with opportunities for self improvement. It is our job to nurture our staff in the special vocations of hope. It is our job to ask people with psychiatric disabilities what it is they want and need in order to grow and then to provide them with the good soil in which a new life can secure its roots and grow. And then, finally, it is our job to wait patiently, to sit with, to watch with wonder, and to witness with reverence the unfolding of another person's life. (p. 8)

According to Deegan, when we fail to engage with love, dignity, and respect, we not only risk diminishing the humanity of another, but also find that our own personhood begins to atrophy (Deegan, 1996, p. 7). The result, Deegan contends, is a breaking of the spirit that robs both clients and helpers of their full humanity (Deegan, 1990). In contrast, Deegan invites practitioners to enter into a "conspiracy of hope" wherein we "refuse to reduce humans beings to illness"; challenge radical power balances between professionals and those labeled as "clients," "patients," or "consumers"; and craft relationships marked by "true mutuality" (1996, pp. 2, 3). It seems her conspiracy of hope is also a conspiracy of love that honors the full humanity of both "client" and social worker.

Deegan's notion of love resonates with the concept of the "Love Paradigm" promoted by long-time group worker Norm Goroff as a means of overcoming the violence of U.S. society (Goroff, 1984, 1988; Reisch & Andrews, 2001, p. 181). Goroff seemed to draw inspiration from Erich Fromm's definition of genuine love as "the productive form of relatedness to others and to onself. It implies responsibility, care, respect, and knowledge, and the wish for the other person to grow and develop. It is fusion under the condition of integrity" (Fromm, 1947, p. 116). According to Fromm, the caring component of love is the "active concern for the life and the growth of that which we love" (Fromm, 1956, p. 22). Responsibility is an act of faith and a practice of responsive dialogue with another (Fromm, 1947). Respect implies the ability to see another as she or he really is (Fromm, 1956). Love is also a pathway to knowledge and meaning connected to one's sense of belonging in the world. In sum, Fromm (1956) describes love as "the active power in man: a power which breaks through the walls which separate man from his fellow men, which unites him with others; loves makes him overcome a sense of isolation and separateness, yet it permits him to be himself, to retain his integrity" (p. 24). According to William DuBois (1983), love recognizes that there is another way of life than force and control. It is a trust in the power of love. It is the truth that love, as if by magic, will awaken love. It is a faith that loves will take us where we need to go.

As DuBois (1983) asserts, Fromm's grasp of love bridges the individual and the sociopolitical realms: "love requires us to re-explore the nature of self and other; it requires us to re-examine the nature of social realities; and it demands that we re-formulate society." DuBois points to the conclusion of *The Art of Loving* (Fromm, 1956) to illustrate this connection of the personal and the political:

> The discussion of the art of loving cannot be restricted to the personal realm of acquiring and developing those characteristics and attitudes which have been described in this chapter. It is inseparably connected to the social realm. . . .

have muted but not silenced a language and practice of love in the pursuit of justice. The critical theoretical perspectives of the present, which render humanism "passé," should be challenged. It is in our fundamental humanism, our cultural meaning-making capacity, our capacity for love, and our decision to act lovingly in the world that we find hope for the future. In order to claim place and voice in the struggle for social justice, we must first (re)claim love as a basis for social work.

NOTES

1. Thanks to Jennifer Stucker for her thoughtful review and comments on this chapter.
2. For a discussion of the dialectics of love and justice in the context of theological ethics, see Niebuhr (1992).
3. Ross notes that Septima Clark was also critical of the oppressive power of religion. However she remained devoted to traditional Christianity throughout her life (Ross, 2003, p. 82).
4. See Reisch & Andrews (2001) for an in-depth account of the silencing of radical social work in the McCarthy era. An examination of this history is beyond the scope of this chapter.
5. The term *praxis* refers to the ongoing systematic process of action and critical reflection.
6. The literacy work of Septima Clark could also be thought of as a form of liberation theology, although the term was coined in reference to the movements informed by a blending of Catholic faith and emancipatory social movements in Latin America in the wake of Vatican II.
7. Thanks to Jennifer Stucker for making this connection. The notion of an approach that embraces head, heart, and hand is borrowed from Kelly and Sewell (1988).
8. For a detailed account of the Caravan of Death, see Verdugo (1989).
9. For documentary accounts of the Caravan of Death, see also the films *Días de octubre* (1991) and *Danza de esperanza* (1989).
10. Personal communication with author.

REFERENCES

Abrams, L., & Curran, L. (2004). Between women: Gender and social work in historical perspective. *Social Service Review* 78(3), 429–46.

Adams, R., Domenelli, L., & Payne, M. (Eds.) (2005). *Social work futures: Crossing boundaries and transforming practice.* New York: Palgrave/Macmillan.

Addams, J. (1910). *Twenty years at Hull House.* New York: Crowell/Macmillan.

Allan, J., Pease, B., & Briskman, L. (Eds.) (2003). *Critical social work: An introduction to theories and practices.* Crows Nest, NSW, Australia: Allen & Unwin.

Allen, P. (1999). *Flores en el Desierto/Flowers in the Desert.* Santiago: Cuarto Propio.

Bailey, R., & Brake, M. (1976). *Radical social work.* New York: Random House.

Berlin, S. (2005). The value of acceptance in social work direct practice: A historical and contemporary view. *Social Service Review* 79(3), 482–510.

Berryman, P. (1987). Liberation theology: Essential facts about the revolutionary movement in Latin America and beyond. New York: Pantheon.

Biestek, F. (1957). The casework relationship. Chicago: Loyola University Press.

Boff, L. (1989). *Faith on the edge: Religion and marginalized existence.* San Francisco: Harper & Row.

Chambon, A., Irving, A., & Epstein, L. (Eds.) (1999). *Reading Foucault for social work.* New York: Columbia University Press.

Dana, B. (1973). Health, social work, and social justice. In B. Ross and C. Shireman (Eds.), *Social work practice and social justice* (pp. 111–128) Washington, D.C.: NASW.

Danza de esperanza (1989). Documentary film directed by Deborah Shaffer and produced by Lavonne Poteet. Santiago: Copihue Productions.

Day, P. (2006). *A new history of social welfare.* 5th ed. Boston: Allyn & Bacon.

Deegan, P. (1996). *Recovery and the conspiracy of hope.* Presentation at 6th Annual Mental Health Services Conference of Australia and New Zealand, Brisbane, Australia.

Días de octubre (1991). Documentary film directed by Hernan Castro and produced by Wolfgang Pens. Santiago.

Dominelli, L. (2002). *Anti-oppressive social work theory and practice.* London: Macmillan.

Dominguez, V. (2000). For a politics of love and rescue. *Cultural Anthropology,* 15(3), 361–393.

DuBois, W. (1983). Love, Synergy, and the Magical: The Foundations of a Humanistic Sociology. Ph.D. Dissertation, Oklahoma State University.

Farmer, P. (2003). Pathologies of power: Health, human rights, and the new war on the poor. Berkeley: University of California Press.

Faver, C. (2004). Relational spirituality and social caregiving. *Social Work,* 49(2), 241–249.

Figueira-McDonough, J., Netting, F.E., & Nichols-Casebolt, A. (Eds.) (1998). The role of gender in practice knowledge: Claiming half the human experience. New York: Garland.

Finn, J. (1998). Tracing the veins: Of copper, culture, and community from Butte to Chuquicamata. Berkeley: University of California Press.

Finn, J. (2001). The women of Vila Paula Jaraquemada: Building community in Chile's transition to democracy. *Community Development Journal,* 36(3), 183–197.

Finn, J., & Jacobson, M. (2003). Just practice: Steps toward a new social work paradigm. *Journal of Social Work Education,* 39(1), 57–78.

Finn, J., & Jacobson, M. (2008). *Just practice: A social justice approach to social work.* Peosta, Iowa: Eddie Bowers Publishing.

Freire, P. (1973). *Education for critical consciousness.* New York: Seabury.

Freire, P. (1974). Pedagogy of the oppressed. New York: Seabury Fromm.

Fromm, E. (1947). Man for himself: An inquiry into the psychology of ethics. New York: Fawcett.

Fromm, E. (1956). *The art of loving.* New York: Harper.

Galper, J. (1975). *The politics of social services.* Englewood Cliffs, N.J.: Prentice-Hall.

Gordon, L. (1988). *Heroes of their own lives: The politics and history of family violence.* New York: Viking Penguin.

Goroff, N. (1984). The love paradigm. Presented at the Sixth Annual Symposium, Advancement for Social Work Groups conference, Chicago.

Goroff, N. (1988). Helping overcome family violence: A social group work approach. Unpublished paper. Toronto.

Guzman Bouvard, M. (1994). *Revolutionizing motherhood*. Wilmington, Del.: Scholarly Resources Press.

Hamilton, G. (1940). *The theory and practice of social casework*. New York: Columbia University Press.

Hamilton, G. (1949). *Helping people: The growth of a profession: Essay in social work and human relations*. Anniversary Papers of New York School of Social Work and Community Service Society of New York. New York: Columbia University Press.

Hamilton, G. (1958). A theory of personality: Freud's contribution to social work. In H. Parad (Ed.), *Ego psychology and dynamic casework: Papers from the Smith College School for Social Work* (pp. 11–37). New York: Family Service Association of America.

Hanmer, J., & Statham, D. (1989). Women and social work: Towards a woman-centered practice. Chicago: Lyceum.

Hill Collins, P. (1990). Black feminist thought: Knowledge, consciousness, and the politics of empowerment. New York: Unwin Hyman.

hooks, b. (1990). Yearning: Race, gender, and cultural politics. Boston: South End Press.

hooks, b. (2000). *All about love: New visions*. New York: William Morrow.

Hope, A., & Timmel, S. (1999). *Training for transformation: A handbook for community workers: Books 1–4*. London, U.K.: Intermediate Technology Publications.

Jordan, J. (2003). Valuing vulnerability: New definitions of courage. Work in Progress Paper 102. Wellesley, Mass.: Stone Center, Wellesley Center for Women, Wellesley College.

Jordan, J., Kaplan, A., Baker Miller, J., Stiver, I., & Surrey, J. (1991). *Women's growth in diversity: More writings from the Stone Center*. New York: Guilford.

Jordan, J., Surrey, J., & Kaplan, A. (2002). Women and empathy: Implications for psychological development and psychotherapy. Work in Progress Paper 2. Wellesley, Mass.: Stone Center, Wellesley Center for Women, Wellesley College.

Kelly, A., & Sewell, S. (1988). *With head, heart, and hand*. Brisbane, Australia: Boolarong.

Kondrat, M. (2002). Actor-centered social work: Re-visioning "person in environment" through a critical theory lens. *Social Work*, 47(4), 435–448.

Margolin, L. (1997). *Under the cover of kindness: The invention of social work*. Charlottesville: University Press of Virginia.

Maturana, H., & Nisis, (1997). *Formación humana y capacitación*. Santiago: Editorial Dolmen.

Maturana, H., & Verden Zoller, G. (2008). Origins of humanness in the biology of love. Exeter, UK: Imprint Academic.

Naples, N. (1998). Grassroots warriors: Activist mothering, community work, and the war on poverty. New York: Routledge.

Niebuhr, R. (1992). *Love and justice: Selections from the shorter writings of Reinhold Niebuhr*, ed. D. B. Robertson. Louisville, Ky.: Westminster/John Knox Press.

Pease, B., & Fook, J. (Eds.) (1999). *Transforming social work practice: Postmodern critical perspectives*. New York: Routledge.

Perlman, H. (1979). *Relationship*. Chicago: University of Chicago Press.

Reid, W. (2002). Knowledge for direct social work practice: An analysis of trends. *Social Service Review*, 76(1), 6–33.

Reisch, M. (2005). American exceptionalism and critical social work: A retrospective and prospective analysis. In I. Ferguson, M. Lavalette & E. Whitmore (Eds.), *Globalisation, global justice and social work* (pp. 157–172). New York: Routledge.

Reisch, M., & Andrews, J. (2001). The road not taken: A history of radical social work in the United States. New York: Brunner Routledge.

Richmond, M. (1922). What is social case work? An introductory description. New York: Russell Sage.

Rimor, M. (2003). If love then justice. Sociological Inquiry, 73(2), 167–176.

Robinson, V. (1978). The development of a professional self: Teaching and learning in professional helping processes: Selected writings, 1930–1968. New York: AMS.

Rogers, C. (1951) Client-centered therapy: Its current practice, implications, and theory. Boston: Houghton Mifflin.

Rogers, C., Gendlin, E., Kiesler, D., & Truax, C. (1967). The therapeutic relationship and its impact: A study of psychotherapy with schizophrenics. Madison: University of Wisconsin Press.

Rose, S. (2000). Reflections on empowerment based practice. Social Work, 45(5), 403–412.

Ross, B. (1973). Professional dilemmas. In B. Ross and C. Shireman (Eds.), Social work practice and social justice (pp. 147–152). Washington, D.C.: NASW.

Ross, R. (2003). Witnessing and testifying: Black women, religion, and civil rights. Minneapolis: Fortress Press.

Ross, R., & Shireman, C. (Eds.) (1973). Social work practice and social justice. Washington, DC: NASW.

Ruddick, S. (1989). Maternal thinking: Toward a politics of peace. Boston: Beacon Press.

Sakamoto, I., & Pitner, R. (2005). Use of critical consciousness in anti-oppressive social work practice: Disentangling power dynamics at personal and structural levels. British Journal of Social Work, 35, 435–452.

Saleebey, D. (1990). Philosophical disputes in social work: Social justice denied. Journal of Sociology and Social Welfare, 17 (2), 29–40.

Saleebey, D. (1993). Theory and the generation and subversion of knowledge. Journal of Sociology and Social Welfare, 20(1), 5–25.

Saleebey, D. (1994). Culture, theory, and narrative: The intersection of meanings in practice. Social Work, 39(4), 351–359.

Saleebey, D. (Ed.) (2006). The strengths perspective in social work practice. 4th ed. Boston: Pearson Education.

Stebner, E. (1997). The women of Hull House: Study in spirituality, vocation, and friendship. Albany: SUNY Press.

Verdugo, P. (1989). Los zarpazos del puma. Santiago: Ediciones ChileAmerica.

8 THE ROLE OF THEORY IN CONDUCTING EVIDENCE-BASED CLINICAL PRACTICE

STANLEY MCCRACKEN AND TINA RZEPNICKI

REALITY IS NOTHING BUT A COLLECTIVE HUNCH.

—LILY TOMLIN

DURING THE 1960S and 1970s, in response to concern about the lack of research demonstrating the effectiveness of social work practice, the empirical practice movement emerged in schools of social work (see Reid, 1994, for a history). Similar movements were occurring in other disciplines, notably psychology and medicine, at the same time. This concern with the empirical basis of practice and attention to the integration of research and practice led to developments in assessment, monitoring, and evaluation of practice; to increased research on treatment effectiveness; to development and demand for treatment guidelines and practice manuals; and to the formulation and refinement of a process for using evidence in clinical practice (Norcross, Beutler & Levant, 2006; Reid, 1994; Sackett, Straus, Richardson, Rosenberg & Haynes, 2000).

Even though there has been considerable growth in the amount of research published in the professional literature, there are wide gaps between clinical research and what is happening in actual practice. It has been found that even when randomized controlled trials (RCTs) support certain interventions, it is several years (if at all) before the results of this research begin to inform individual clinical practice (Eddy, 2005). Evidence-based medicine (EBM) and evidence-based practice (EBP) were developed in response to this research-practice gap and to the need for a method to identify and use research for clinical decision making in real time (Sackett et al., 2000; Shlon-sky & Gibbs, 2004). Current progress in EBP has been enabled by developments in other areas, such as availability of electronic databases of research literature and powerful search engines to search these databases; access to high-speed Internet connections and relatively inexpensive and powerful computers to enable one to conduct searches from practice settings; availability of meta-analyses, systematic reviews, and other study syntheses; access to electronic versions of journal articles that allow these articles to be directly downloaded; and development of techniques for efficiently and effectively searching the literature and identifying relevant studies (Gibbs, 2003).

Writing on EBP has addressed the suitability and appropriateness of EBP for clinical practice, the kinds of research that should be used as evidence for practice, and the relative importance of different factors for therapy outcome—for example, techniques, principles, relationship, or other common factors (Chorpita, Becker & Daleiden, 2007; Norcross et al., 2006). Surprisingly little has been written on the role of theory in EBP (Green, 2000). In fact, one might ask whether it is possible to conduct EBP without considering theory. We would argue that, depending on how narrowly one defines theory, it might be possible to conduct EBP without explicitly considering theory. However, we believe that there are advantages to explicitly considering practice theory when using EBP in clinical practice. In other words, we believe that practice should be based on all three elements—practice experience, research, *and* theory (see Marsh, 2004). In this chapter we discuss the relevance of theory for the practitioner of EBP.

WHAT DO WE MEAN BY THEORY?

For purposes of this chapter we broadly define theory as a systematic way of understanding events, phenomena, and situations. Theory includes a range of explanatory or predictive propositions, such as models, perspectives, approaches, and frameworks, and should be applicable to a broad range of situations (Berlin & Marsh, 1993; National Cancer Institute [NCI], 2005). Theories can be formal knowledge structures that are subject to evaluation by researchers, scholars, and practitioners, or they can be personal knowledge structures that help practitioners organize and understand the clinical phenomena they encounter in practice. Schemas (cognitive structures that contain information about the attributes of a concept and the relationships between these attributes) are another, less formal knowledge structure that guide practice (Berlin & Marsh, 1993). While schemas are produced and shaped by personal and clinical experience, they also shape experience by influencing what the practitioner sees and attends to, the meaning that is given to these events, and actions that are taken as a result of these events. Berlin and Marsh (1993) describe theories as the "schema of experts" (p. 11). Theories (both formal and personal) can be implicit or explicit, and they can be used to understand the reasons why a problem exists or to predict how and under what conditions change occurs.

Theories may be tested either formally, through experimentation and logical argument, or informally, through systematic feedback from direct experience. If theories are not tested, they remain abstract ideas unconnected to the dynamics of human interaction. Research and testing provide a measure of quality control of these ideas by producing data from observations and comparing these data with the theories (Berlin & Marsh, 1993; Stiles, 2006). Data from these observations change the ideas and the theories. Stiles (2006) uses a diffusion metaphor to describe the process by which new observations permeate the theory, "the ideas change to accommodate the observations, and aspects of the observations become part of the theory. . . . Thus, the theory is modified by the observations to become more general, more precise, and more realistic" (p. 58). To be tested, theories must be explicit. Implicit theories are impermeable to evidence because inconsistencies between theory and observations remain hidden. Mindful practice (Epstein, 1999) and logic modeling (Alter & Egan, 1997; Renger & Hurley, 2006) are two tools that practitioners can use to make implicit practice theories explicit.

Mindful practice, a prerequisite of critical self-reflection, raises tacit personal knowledge, including schemas, and deeply held values to awareness. As in other applications of mindfulness (Baer, 2003), the mindful practitioner attends in a nonjudgmental way to her own everyday physical and mental processes in order to act with clarity and insight (Epstein, 1999). We propose that awareness of one's schemas is an important component of becoming a good observer. Awareness of one's personal theories and preconceptions allows one to loosen up these preconceptions in order to see the unexpected—to develop what is known in Zen as beginner's mind (Berlin & Marsh, 1993; Suzuki, 1980).

Logic modeling is another tool that can be used to make explicit one's practice theories. A logic model helps one analyze and intervene in social problems by providing a visual map of the relationship between antecedent conditions (problems), the desired outcomes (results, changes, goals), actions taken to accomplish these goals (intervention, program), and the resources needed to accomplish the goals (Alter & Egan, 1997; W. K. Kellogg

Foundation, 2004). A theory-based logic model makes explicit the underlying assumptions and the rationale (change theory) of the intervention and how the various components are connected (Rubin & Babbie, 2007). While the theories underlying an intervention (or a program) may remain implicit, all interventions are based on some idea of the mechanisms underlying that change and how the components of the intervention affect those mechanisms (Marsh, 2004). Failure to specify these ideas entails several risks: failing to implement the intervention in a manner, intensity, or duration necessary to affect mechanisms required for change; failing to identify and monitor appropriate indicators of change; failing to identify and monitor indicators of harm or adverse iatrogenic effects; or modifying core rather than peripheral elements of the intervention when adapting the treatment to one's client or practice setting.

The final distinction to be made is between explanatory and change theories. *Explanatory theories* describe the reasons a problem exists; *change theories* spell out the concepts that can be translated into the intervention. Explanatory theories explain how people develop and how problems occur; they elucidate the nature of the problem and help to identify the range of factors that the practitioner might try to modify. Change theories explain how problems and people change, and they guide the development and implementation of the intervention (Berlin & Marsh, 1993; Green, 2000). While much of our discussion of EBP will focus on change theories, explanatory theories are quite useful for some components of EBP.

WHAT DO WE MEAN BY EVIDENCE-BASED PRACTICE?

Evidence-based practice has had two general meanings: one focusing on the *process* of asking questions about practice, and the other focusing on the *product* of this questioning—that is, interventions based on this research. These interventions are variously called evidence-based guidelines (Eddy, 2005; Rosen & Proctor, 2003), evidence-based practices (Mullen & Streiner, 2004), or empirically validated/supported treatments (Chambless, 1998). Evidence-based process is an approach to using data to make decisions about the care of clients and has been referred to as evidence-based medicine, or EBM (Sackett, Rosenberg, Muir Gray, Haynes & Richardson, 1996); evidence-based individual decision making (Eddy, 2005); and evidence-based process (Mullen & Streiner, 2004). Our discussion will focus on EBP as process. We view EBP as an orientation to practice that values evidence as a resource for clinical decision making, while recognizing that evidence alone is never sufficient to make a clinical decision (Berlin & Marsh, 1993; Guyatt & Rennie, 2002; Weisz & Addis, 2006). Specifically, EBP is the integration of client clinical state and circumstances, and client preferences and actions, with the best available evidence (research literature and systematic data from practice) (Sackett et al. 1996; Gellis & Reid, 2004). These three sets of variables are integrated by clinician expertise and occur in a specific practice and community context (Haynes, Devereaux & Guyatt, 2002; Regehr, Stern & Shlonsky, 2007). This interaction is illustrated in Figure 8.1. EBP is implemented in a series of steps that begin with motivation to use EBP and definition of a problem, and end with implementing an intervention and gathering data on the effect of the intervention (Sackett, Straus, Richardson, Rosenberg & Haynes, 2000; Gibbs, 2003). These steps are as follows:

1. Become motivated to use EBP.
2. Convert the need for information into an answerable question.
3. Track down with maximum efficiency the best evidence with which to answer that question.
4. Critically appraise that evidence for its validity and usefulness.
5. Integrate the critical appraisal with practitioner clinical expertise and with the client values, preferences, and clinical circumstances, and apply the results to practice.
6. Evaluate the outcome.

In the remainder of this chapter we discuss the role of theory at each of these steps. Before doing this, we identify two important assumptions that we make about knowledge. First, knowledge from research based on the scientific method and from data systematically collected from practice are both useful to practitioners working in real-world settings. Useful information can be generated by a variety of research designs, depending on the research question, the level of control that can be achieved, and the preexisting state of knowledge in that area. This includes information from randomized controlled trials, case studies and single-subject designs, quasi-experimental research, survey research, and qualitative studies; from efficacy, effectiveness, and implementation research; and from study syntheses, such as meta-analyses and meta-syntheses. Thus, we regard data as an important source of information for clinical decision making.

Second, knowledge is to varying degrees contextual, and knowledge gathered from research and practice is a representation of reality and not reality itself—both researchers and practitioners interpret and bring meaning to

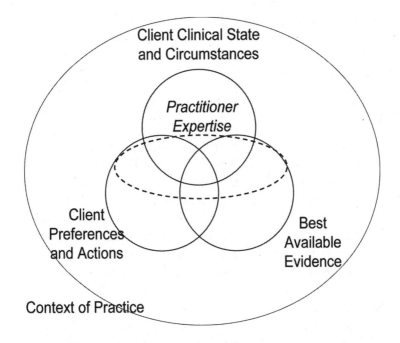

FIGURE 8.1 A Model of Evidence-Based Practice

SOURCE: MODIFIED FROM HAYNES, DEVEREAUX & GUYATT (2002)

observation and experience. As we have mentioned, we believe that one's view of reality is shaped by experience. Our assumption that knowledge is contextual means that evidence from one study investigating the use of an intervention in a particular setting with a given group of subjects and a specific set of problems may or may not generalize to a different setting or group of clients and problems, though it is a good place to start. Thus, evidence from research and from practice, while useful, must be held lightly. One should remain skeptical when applying both evidence and theory. Evidence is contextual and may not apply to a new client, situation, or setting, and theory is hypothetical and subject to falsification (Gomory, 2001). We acknowledge that our assumptions are based in two contradictory camps: generally logical positivist, in that we believe that knowledge can be gained from observation, experience, and the scientific method; and generally postmodern, in that we believe knowledge is contextual and a representation of reality (Fischer, 1993; Marsh, 2004). We believe that, though contradictory, this is a realistic and clinically useful mindset, since it allows for the inclusion of research in clinical decision making while recognizing that knowledge from any source is tentative.

STEP 1. BECOMING MOTIVATED TO USE EBP

The transtheoretical, or stages of change, model is a useful way of thinking about motivation to use EBP. The transtheoretical model describes the process of change that an individual goes through in deciding to make significant changes in behavior (Prochaska, DiClemente & Norcross, 1992). Originally developed to provide a way of thinking about and addressing change in clinical situations, particularly substance abuse, it has been applied to practitioners' decisions to learn and use new interventions, such as EBP (Corrigan & McCracken, 1997). Briefly, as applied to the decision to use EBP as an approach to clinical practice, this model suggests that an individual goes through a series of stages or steps in deciding to use EBP. In the first stage, called precontemplation, the staff person sees no problem with the current method of practice and is not even considering adopting EBP. An individual in the second stage, called contemplation, sees both costs and benefits to the current approach to practice and to EBP. It is not clear to the individual in this stage whether EBP is any better than what she is currently doing or whether the effort needed to learn and use EBP is worth any benefit that might be realized from the change. Thus, there is no intention to change—at this time. In the third stage (preparation), the individual sees benefits to using EBP and believes that the benefits are worth the effort of learning the methods of EBP. An individual at this stage may have started gathering information by reading and talking with others about EBP. In the fourth stage (action) the individual is learning and using EBP, and in the fifth stage (maintenance) the individual is continuing to use the innovation and EBP has become the norm. Even after the individual has started using EBP, she may decide to stop using the innovation and return to the former method of practice. This decision may be made for various reasons, including failing to see any benefit to using EBP in practice, lack of organizational support for EBP, or too much effort required to continue use of EBP (Massatti, Sweeney, Panzano, & Roth, 2008). For staff considering a change in practice, the primary consideration is whether a new approach to practice will enhance practice in some way (by making it more effective, more acceptable, more enjoyable, more efficient, or easier) and whether the potential benefits of a new method of practice outweigh the costs of adopting this new approach.

An important factor in considering whether an evidence-based approach to practice will enhance one's practice is whether one views systematically gathered evidence and in particular, evidence gathered from treatment research, as a source of practice knowledge. "Does the research address issues of importance to my clients and my practice? If so, can I apply these results to my practice, and if I do, will my clients benefit and will my practice be enhanced?" A practitioner may be skeptical about the generalizability of clinical research, particularly from randomized controlled trials (RCTs), to community practice. One may view the entire argument for an empirical approach to practice as resting on questionable assumptions or may question the degree to which laboratory-validated treatments can be translated into community practice because of the uniqueness of the setting, the clients, or the practitioner relationship (Witkin, 1991; Franks, 2004; Westen, 2006). One may question whether there is any evidence to support the contention that EBP actually improves practice outcomes (Wampold, 2006). Finally, one may view one's supervisor or colleagues, rather than the research literature, as the best sources of information about clinical practice (Mullen & Bacon, 2004). Even if one felt that using EBP might enhance one's practice, there might be barriers to using EBP, thus making the cost outweigh the benefit.

Staff in community programs identify several potential barriers to using EBP; these include attitudes about research (lacking relevance to client population and practice situation, biased, skewed toward certain kinds of interventions); beliefs about EBP (rigid, stifling creativity, limited to certain kinds of interventions, time-consuming, lacking access to relevant information); concerns about how it might be implemented in the agency (imposed without staff input, would control rather than guide practice, would not recognize the work they already are doing); and finally, loyalty to a particular theoretical perspective—with the implication that EBP must not reject that approach outright (McCracken, Steffen & Hutchins, 2007). Thus, becoming motivated to use EBP is a complex interaction of personal practice theories, professional values and allegiances, views about research, and organizational barriers.

STEP 2. CONVERTING THE NEED FOR INFORMATION INTO AN ANSWERABLE QUESTION

A well-designed practice question contains four elements: the client and problem, the action to be taken (intervention, assessment), an alternative action (alternative intervention, wait list, treatment as usual), and the desired outcome (Gibbs, 2003; Sackett et al., 1996). While the practitioner's need for information is determined by the client's clinical condition and situation, how one views that condition and situation, and thus how one frames each of the elements of the practice question, are influenced by one's practice theory.

It is rare that all the potentially relevant characteristics of a particular client will be present in any given study, and thus a practitioner must prioritize the characteristics of the client in formulating a search question. It is unlikely, for example, that one would find literature as specific as the treatment of chronic depression in a forty-year-old, Mexican, Roman Catholic, divorced, high school teacher and single mother living in an upper-middle-class residential neighborhood in Chicago. Practice theory will influence how one prioritizes and chooses client characteristics for the search. Similarly, practice theory influences how the practitioner formulates the client's clinical condition and outcomes (problems and goals). For example, how a practitioner formulates the client problem for the search question will depend on answers to such questions as what is the role (if any) of psychiatric diagnosis in marital problems; are symptoms of anxiety or disrupted attachment more important in working with an abused child in foster care; or what is the role of sexual orientation in the development and treatment of a drinking problem.

Client preferences are a major determinant of the outcomes selected for the search question, but how those preferences are framed in the question will, once again, be influenced by one's practice theory. For example, a veteran with posttraumatic stress syndrome (PTSD), a drinking problem, and outbursts of anger and abusive behavior may have a goal of holding down a job and reuniting with his wife and child. The practitioner may frame the search in terms of PTSD and alcohol dependence, anger and abusive behavior, employment, family relationships, or some combination. It is unlikely, however, that the practitioner will find substantial literature that considers all these facets of the case; it also is unlikely that the practitioner would intervene in all these areas simultaneously, whether or not he conducted a literature search. Practice theory will influence the decision to focus the search on the eventual (or distal) outcomes of strengthening employment and marital stability or on intermediate (proximal) goals of reducing anger and aggression, drinking, or symptoms of PTSD.

Practice theory also will influence what actions and alternative actions are being considered for the search question. This includes decisions about the level at which the intervention should take place, the modality of service delivery, and the specific interventions being considered. The problem of delinquency illustrates this issue. The practitioner's theory of

practice will influence whether she looks for policy studies in juvenile justice, research on community change strategies, outcomes of interventions
designed to increase attendance and involvement with school, effectiveness of parent-training or family-based interventions, or effectiveness of
individual interventions for working with the youth. We would not want
to give the impression that practice theory is the only factor that influences the structure of the search question. Client preferences, practitioner expertise, and practice context also inform the decision to pose the
question in a particular way. In the delinquency example, it is unlikely
that a practitioner would include policy, community change, or family
intervention strategies in the search if she is working as a school social
worker whose role is limited to interventions in the classroom or directly
with the student.

Guyatt and Rennie (2002) distinguish two types of questions practitioners ask in clinical practice. *Background questions* provide basic information
about client characteristics and different kinds of problems, and often involve
explanatory theories. For example, background questions might address
developmental and cultural issues; the epidemiology, proposed etiology, and
course of development of a particular problem or disorder; or social problems
leading to or resulting from problems of different sorts. *Foreground questions*
address the specific clinical issue at hand and involve change theories, or
what Marsh (2004) refers to as problem-service matching theories. Problem-
service matching theories describe the interaction between an intervention
and the specific client and problem characteristics. They address the need to
tailor the intervention to the client and problem (Marsh, 2004). Foreground
questions are framed very specifically—for example, what is the most effective intervention to reduce separation anxiety in a sexually abused, five-
year-old girl; or what is the most effective treatment to reduce aggression
and psychotic symptoms in a seventy-five-year-old man with Alzheimer's
disease, living in a nursing home. Because of the nature of the literature in
most areas, it often is necessary to formulate both a background question
and a foreground question in order to triangulate on a problem. For example,
there is a paucity of literature considering the effect of culture and ethnicity, gender, or sexual orientation on treatment outcome (Comas-Diaz, 2006;
Norcross, Beutler & Levant, 2006). It may be necessary for the practitioner
to formulate a foreground question regarding treatment of a client's clinical
condition to identify an intervention that might be used to treat a particular problem, and a background question on client characteristics that would
provide information that may be used to adapt the intervention to the characteristics of one's client (McCracken & Marsh, 2008).

STEP 3. TRACKING DOWN WITH MAXIMUM EFFICIENCY THE BEST EVIDENCE WITH WHICH TO ANSWER THAT QUESTION

Much of what was said in the previous step about the role of theory in converting the need for information into an answerable question could be applied to tracking down the best evidence to answer the question. For example, the practitioner's choice of search terms and synonyms for these terms could be influenced by theory as well as by the thesaurus in the database. The theoretical element unique to this step lies in the decision about what sorts of research counts as evidence to support an intervention and how to prioritize and weight evidence from various sources. While evidence from replicated RCTs is at the top of the hierarchy of evidence in EBM (Guyatt & Rennie, 2002), there remains disagreement about the sort of evidence that should guide psychology and social work practice (Magill, 2006; Gellis & Reid, 2004; Norcross et al., 2006). For example, case studies typically are placed at the lowest level of the hierarchy of evidence in EBM. However, Stiles (2006) argued that case studies actually have advantages for psychotherapy because they can examine complex clinical phenomena in context. Others have argued for the value of single-participant, qualitative, and effectiveness research both from the literature and from one's own practice as evidence for clinical practice (Borkovec & Castonguay, 2006; Gellis & Reid, 2004; Hill, 2006; Hurst & Nelson-Gray, 2006). Even if a practitioner values evidence for clinical decision making, the nature of the evidence that is valued will be influenced by practice theory.

One final point is that the EBP practitioner is enjoined to "*look first for that which disconfirms your beliefs; then look for that which supports them. Look with equal diligence for both. Doing so will make the difference between scientific honesty and artfully supported propaganda*" (Gibbs, 2003 p. 89; original emphasis). While this commitment is in accord with the principle of falsifiability of one's hypothesis, it is driven less by that principle than by the ethics of EBP.

STEP 4. CRITICALLY APPRAISING THAT EVIDENCE FOR ITS VALIDITY AND USEFULNESS

The actual appraisal of the evidence for its validity is less influenced by practice theory than is the appraisal of the evidence for its usefulness in a particular practice situation. While one's practice theory guides the selection about what sort of evidence to use to inform practice, once that decision is made, evaluating the validity of that research is less a matter of theory than of knowledge of research methods. There are several checklists the practitioner can use as guides in evaluating the validity of different kinds of research (e.g., Gibbs, 2003; Moher, Schulz & Altman, 2001).

Practice theory has much more influence on the decisions about the usefulness of the evidence for the particular clinical question that led to the search in the first place. Regardless of what sort of study is being reviewed, it is highly unlikely that that there will be a perfect match between the subjects and conditions of the study and the practitioner's client. The practitioner's view about whether his clients are so different that the results would not apply will be influenced by how he prioritizes the client and subject characteristics, in much the same way as when formulating the practice question. Furthermore, even though evidence from studies and syntheses identified in the electronic search is of high quality, it may or may not clearly identify a single intervention to use with one's client. Even if one intervention is more strongly supported than another, there are times when the practitioner may select an intervention with less evidence of effectiveness than one with more effectiveness, if he determines that there is a better fit with certain client characteristics. For example, a practitioner working in a large family service agency chose child-parent psychotherapy (CPP; Lieberman, Van Horn & Ippen, 2005) rather than cognitive behavioral therapy (CBT; Toth, Maughan, Manly, Spagnola & Cicchetti, 2002) to work with a sexually abused preschool child in spite of greater evidence supporting the latter approach. She chose CPP over CBT largely because of the child's age (four years old) and her belief that the child's attachment problems were more relevant in choosing an intervention than her anxiety symptoms; this determination was based on her case formulation and influenced by her practice theory (McCracken & Marsh, 2008). Practitioners must consider the magnitude and precision of the effect of the study, determine the likelihood of benefit, balance the potential benefit versus harm, assess the feasibility of the intervention both with the client and in one's practice setting (Guyatt & Rennie, 2002; Straus, Richardson, Glasziou & Haynes, 2005). Both one's beliefs about the problem (explanatory theory) and one's beliefs about how problems are resolved (change theory) will influence one's view of the relevance of one set of studies over another.

STEP 5. INTEGRATING THE CRITICAL APPRAISAL WITH PRACTITIONER CLINICAL EXPERTISE AND WITH CLIENT VALUES, PREFERENCES, AND CLINICAL CIRCUMSTANCES, AND APPLYING THE RESULTS TO PRACTICE

This step includes two components—integrating the intervention with client characteristics, and applying the results. Some formulations of EBP divide this into two steps: considering the client's unique values, needs, and preferences; and applying the empirically informed intervention to practice (Magill, 2006). We would suggest that the second of these consists of several components: deciding whether the intervention (supported by evidence and acceptable to the client) should be applied as is or adapted to the specific characteristics of the client and the practice situation; modifying the intervention to fit the client and the practice environment; and implementing the intervention.

Up to this point we have focused on the practitioner's practice theory. Of course, clients also have explanatory and change theories in addition to needs, values, expectations, and preferences; integrating the critical appraisal of the evidence requires consideration of the client's theoretical constructs (Kleinman, 1988). The client's theoretical constructs are influenced by a variety of factors, such as culture (both background and contemporary), family, education, and previous experience with formal and informal health care systems. At times the practitioner may choose to work within the client's theoretical framework—for example, when a therapist, working with an addicted client, frames a cognitive-behavioral approach in twelve-step language. At other times, the practitioner will attempt to modify or expand the client's framework—for example, by providing a biological or interpersonal explanation of depression to a client who feels his problem is related to poor nutrition. The practitioner may even use an approach like motivational interviewing to influence the client's view about whether there is a problem and what is the nature of the problem (McCracken & Corrigan, 2008; Miller & Rollnick, 2002). Discussing the evidence with the client involves not only presenting information about the effectiveness of an intervention but also explaining why the therapist thinks the intervention is worth considering and why it might be likely to work with that client. An important component of implementing the intervention is providing the client with an explanatory system for his problems and reasons why the intervention will help (Zeiss, Lewinsohn & Munoz, 1979).

Once the decision has been made to use a particular intervention, the practitioner with the client must decide whether to implement the intervention as described in the literature or in a treatment manual or to adapt it in some way to fit better with the client or the practice environment. There is risk both in adapting and failing to adapt an intervention (Proctor & Rosen, 2006). The risk of adapting is that the intervention may be less effective if one does not maintain fidelity to the intervention. The risk of failing to adapt is that there may be elements of the intervention that make it inappropriate for a particular client or not feasible in a particular practice situation. Denis and colleagues (Denis, Hebert, Langley, Lozeau & Trottier, 2002) note that there is a tacit assumption that an intervention will be implemented as a unit. However, they observed that interventions are composed of a hard core that is relatively fixed and a soft periphery related to different ways in which it might be adapted to specific practice situations. Since many of the interventions that are of interest to social workers are complex packages consisting of multiple components, and since there are relatively few dismantling studies that identify the relative contribution of the different components to the effectiveness of the intervention, the practitioner is left to her own devices in making decisions about how to adapt the intervention to a specific clinical situation. *Fidelity measures* identify the elements of the intervention deemed important by theory, by research, or both. They may focus solely on practitioner behaviors, or they also may address structural components of the program, such as location of the intervention, duration of services, or caseload (Bond, Williams, Evans et al., 2000). A fidelity assessment may or may not provide help when attempting to modify the intervention. Even when a fidelity assessment has been constructed for the intervention, the assessment is more likely to provide information about whether the different elements of the intervention are carried out correctly than about the relative importance of each element or how an element might be modified and still maintain the spirit of the intervention. Familiarity with the theory upon which the intervention is based is helpful to the practitioner seeking to make decisions about adapting the intervention. Knowing the theory may help the practitioner distinguish between the core elements that should not be modified and the peripheral elements that may be changed and still maintain theoretical fidelity. Whether or not the practitioner modifies the intervention, he will need to evaluate whether the intervention is effective with his client and practice situation.

Understanding the theoretical basis of an intervention also is helpful when implementing the intervention and may help the practitioner avoid the Type III error (rejecting the effectiveness of an intervention when the intervention itself was not adequately designed or delivered) (Green, 2000). Familiarity with this theoretical foundation can help the practitioner know when she has identified and addressed the combination of variables necessary for an intervention to have the desired effect and when the necessary elements of the intervention are in place. This information is important not only during initial implementation but also when deciding to move from one phase of treatment to another and when troubleshooting interventions that are not having the desired effect. For example, does the proposed mechanism of change require mastery of one set of skills before proceeding to a different set (for example, must a client be able to identify a maladaptive thought before being able to challenge that thought)? In some situations there may be empirical evidence from a dismantling study that provides an answer to that sort of question.

However, it is more likely that the practitioner will not have access to this sort of information when implementing a novel intervention, and instead will have to rely on a combination of theory and careful observation of the client to provide some indication of this answer. Unfortunately, theoretical knowledge may not be adequately supplied by the evaluation studies, since few reports fully document the theoretical analysis underlying the intervention or how that analysis was translated into action (Green, 2000). Guidelines and treatment manuals are more likely to explicate the theoretical formulation of the problem or the underpinnings of the treatment, though there is considerable variability among manuals in regard to this theoretical clarity. Thus the practitioner may need to supplement what is spelled out in the manual with what she knows from other sources.

For the purposes of intervention planning and evaluation, it is useful to create a logic model that makes explicit the change strategies selected, including underlying assumptions, key elements, desired outcomes, and measurement approaches. Its application is described in the next step.

STEP 6. EVALUATING THE OUTCOME

The primary goal of this step is to evaluate whether the intervention is having the desired effect (whether it is effective, acceptable, and not harmful) and whether it should be continued, modified, or discontinued in favor of an alternative. We would argue that this step has benefits for the evidence-based practitioner as well as for the client. If thoughtfully designed and implemented, this step brings together all the previous elements of EBP and has the potential to contribute to practice knowledge, skills, and theory of practice. In previous steps the practitioner has made choices about interventions informed by relevant research, client preferences, his own expertise, and the context in which the intervention will occur. Practice theory helps inform decisions regarding essential elements and adaptations of the selected intervention, particularly when empirical support is limited, samples do not resemble the target client/population, or the research settings are very different from the practice setting. The elements of intervention must hang together conceptually and be linked to desired program/individual client outcomes, producing a coherent rationale for the intervention and a theory of change for the situation at hand. Although there is no guarantee that the proposed intervention will be effective, it is likely that weak links among elements will result in poor outcomes. If there are weak links among available resources, chosen methods, and the desired outcomes, a need to rethink choices will become obvious. The logic model is a tool that allows the practitioner to depict the explicit relationship between interventions and outcomes and how outcomes are related to each other. It serves as a blueprint against which actions and outcomes can be measured and for building practice knowledge.

A sound logic model reveals a coherent and informed theory of change. The practitioner brings together practice theory, empirical knowledge, client preferences, and organizational supports in a graphic model that specifies all elements of the intervention and the pathways by which they will lead to desired outcomes. It represents the results of critical thinking to select the best and most relevant knowledge and adapts it in ways that make sense for the current situation. Based on Bennett's theory of action (1979), the application of logic models has been emphasized in the fields of program evaluation (Bickman 1987; Bickman and Peterson, 1990; Chen, 1990; Patton, 1997; Weiss, 1997) and social work (Alter and Egan, 1997; Alter and McMurty, 1997; Mullen and Magnabosco, 1997; Savaya and Waysman, 2005).

As a visual map, the logic model permits careful examination of the planned intervention, inviting challenges to the underlying logic, strategies, and their connections to intended results, before implementation is under way. Its specificity helps to create a shared understanding of the plan that makes sense conceptually and practically, so that the plan can be successfully implemented and progress tracked. While the logic model serves as a blueprint for action, it should not be used rigidly. Intervention is a fluid process, and changing conditions or lack of progress may require revised plans (Pollio, 2006).

Several logic model formats are available, but most resemble a flow chart illustrating a logical sequence of events. At a minimum, logic models include a brief description of the problem to be addressed, resources required for the intervention (for example, staff, services, office space, supplies), methods/strategies to be implemented, and desired outcomes. Desired outcomes may be immediate results, such as increases in knowledge or skill; intermediate, such as changes in behavior; or long-term, such as improvements in family relationships.

Figure 8.2 is a logic model created by a social work intern to depict the plan that she and her four clients developed to improve their ability to get along as roommates in a residential care facility. The intervention emerged from a careful review of the research literature, client interests and abilities, and agency philosophy. As can be seen, the objectives of intervention represent a mix of emotional, cognitive, and behavior changes. Intervention strategies, drawn from both psychodynamic and behavioral practice theory, appear to be appropriate, although one might argue that it would have made more sense to engage a single theoretical framework.

The intern's theory of change was heavily influenced by both the research she found and her understanding of contemporary psychodynamic theory. Several assumptions were essential to the development of a coherent intervention strategy. First, she assumed that the interpretive process of psychodynamic therapy would help redefine the clients' self-concept, enhancing their well-being. It was expected that by developing a stronger and more cohesive sense of self, the roommates would be better able to control their reactions to each other, to feel better about themselves, and to experience a decrease in anxiety. Second, reflective exercises offered an opportunity for the clients to practice observing themselves and their roles and responsibilities as roommates, and to see how others viewed them. They would be drawn out of their isolated selves, become more self-aware and more aware of each other, and with coaching, would develop the skills to better cope with each other. Thus, the most effective intervention would integrate psychodynamic and behavioral-based approaches. Finally, due to the cognitive limitations exhibited by the four roommates, the work called for careful use of language, concrete examples and methods, interesting activities to capture their attention, repetition and reinforcement techniques, avoidance of memory overload, and consistent structure and framing in each session.

What is most valuable here is that specific interventions are linked to specific results, allowing the practitioner to determine not only whether intervention is successful in achieving case objectives, but also whether any components are not effective and require modification. In this case, the logic model identifies outcome measures, most of which are individualized rating scales completed by the clients, in addition to incident reports submitted by the residence director. The logic model may also include identification of strategies for monitoring implementation, as well as a brief description of underlying assumptions of the change process, although this one does not.

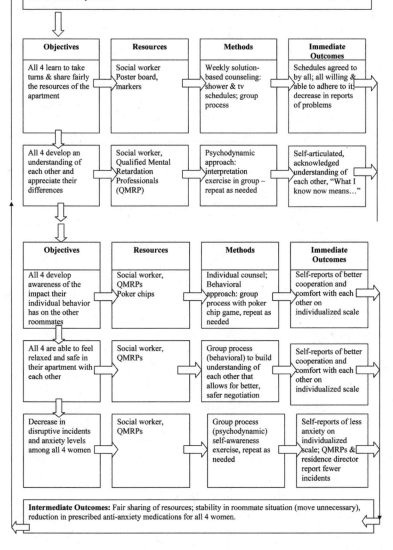

Problem: 4 female roommates with developmental disabilities in the mild to moderate range share an apartment in a supervised residential facility. Events occur among the 4 in their apartment that causes them to have outbursts with each other or to display frustration. The stress is sometimes internalized and results in anxiety which they personally speak to or is observed in their movements, such as picking at their fingers or rocking.

Long-term Outcome (Goal): The 4 roommates will have the ability to get along and to negotiate their differences with each other in daily living, fair sharing of resources in the apartment, and live in a supportive environment that adds to their quality of life and to their sense of refuge and safety within the confines of their apartment.

Objectives	Resources	Methods	Immediate Outcomes
All 4 learn to take turns & share fairly the resources of the apartment	Social worker Poster board, markers	Weekly solution-based counseling: shower & tv schedules; group process	Schedules agreed to by all; all willing & able to adhere to it; decrease in reports of problems
All 4 develop an understanding of each other and appreciate their differences	Social worker, Qualified Mental Retardation Professionals (QMRP)	Psychodynamic approach: interpretation exercise in group – repeat as needed	Self-articulated, acknowledged understanding of each other, "What I know now means…"

Objectives	Resources	Methods	Immediate Outcomes
All 4 develop awareness of the impact their individual behavior has on the other roommates	Social worker, QMRPs Poker chips	Individual counsel; Behavioral approach: group process with poker chip game, repeat as needed	Self-reports of better cooperation and comfort with each other on individualized scale
All 4 are able to feel relaxed and safe in their apartment with each other	Social worker, QMRPs	Group process (behavioral) to build understanding of each other that allows for better, safer negotiation	Self-reports of better cooperation and comfort with each other on individualized scale
Decrease in disruptive incidents and anxiety levels among all 4 women	Social worker, QMRPs	Group process (psychodynamic) self-awareness exercise, repeat as needed	Self-reports of less anxiety on individualized scale; QMRPs & residence director report fewer incidents

Intermediate Outcomes: Fair sharing of resources; stability in roommate situation (move unnecessary), reduction in prescribed anti-anxiety medications for all 4 women.

FIGURE 8.2 Logic Model Example: 4 Roommates

(COURTESY OF CATHERINE HOLMQUIST)

Assumptions of theory are represented in this logic model by how the elements (problem conditions to be addressed, necessary resources, methods, outcomes) are described.

Ideally a collaborative process, construction of a logic model proceeds most easily when, after identifying the problem(s) to be addressed, the practitioner and client work backward from the more distal outcomes (for example, ability to get along with roommates and negotiate differences, changes in family relationships, graduation from high school) to those that are most immediate (direct results expected from the intervention effort—for example, adherence to shower schedule, lower score on anxiety scale, increased parenting skill, or improved grades), then to the specific strategies to be implemented (how these outcomes will be achieved) , and finally to the resources required to carry out the interventions (how the interventions will be implemented). By identifying necessary resources, the practitioner will know whether or not the planned intervention is realistic and feasible.

Choices are necessarily made by the practitioner and client about the outcomes that are most important to monitor. Because clients' problems and intervention programs are often complex, it may not be necessary to track progress on every one, but instead to select outcomes that are of highest priority or most representative of changes desired. Tracking change in the most immediate outcomes over time allows the practitioner, client, and other stakeholders, such as the practitioner's supervisor, to know whether intervention is having the intended effects. If little or no progress is made, one reason might be that links between the interventions and desired outcomes are weak. This may be an indication that the theory of change depicted in the logic model is flawed and needs adjustment. Another possibility, of course, is that the intervention was not implemented as intended. For this reason, it is also useful to monitor program implementation.

Central to the logic model are program components—the resources that will be brought to bear on the problem situation and the specific interventions. The monitoring of these elements allows the practitioner to know whether resources are sufficient to deliver the intervention and to what extent the intervention program, as implemented, resembled the plan. Intervention fidelity may be measured if the program is manualized and a fidelity measure is available. Otherwise, the practitioner can choose program elements logically and theoretically expected to be the most important and collect data on their application. When linked to outcomes, data on program implementation provide evidence regarding the soundness of the practice theory represented in the logic model.

Several major benefits accrue from using a logic model for planning and guiding the evaluation of an intervention program. First and foremost, it ensures that the program is grounded in a theory of change, and that the theory of change is explicit and thus is falsifiable/modifiable. By requiring the specification of its constituent elements, the logic model permits the quantification and measurement of key indicators of program implementation and outcomes. Measurement of the processes and outcomes of service is essential for knowing whether intervention is effective. Furthermore, it contributes to the development of intervention knowledge, to the strengthening of the practitioner's repertoire of skills, and to the refinement of the practitioner's general theory of practice and the specific theory being applied to the client.

CONCLUSION

In this chapter, we argue that EBP draws strength from theory. Not only does theory make a valuable contribution to understanding human behavior, it also provides guidance for intervention. This is important, particularly in a professional environment in which empirically supported interventions are in short supply. In addition, EBP provides an opportunity for the practitioner to develop and make explicit a theory of change for a specific situation or client target group. We contend that EBP is most effective when research, practice experience, and theory are combined every step of the way.

We define *theory* as a systematic way of understanding events, phenomena, and situations. Theories can be formal knowledge structures that are subject to evaluation by researchers, scholars, and practitioners. They can also be informal, personal knowledge structures that we refer to as schemas, which allow practitioners to filter and organize information to better understand human experience. Although the use of theory in practice may be explicit or implicit, we suggest that it is advantageous for practitioners to use theory mindfully and explicitly.

Evidence-based practice provides a framework for systematically applying theory to practice, in combination with the best available evidence, practitioner expertise, client preferences, and clinical circumstances. Our definition of EBP is not limited to the use of empirically supported guidelines gleaned from the social science literature. We consider EBP to be a process through which selected interventions are adapted as necessary, and then implemented, and data are collected to inform real-time case decision making. In this chapter we explored how theory can enhance EBP at each stage of intervention:

(1) becoming motivated to use evidence-based practice; (2) posing an answerable question; (3) tracking down the best available evidence to answer the question; (4) critically appraising the evidence; (5) integrating the appraisal with practitioner expertise, client values, preferences, and clinical circumstances, and applying the results; and (6) evaluating the outcome.

To the question, "Is evidence-based practice atheoretical?" we answer a resounding *no!* Not only is every step informed by theory, but the practitioner is encouraged to make the application of theory explicit and to use theory mindfully to guide case decision making. Last, but certainly not least, practitioners can build knowledge for their own professional development, as well as for the field, by being able to demonstrate that the change theory on which an intervention or program is based is clear and specific, and is, if effective in producing desired outcomes, replicable.

REFERENCES

Alter, C., & Egan, M. (1997). Logic modeling: A tool for teaching critical thinking in social work practice. *Journal of Social Work Education*, 33(1), 85–102.

Alter, C., & McMurty, S. (1997). Logic modeling: A tool for teaching practice evaluation. *Journal of Social Work Education*, 33(1), 103–117.

Baer, R. W. (2003). Mindfulness training as a clinical intervention: A conceptual and empirical review. *Clinical Psychology: Science and Practice*, 10, 125–143.

Bennett, C. F. (1979). *Analyzing impacts of extension programs*. ESC-57. Washington, D.C.: U.S. Department of Agriculture, Science & Education Administration.

Berlin, S. B., & Marsh, J. C. (1993). *Informing practice decisions*. New York: Macmillan.

Bickman, L. (1987). The functions of program theory. In L. Bickman (Ed.), *Using program theory in evaluation* (pp. 5–18). New Directions for Program Evaluation 33. San Francisco: Jossey-Bass.

Bickman, L., & Peterson, K. A. (1990). Using program theory to describe and measure program quality. In L. Bickman (Ed.), *Advances in program theory* (pp. 61–72). New Directions for Program Evaluation 47. San Francisco: Jossey-Bass.

Bond, G., Williams, J., Evans, L., Salyers, M., Kim, H. W., Sharpe, H., & Leff, H. S. (2000). *Psychiatric rehabilitation fidelity toolkit*. Cambridge, Mass.: Human Services Research Institute.

Borkovec, T. D., & Castonguay, L. G. (2006). Effectiveness research. In J. C. Norcross, L. E. Beutler & R. F. Levant (Eds.), *Evidence-based practices in mental health: Debate and dialogue on the fundamental questions* (pp. 89–96). Washington, D.C.: American Psychological Association.

Chambless, D. L. (1998). Empirically validated treatments. In G. P. Koocher, J. C. Norcross & S. S. Hill (Eds.), *Pscyhologists' desk reference* (pp. 209–219). New York: Oxford.

Chen, H. T. (1990). *Theory-driven evaluations*. Newbury Park, Calif.: Sage.

Chorpita, B. F., Becker, K. D., & Daleiden, E. L. (2007). Understanding the common elements of evidence-based practice: Misconceptions and clinical examples. *Journal of the Academy of Child and Adolescent Psychiatry*, 46, 647–652.

Comas-Diaz, L. (2006). Cultural variation in the therapeutic relationship. In C. D. Good-heart, A. E. Kazdin & R. J. Sternberg (Eds.), *Evidence-based psychotherapy: Where practice and research meet* (pp. 37–61). Washington, D.C.: American Psychological Association.

Corrigan, P. W., & McCracken, S. G. (1997). *Interactive staff training: Rehabilitation teams that work*. New York: Plenum.

Denis, J., Hebert, Y., Langley, A., Lozeau, D., Trottier, L. (2002). Explaining diffusion patterns for complex health care innovation. *Health Care Management Review*, 27, 60–73.

Eddy, D. M. (2005). Evidence-based medicine: A unified approach. *Health Affairs*, 24, 9–16.

Epstein, R. M. (1999). Mindful practice. *Journal of the American Medical Association*, 282, 833–839.

Fischer, J. (1993). Empirically-based practice: The end of ideology? *Journal of Social Service Research*, 18, 19–64.

Franks, V. (2004). Evidence-based uncertainty in mental health nursing. *Journal of Psychiatric and Mental Health Nursing*, 11, 99–105.

Gellis, Z., & Reid, W. J. (2004). Strengthening evidence-based practice. Brief Treatment and Crisis Intervention, 4, 155–165.

Gibbs, L. E. (2003). Evidence-based practice for the helping professions: A practical guide with integrated multimedia. Pacific Grove, Calif.: Brooks/Cole-Thompson Learning.

Gomory, T. (2001). A fallibilistic response to Thyer's theory of theory-free empirical research in social work practice. *Journal of Social Work Education*, 37, 26–50.

Green, J. (2000). The role of theory in evidence-based health promotion practice. *Health Education Research*, 15, 125–129.

Guyatt, G., & Rennie, D. (Eds.) (2002). *Users' guides to the medical literature: Essentials of evidence-based clinical practice*. Chicago: American Medical Association.

Haynes, R. B., Devereaux, P. J., & Guyatt, G. H. (2002). Clinical expertise in the era of evidence-based medicine and patient choice. *Evidence-Based Medicine*, 7, 36–38. http//ebm.bmj.com/cgi/content/full/7/27/36 (accessed 24 November 2006).

Hill, C. E. (2006). Qualitative research. In J. C. Norcross, L. E. Beutler & R. F. Levant (Eds.), *Evidence-based practices in mental health: Debate and dialogue on the fundamental questions* (pp. 74–81). Washington, D.C.: American Psychological Association.

Hurst, R. M., & Nelson-Gray, R. (2006). Single-participant (S-P) design research. In J. C. Norcross, L. E. Beutler & R. F. Levant (Eds.), *Evidence-based practices in mental health: Debate and dialogue on the fundamental questions* (pp. 64–73). Washington, D.C.: American Psychological Association.

Kleinman, A. (1988). *Rethinking psychiatry: From cultural category to personal experience*. New York: Free Press.

Lieberman, A. F., Van Horn, P., & Ippen, C. G. (2005). Toward evidence-based treatment: Child-parent psychotherapy with preschoolers exposed to marital violence. *Journal of the American Academy of Child & Adolescent Psychiatry*, 44, 1241–1248.

Magill, M. (2006). The future of evidence in evidence-based practice: Who will answer the call for clinical relevance? *Journal of Social Work*, 6, 101–115.

Marsh, J. C. (2004). Theory-driven versus theory-free research in empirical social work practice. In H. E. Briggs & T. L. Rzepnicki (Eds.), *Using evidence in social work practice: Behavioral perspectives* (pp. 20–35). Chicago: Lyceum.

Massatti, R. R., Sweeney, H. A., Panzano, P.C., & Roth, D. (2008). The de-adoption of innovative mental health practices (IMHP): Why organizations choose not to sustain an IMHP. *Administration and Policy in Mental Health*, 35, 50–65.

McCracken, S. G., & Corrigan, P. W. (2008). Motivational interviewing for medication adherence in individuals with schizophrenia. In H. Arkowitz, H.A. Westra, W.R. Miller, & S. Rollnick (Eds). *Motivational Interviewing in the Treatment of Psychological Problems.* (pp. 249–276). New York: Guilford.

McCracken, S., & Marsh, J. (2008). Practitioner expertise in evidence-based practice decision making. *Research in Social Work Practice,* 18, 301–310.

McCracken, S., Steffen, F., & Hutchins, E. (2007, January). *Implementing EBP in a large metropolitan family service agency: Preparing the organization for change.* Paper presented at the annual conference of the Society for Social Work and Research, San Francisco.

Miller, W. R., & Rollnick, S. (2002). *Motivational interviewing: Preparing people to change addictive behavior,* 2d ed. New York: Guilford.

Moher, D., Schultz, K. F., Altman, D., for the CONSORT Group. (2001). The CONSORT statement: Revised recommendations for improving the quality of reports of parallel-group randomized trials. *Journal of the American Medical Association,* 285, 1987–1991.

Mullen, E. J., & Bacon, W. (2004). Implementation of practice guidelines and evidence-based treatment: A survey of psychiatrists, psychologists, and social workers. In A. R. Roberts & K. R. Yeager (Eds.), *Evidence-based practice manual: Research and outcome measures in health and human services* (pp. 210–218). New York: Oxford.

Mullen, E., & Magnabosco, J. (1997). *Outcomes measurement in the human services: Cross-cutting issues and methods.* Washington, D.C.: National Association of Social Work Press.

Mullen, E. J., & Streiner, D. L. (2004). The evidence for and against evidence-based practice. *Brief Treatment and Crisis Intervention,* 4, 111–121.

National Cancer Institute (2005). *Theory at a glance: A guide for health promotion practice.* 2d ed. http://www.cancer.gov/PDF/481f5d53–63df-41bc-bfaf-5aa48ee1da4d/TAAG3.pdf (accessed 1 December 2007).

Norcross, J. C., Beutler, L. E., & Levant, R. F. (Eds.) (2006). *Evidence-based practices in mental health: Debate and dialogue on the fundamental questions.* Washington, D.C.: American Psychological Association.

Patton, M. Q. (1997). *Utilization-focused evaluation.* 3d ed. Thousand Oaks, Calif.: Sage.

Pollio, D. E. (2006). The art of evidence-based practice. *Research on Social Work Practice,* 16, 224–232.

Prochaska, J. O., DiClemente, C. C., & Norcross, J. C. (1992). In search of how people change: Applications to addictive behavior. *American Psychologist,* 47, 1102–1114.

Proctor, E. K. & Rosen, A. (2006). Concise standards for developing evidence-based practice guidelines. In A. R. Roberts & K .R. Yeager (Eds.), *Foundations of evidence-based social work* (pp. 93–102). New York: Oxford.

Regehr, C., Stern, S., & Shlonsky, A. (2007). Operationalizing evidence-based practice: The development of an institute for evidence-based social work. *Research on Social Work Practice,* 17, 408–416.

Reid, W. J. (1994). The empirical practice movement. *Social Service Review,* 68, 165–184.

Renger, R., & Hurley, C. (2006). From theory to practice: Lessons learned in the application of the ATM approach to developing logic models. *Evaluation and Program Planning,* 29, 106–119.

Rosen, A., & Proctor, E.K. (Eds.). (2003). Developing practice guidelines for social work intervention: Issues, methods, and research agenda. New York: Columbia University.

Rubin, A., & Babbie, E. (2007). Essential research methods for social work. Belmont, Calif.: Thompson Brooks/Cole.

Sackett, D. L., Rosenberg, W. M. C., Muir Gray, J. A., Haynes, R. B., & Richardson, W. S. (1996). Evidence-based medicine: What it is and what it isn't. *British Medical Journal*, 312, 71–72.

Sackett, D. L., Straus, S. E., Richardson, W. S., Rosenberg, W., & Haynes, R. B. (2000). *Evidence-based medicine: How to practice and teach EBM.* 2d ed. Edinburgh: Churchill Livingstone.

Savaya, R., & Waysman, M. (2005) The logic model: A tool for incorporating theory in development and evaluation of programs. *Administration in Social Work*, 29(2), 85–103.

Shlonsky, A., & Gibbs, L. (2004). Will the real evidence-based practice please stand up? Teaching the process of evidence-based practice to the helping professions. *Brief Treatment and Crisis Intervention*, 4, 137–153.

Stiles, W. B. (2006). Case studies. In J. C. Norcross, L. E. Beutler, & R. F. Levant (Eds.), *Evidence-based practices in mental health: Debate and dialogue on the fundamental questions* (pp. 57–64). Washington, D.C.: American Psychological Association.

Straus, S. E., Richardson, W. S., Glasziou, P., & Haynes, R. B. (2005). *Evidence-based medicine: How to practice and teach EBM.* 3d ed. Edinburgh: Elsevier.

Suzuki, S. (1980). *Zen mind, beginner's mind.* New York: Weatherhill.

Toth, S. L., Maughan, A., Manly, J. T., Spagnola, M., & Cicchetti, D. (2002). The relative efficacy of two interventions in altering maltreated preschool children's representational models: Implications for attachment theory. *Development and Psychopathology*, 14, 877–908.

Wampold, B. E. (2006). Not a scintilla of evidence to support empirically supported treatments as more effective than other treatments. In J. C. Norcross, L. E. Beutler, & R. F. Levant (Eds.), *Evidence-based practices in mental health: Debate and dialogue on the fundamental questions* (pp. 299–308). Washington, D.C.: American Psychological Association.

Weiss, C. (1997) Theory-based evaluation: Past, present, and future. In D. Rog & D. Fournier (Eds.), *Progress and future directions in evaluation: Perspectives on theory, practice, and methods* (pp. 41–55). New Directions for Program Evaluation 76. San Francisco: Jossey-Bass.

Weisz, J. R., & Addis, M. E. (2006). The research-practice tango and other choreographic challenges: Using and testing evidence-based psychotherapies in clinical care settings. In C. E. Gooheart, A. E. Kazdin, & R. J. Sternberg (Eds.), *Evidence-based psychotherapy: Where practice and research meet* (pp. 179–206). Washington, D.C.: American Psychological Association.

Westen, D. (2006). Patients and treatments in clinical trials are not adequately representative of clinical practice. In J. C. Norcross, L. E. Beutler, & R. F. Levant (Eds.), *Evidence-based practices in mental health: Debate and dialogue on the fundamental questions* (pp. 161–171). Washington, D.C.: American Psychological Association.

Witkin, S. L. (1991). Empirical clinical practice: A critical analysis. *Social Work*, 36, 158–163.

W. K. Kellogg Foundation (2004). *W. K. Kellogg Foundation Logic model development guide.* Battle Creek, Mich.: Kellogg Foundation.

Zeiss, A. M., Lewinsohn, P. M., & Munoz, R. F. (1979). Nonspecific improvement effects in depression using interpersonal skills training, pleasant activity schedules, or cognitive training. *Journal of Consulting and Clinical Psychology*, 47, 427–439.

9 PRACTICE THEORY

Ideas Embodied in a Wise Person's Professional Process

MALCOLM PAYNE

A FEW WEEKS ago, I was covering for the social work team in the hospice where I work, and received a telephone call from a young doctor asking for a social worker to assist him. He explained that he wanted me to participate in a potentially difficult interview. He was about to meet with Carol, the wife of a patient who had recently returned from hospital after intensive treatment for an infection. The patient was in the final stages of a degenerative neurological illness, and had become progressively paralyzed over a period of some years. The hospital informed the hospice medical team that they would not consider it worthwhile to repeat the treatment. The patient had returned to the hospice ward, and after being stable for a few days, he had begun to deteriorate again. Carol and a friend were present on the ward and had asked to see the doctor. He surmised that he would need to discuss with her the reality that the patient was moving rapidly toward the end of his life, building on quite a lot of advance information given to patients and their families when they come to the hospice. A nurse accompanied us in the interview, held in a lounge near the patient's room. The doctor was a high-status South Asian man; the nurse and I were, respectively, a local woman and man, both white; the patient and her friend were of African Caribbean origin. I said to the doctor, whom I knew slightly but had not worked with before: "I imagine you'll start by asking her how she sees her husband's condition," and he replied: "Yes, the usual approach."

We all introduced ourselves, and the doctor took the lead in the interview. He asked Carol how she thought her husband was. She described his deteriorating condition over the previous two days, and said her husband had stopped talking about going home, and had asked to see the children; he was talking less and seemed quite withdrawn. She was disappointed that the hospital treatment had not improved his condition and asked what we were going to do now. The doctor set off on his explanation about the hospital's decision not to try further treatment, and he and the nurse explained how they would try to maintain the patient's alertness and keep him comfortable. During this lengthy exchange, Carol collapsed with a wail into her friend's arms and said, through the tears: "Oh God, I've just realized; you're trying to tell me you think he's going to die, aren't you?" There was further explanation from the doctor and the nurse, and discussion about how Carol felt about what was happening and what might happen. As part of this conversation, Carol began to see that her husband's changed demeanor meant that he had also realized and accepted that he was going to die soon.

This part of the conversation naturally came to an end, and at this point I intervened for the first time since the introductions. I said: "Can I just take you back to something you said earlier? You said your husband was asking to see the children. I got the impression that was a bit unusual. Do they know about his illness? Have they been coming to see him since he's been here?" Carol explained that because he had been ill for many years, and had been in and out of hospitals many times, the children did not usually come to visit him; they expected him to return home and continue life as before. But because he had asked, she had arranged for them to come into the hospice that afternoon (it was a school day). I asked about the children. They were aged ten and twelve. Had she talked with them about his death? She had talked with them about how he had been getting worse, but she and they had not really been thinking about the possibility of his death.

In a way, this is surprising, because this was the first time he had been in the hospice, and most people in the United Kingdom think that admission to a hospice means that you are very close to death. The situation is different in the United States, where some hospice services care for people as in-patients for quite long periods. However, Houghton (2001), describing his own experience of serious illness, says that although he was aware of the likelihood of impending death, this was not a major factor in his daily thinking. As his condition changed, the closeness of death became an increasingly present part of his daily thoughts. I asked if Carol felt okay about talking this over with her children; she thought so. I offered to talk to her again later that day or on another day if she wanted to discuss it; she could ask the nurses to call me.

Further closing conversation took place, with the aim of reassurance and confidence-building. The meeting ended after about an hour, and I left a note for the ward social worker about the event. I also talked it over with the doctor, who felt the meeting had achieved his aims. I had no more personal involvement with the situation, but the ward social worker picked up contacts with both the wife and her husband, who died less than two days later.

COMMENTARY

This is an account of a situation in which a social worker was involved in helping someone with social and psychological needs, in a multiprofessional health and social care agency. The situation is in several respects typical of many social work actions, in the following ways:

- The agency's role and aims, to provide care for dying people and their families, set the subject and form of the intervention.
- The agency has established treatment traditions, informed but not centrally created by social work, about how to deal with difficult emotional issues around death and dying.
- The intervention is set up hurriedly in response to a client's request, with the aim of informing her further interactions with her husband, not planned with a social work purpose.
- As the social worker involved, I was not centrally part of the multiprofessional team that would normally work with the patient, and so occupied a limited role. Had I been the ward social worker, I might already have developed a relationship with the wife, who was a regular visitor, and have talked with her about her children's involvement with and reaction to the present situation. If that had been so, after the meeting I might have taken time with her to rehearse how she was going to work with the children now. I would have made sure to talk with her and perhaps them after they had visited their father. The social work team has a policy of helping parents work through the experience of a parental death with children, rather than intervening with the children directly, because this supports continuing parenting in the future. However, I might well have worked directly with the children in a planned way if that had been required.

- Another professional, the doctor, takes the lead and sets the parameters of the interaction.
- The form of the intervention is explicitly set by the evidence in the healthcare literature about "giving bad news."

THE CRITIQUE OF PRACTICE THEORY

All these factors, and others, mean that social work operates within a service that is often not centrally a social work setting. This does not fit with the assumptions of practice theory. *Practice theory* is an aspect of social work theory concerned with how to do social work, in which ideas are developed to prescribe particular models of practice or ways of practicing (Payne, 2005a). Practice theory includes formal and informal sets of ideas. Formal practice theory is written, usually published, evidence and analysis worked out in a rational structured form, which offers general ideas that may be applied deductively to particular practice situations; that is, the ideas are applied to the situation rather than the situation generating ideas. Informal practice theory draws on ideas and experience gained in life and practice. It is applied inductively—that is, the theory derives from particular situations and is generalized to other relevant practice situations. This requires decisions about similarities and differences between situations to decide if the generalization is relevant. Practice theory is not the only form of social work theory: there are also theories of what social work is and of psychological and social knowledge about the client's world (Sibeon, 1990).

Practice theory does not generally prescribe how actions should be mediated by the demands of a particular agency, or by the situation that leads to the intervention. It does not deal with the general exigencies of working in an organization with several professions or with organizational factors that affect the service. This interaction fitted that picture. The knowledge on which it was based is primarily research about how healthcare professionals should deliver "bad news" to patients. The interview was not highly planned, and although it was emotionally charged, it is a commonplace one in a hospice, so its content and approach mainly reflected the norms of professional work in palliative and end-of-life care, rather than social work practice theory.

Social work practice situations that make it impossible to implement practice theory are commonplace. Many practitioners and their managers consequently question the value or relevance of the knowledge and ideas they are taught in social work education, and claim that their work is eclectic, drawing on experience of similar situations in their experience, rather than theoretical and empirical evidence of what is effective (Marsh & Triseliotis, 1996; Payne, 2005a, chapter 1). Studying practice theory then becomes a general intellectual basis for the creation of an individual mode of practice. It might be used in a planned way in a few specific cases, but most of the time social workers use social work skills to deliver a good-quality, caring agency service. This has led to the situation where, mainly in the United States, elite social workers have been criticized for withdrawing into private practice, engaging in a form of psychotherapy that allows them to use the practice theory in which they were trained, in controlled circumstances (Specht & Courtney, 1994). In the United States and the rest of the world, they may move to specialized settings that allow a greater measure of control over the circumstances of their work; in many countries such settings are exceptional, since most social work is carried out in state-provided or state-funded social care services. This leaves the vast majority of people who might benefit from social work receiving "untheorized," less structured and planned practice than might be desirable. It means that practice is informed by specialist considerations of particular identified social needs and agency interests and political policy. Moreover, it weakens social work as a distinctive practice within the social arena and as an intellectual discipline, because it cannot be shown that its theory is integrated with and relevant to its practice in the most common settings.

Some commentary in the social work literature tries to incorporate into social work thinking informal theoretical ideas, such as "practice wisdom" (O'Sullivan, 2005; Sheppard, 1995; Krill, 1990), which affirm the value of experience and draw on a long history of social work being seen as an art rather than a science. Challenging this turn in thinking, worldwide movements to develop practice prescriptions seek an evidence-based or research-minded practice theory. This has led to a debate. On one side, proponents of positivist research assumptions argue that knowledge about human beings may and should develop explanatory theory that can reliably and universally prescribe professional actions. On the other side, proponents of interpretivist research assumptions argue that knowledge about human beings is also mediated and interpreted by the historical and social contexts, and cannot be universally used to guide human action (see Borden, this volume, chapter 1; Brechin & Sidell, 2000).

Current practice theory, in summary, has two major weaknesses. First, it is universalist, because it assumes that social workers can act according to research-based behavioral prescriptions. On the contrary, social workers need to understand and respond to the variations in social and historical contexts in which they operate. Second, current practice theory focuses on behavior and social change. On the contrary, much social work is concerned with maintenance, care, and support. Although this may be idealized as being concerned with behavioral change, this is a misrepresentation of what the participants conceive themselves as doing.

This chapter explores two approaches to these weaknesses. First, it argues that we need to understand how social workers may incorporate flexibility in social and historical contexts within their practice. Second, it suggests that research focused on five elements of care and support carries the potential to establish helpful additional elements of practice theory relevant to important current roles in social work.

EMBODYING KNOWLEDGE AND EXPERIENCE IN A "WISE PERSON"

As in Carol's case, when social workers are called to participate in an agency's work, their actions are not formally prescribed by research, but developed by their personal response to the agency's requirements in each situation. Their agency and the multiprofessional network of services partly define the practice identity of social work. In the hospice, social work is distinguished from cognate professions, such as creative arts and spiritual care, as being concerned with the social understanding and coping of patients' families and social networks (Payne, 2004). More widely, social workers create a professional identity by the roles they take in interaction with professional colleagues (Payne, 2006b). In the interview with Carol, I fulfilled the hospice and broader perception of social work by being prepared to respond to the doctor's wish to have support in case of potentially complex emotional reactions and by focusing on how the family might cope with the situation. Thus, the call for and arrival of social workers designates them with wisdom in particular areas of social functioning.

The social expectations mean that, while social workers are not necessarily wise, when called on in their profession, people expect them to be an appropriate kind of person for the role, to be a "wise person" in matters that agency and client assume to be within the province of social work. This means that the person who is present as a social worker in a social situation has to incorporate within herself and demonstrate in her performance the knowledge, values, and understanding that allow her to do the work well (Payne, 2007). In practice situations, social workers' professional identity becomes their personhood; this happens in four main ways.

First, they follow a pathway into social work through which they gradually come to see themselves as a social worker or which generates experiences that lead them toward social work. They gain initial and partial impressions of social work through reading about or encountering social workers; they might have early experiences in helping, perhaps have learning experiences in cognate academic subjects, and also have early work experiences. The particular experiences and the order in which they come to them will create them as professional social workers, and shape them in particular ways to become unique practitioners. Someone entering training as a social worker with experience as a police officer, say, is likely to approach education and practice differently from someone with experience as, say, a nurse. Their continuing pathway through their qualifying and postqualifying professional education will draw on and adapt this background. Their education interacts with their life history and with their current experience during their practice learning and in their noneducation experiences of life (Payne, 2005b).

Second, they incorporate within themselves a particular balance among three perspectives on social work practice (Payne, 2006a). Social work is a territory bounded by three interacting roles:

- A social order role in which people are helped with problem solving and services organized and managed as a way of maintaining social cohesion by responding to people's difficulties in managing their lives
- A therapeutic role that promotes social well-being by empowering people to develop and fulfill themselves in their social relationships
- A transformational role in which people are helped to cooperate and provide mutual support to each other to reduce oppression and discrimination that creates inequalities and failings for particular groups within society

Each welfare regime (that is, the political and social administration within which social work is defined in each country or state), each agency, each social worker creates a balance among these. This is expressed in how practice actions are taken in every particular situation and interaction (Payne, 2006a). So, in Carol's case, I was mainly concerned to ensure that the family could deal with the problems of the husband's turn for the worse in his illness. However, by helping the family to manage the situation and experience satisfactory participation in the death, I would be promoting their well-being and strengthening their capacity to deal with further difficulties in the future. I was conscious of a transformational role, in that I think I was the only person present who explicitly held a concern that the ethnic differences between the professionals and Carol and her friend should not interfere with the help she received. My failure to raise explicitly the issue of potential ethnic and faith requirements as death approached is a weakness in my contribution to the interview. Although in this particular situation, I do not think it was an issue, failure to raise it routinely means that it becomes exceptional to confirm to service users the importance that we give to the issue as professionals and as an agency, and the exceptional becomes difficult or is avoided. To raise it routinely affirms our care for this issue, and reduces any potential apprehension that the organization will be prejudiced, particularly when service users are being dealt with by people from a different ethnic background.

Third, as social workers progress through their career, they work out issues in particularly problematic case situations. In doing so, they come to a particular way of dealing with the complexities in implementing social work values. Social work values are sometimes presented as a set of prescriptions for action, mainly in the process of socializing and educating social workers (Payne, 2006, chapter 4). When we practice, this may present difficulties, since generalized ethical prescriptions do not adequately reflect the complexities that social workers deal with. For example, my gentle questioning of how Carol had informed her children reflected experience that many parents have difficulty in talking with children about a relative's illness and death. The hospice has a treatment policy of trying to counter this, founded on experience and research that this often leads to current anxiety and guilt among children, future difficulties in bereavement, and a breakdown of trust between parent and child. It is also founded on the human rights of the child for such openness. However, equally, the parent has the right to follow the course that he or she thinks best. Thus, rights often clash; it is difficult both to enforce and to implement them. Moreover, rights to and interests in confidentiality and privacy interact with rights to and interests in openness and transparency. All the conventional elements of social work values, represented in codes of ethics, reveal all these complexities in practice. Gaining experience of these value complexities and handling them in particular settings are an important way in which social workers develop personas as "wise persons" in the issues that they regularly face.

Finally, a variety of knowledges are used in practice, which are then mediated through the situational knowledge, which refers to knowledge gained from and about the specific situation in which the service user is dealt with. Pawson and colleagues (2003) refer to several types of knowledge:

- *Organizational knowledge,* about government and agency organization and regulation
- *Practitioner knowledge,* drawn from experience of practice, which tends to be tacit, personal, and context-specific
- *User knowledge,* drawn from users' knowledge of their lives, situation, and use of services
- *Research knowledge,* drawn from systematic investigation disseminated in reports
- *Policy community knowledge,* drawn from administrators, official documentation, and analysis of policy research

All these are then filtered through the agency's requirements.

In summary, then, social workers build a persona of wisdom, which enables them to perform the roles required of social workers by both the profession and the agency. They do this through their experiential pathway into social work and its education and practice; through incorporating within themselves balances between social order, therapeutic, and transformational elements of social work territory; through incorporating resolutions of social work value complexities; and through filtering various kinds of professional knowledge via the situational requirements of the agency, its service users, and its aims.

THE CONTENT OF PRACTICE WISDOM

What does this wisdom consist of? I want to draw attention to work on five areas of practice that are neglected in practice theory, because of its focus on universal knowledge for behavioral and social change. These elements of practice theory, instead, focus on flexible responses to complexities:

- *Emotional labor and intelligence,* important for the capacity to achieve the social work role of emotional responsiveness
- *Caring,* a neglected aspect of social work, increasingly important as social work shifts from short-term behavior change toward long-term care
- *Resilience,* important because long-term care means increasing people's capacity to maintain motivation and forward movement in adversity over long periods
- *Support,* important for standing alongside people and seeing them through long-term adversities
- *Process,* important for understanding how these elements fit together as part of a long-term care service

EMOTIONAL LABOR AND INTELLIGENCE

One of the roles of social work is to respond to the emotional consequences of social events in people's lives. The doctor recognized this in Carol's case. He was concerned about her emotional reaction when he presented the "bad news" of her husband's impending death, and he called on a social worker to deal with that concern. In this way, the social worker was called upon to be the person who would focus on emotional and social consequences of what took place, who was wise in and able to do the "emotional labor" in the interview.

The concept of emotional labor (Hochschild, 1983; James, 1989) implies that dealing with emotional issues in life is often hard work, requiring effort, skill and experience. Emotional labor is always potentially an aspect of work that involves contact with people. It will always be created and affected by the immediate conditions in which the work has to be undertaken and external controls that affect the work. In particular, like physical labor, it is subject to divisions of labor; that is, people in relationships will divide up among them the effort required to carry out emotional labor.

James (1993/2004) has examined the emotional labor involved in disclosure of cancer; the labor arises from the potentially serious physical and social consequences, including the likelihood of death. Her research shows that a wide range of people, both professionals and family members, are involved in managing the emotional consequences of disclosures. She suggests that in any situation, there are different levels of involvement with the feelings generated by the situation, which arise from competing forms of status and knowledge.

Divisions of emotional labor are affected by the depth of feelings generated, the public context in which feelings are expressed and regulated, and the distance brought about by hierarchies of those involved.

Thus, a senior professional giving information to a patient's relative who has no close relationship with the people involved, and operating in a public setting, such as a meeting or case conference, will carry less of the emotional labor than, say, a nurse who provides daily intimate physical care in the patient's private room. In turn, the nurse is likely to carry less of the labor than the daughter of a dying patient, who has had a close personal relationship with the patient for many years, has been involved in the earlier stages of the illness, and has experienced the patient's physical deterioration. Looking back at the interview with Carol, the high-status males with less emotional investment in her life took on their responsibility for information- and advice-giving roles, but the emotional labor was carried primarily by Carol, who had the closest relationship with the dying man, by her friend, and also probably by nurses and healthcare assistants in daily contact on the ward. The doctor took on the emotional labor of his concern for the emotional and social issues, and I took on the emotional labor of focusing on these issues and the social consequences. More emotional labor would have been taken by the ward social worker when she returned. Research on emotional labor suggests that enabling practitioners to maintain continuing close personal engagement with clients in the setting where their emotional labor takes place should be an important priority for social work management.

Similarly, recent research suggests that "emotional intelligence" is a crucial ingredient that distinguishes good from average performance in management. Morrison (2007) suggests that this has application to social work practice. Such ideas have a long history. Thorndike (1921) coined the term "social intelligence" to refer to acting wisely in human relationships, and Goleman (1996) identified the importance of emotional intelligence in parenting and many other social situations. It comprises an interaction between self-awareness and self-management (intrapersonal intelligence), and awareness of others and capacity to manage relationships with others (interpersonal intelligence) (Morrison, 2007, p. 251). People with emotional intelligence have developed skills in perceiving and identifying feelings in others. They integrate emotions with thinking in a way that facilitates effective cognition and demonstrate a preparedness to think about their own and other people's feelings and manage their own emotions and emotions collectively with others. Social workers who have developed emotional intelligence are likely to be better able to engage with others, carry out social work assessments, make decisions, and collaborate with others. As professionals, they are likely to be better able to deal with stress, build resilience to adversity, and cope better with difficulties in their practice (Morrison, 2007).

CARING

Social work is a crucial part of social arrangements that provide care for people. There has always been a problem providing enough care of the right quality for those who need it. A "care deficit" (Hochschild, 1995)—that is, a gap between the amount and type of care that people might ideally want or need, and what they get—has been commonplace throughout history. Social workers, therefore, have an important role in planning and rationing inadequate provision in care services, through activities such as case management. There may also be a question of a balance between quality and quantity. For example, people may prefer to have very sensitive, intimate care occasionally, or care of a particular kind. One man put up with the female staff in his care home, but preferred the one male carer on the staff. This suggests that it may be possible to improve the experience of caring for people where resources are not good enough by improving quality in a way that connects with the wishes of the service users.

We may care for ideas, and care for people (Mayeroff, 1971). There are both emotional and practical aspects of caring for people: caring about them, and tending them (Parker, 1989). Mayeroff (1971) tries to identify generic characteristics of caring. He starts from the principle: "To care for another person, in the most significant sense, is to help him grow or actualize himself" (p. 1). He goes on to say: "To help another grow is to help him care for something outside himself and to be able to care for himself" (p. 6). Mayeroff's focus on helping people toward self-actualization proposes a direction and priorities in carrying out caring tasks, and a way of deciding what to do; he goes on to analyze elements of caring in some detail. Noddings (1984) criticizes Mayeroff's (1971) view, arguing that caring must involve a connectedness between the care giver and the care receiver, with the care giver concerned for the receiver's well-being and receptive to his or her needs and wishes. Connectedness between people is characteristic of the "ethics of care" approach of Gilligan (1993) and Tronto (1993). Tronto argues that to be ethical, care must involve attentiveness to the needs of the cared-for person, responsibility for taking action to meet his or her needs, competence in doing so, and responsiveness to needs that may lead to risk.

McBeath and Webb (1997) trace ideas about caring to Enlightenment thinkers, who proposed the ethical assumption of a moral duty to reduce suffering and the concept of a free person, who is able through reason to determine his or her own course of action. Western societies have developed practical arrangements that use the concept of care to describe what they are doing. These, in turn, have led Western societies to institutionalize a professionalized practice to meet the need to reduce suffering through a variety of public and social service professions, such as medicine, nursing, social work, and counseling. Halmos (1965, 1970), in an influential series of books, showed that professions working with people became increasingly socially important in a society that sought to provide personal service to help individuals. Gilligan's (1993) research on the moral development of children argues that solidarity in society means that people have an "ethics of care"—that is, we see it as a moral good if people care for each other. She suggests that women are socialized to value interdependence, while men are socialized to value fairness. An important study by Batson and colleagues (1997) confirms this in adults.

Foucault (1986) emphasized that individual self-actualization as a social priority gives importance to the individual in Western society, and values private over public and community life. Dalley (1988) drew attention to the way in which the ideas of community and family interact, in her study of caring. Ideas—for example, about duty, community, and family—are part of what leads us to care for people. She argues that when people talk about community and family as the basis for caring in society, they are often working from an ideology of "familism"—that is, they believe that a social construct, the family, underlies all other relationships within society. Beliefs that we are born into "families" and that we rely on and return to relationships within families are examples of familism. Following on from this, families are seen as part of wider groups, communities, which share interests because they share certain characteristics. Examples of such characteristics are ethnic minority or religious identities or identity that comes from living or growing up in a particular locality. We are possessive about our families and communities: it is "my" family and "my" hometown. Coming from this "possessive familism," we see it as our duty to care for others in the family and as their duty to care for us. Dalley (1988) argues that to avoid imposing the assumption of familism to apply social pressure on women to provide caring within families and communities, we should see it as a role of the state to organize caring as a collective responsibility. However, subsequent evidence (for example, Finch & Mason 1993) suggests that there are complex negotiations within families about duties to care, and men often accept caring roles in particular circumstances.

These arrangements require relationships between individuals as private citizens, state institutions, and economic markets. Because of this, the state and the market intervene in hitherto private lives and make public the private and individual relationships that are part of care. Although the social assumption has been that care is part of a private relationship, if it requires involvement from public services and economic markets, it is increasingly regulated by outsiders. Social workers are at the interface of this social tension between privacy and intervention; it is one of the things that makes the job difficult.

We can see, therefore, that social work is a profession that incorporates social caring into its practice, but the content of this aspect of social work has not been adequately researched and theorized.

What activities would practical, professional caring consist of? First, caring is partly about providing for physical needs, about bodies; this is often the role of nursing professionals. That is not all it is about, but you are not caring if you do not respond to physical need. People have to be fed, enabled to rest and sleep, enabled to carry out bodily functions such as urination and defecation, enabled to exercise and do things with their body. They need bodily communication, to see, hear, and feel things, and the communication of affection and intimacy, and sometimes sexual activities. Many of these physical needs are bound up with social interaction. We sometimes eat alone, but meals are social occasions, and there are social rules about urination and defecation. Also, people sleep together—that is, they share rooms or feel lonely or relieved when they do not—they need other people to experience intimacy and sexual relations. Therefore, although an illness or disability may lead to problems in meeting some of these physical needs, they are essentially natural needs of every human being.

Second, people are, after childhood, normally self-caring in meeting these needs. Even when they cannot self-care all the time, it is rare for someone to need caring for everything all the time. Third, and connected with this, people's ideas about what is caring come from family and cultural expectations. This is because they are such a natural and universal aspect of everybody's lives that everyone assumes that the way it is in their culture or family is the way it should be. Their idea of caring is integral to who they are as human beings, and to their social background and culture. That is another way in which caring is "social." Our understanding of it comes from our closest interpersonal relationships and from the depths of our cultural background.

Fourth, again connected with the cultural basis of caring, caring is so personal that it has to be a lived experience. If it is a natural human relationship, having difficulty in gaining care may seem unnatural, and this may generate anger or guilt when a service cannot provide something that a user or family sees as caring. It involves a sequence in which we become knowing about someone and their needs, we make special efforts to be with them, we do things to and for them, and we enable them to do things themselves. Knowing, being, doing, and enabling emphasize the human interaction aspect of caring, although of course we can give these activities jargon labels, such as "assessment" and "intervention."

A related idea is the concept of "caring presence." Engebretson (2000) explores a range of nursing writing that emphasizes a noninstrumental "overt physical presence" (p. 243), by being open, receptive, ready, and available, as an important part of caring. This involves several elements:

- An orientation to time that focuses on the present, rather than future or past
- Use of silence as part of communication and interaction, conveying sincerity and paying attention to the person as a whole, rather than using words to concentrate on cognitive or thinking aspects of the relationship

- Being physically present with someone and doing things with them, as well as psychological presence in focusing on both people being together
- Focusing on immaterial and immeasurable things, not just those that can be measured and described
- Concentrating on detail and subtle aspects of the relationship

Formulations such as these allow us to see something of what research is required to provide an adequate foundation for caring in practice theory.

RESILIENCE

The idea of resilience is closely linked to attachment theory, which in turn comes from psychoanalytic ideas. Attachment therefore reflects the focus of psychoanalysis on the interaction of people's internal emotional responses and external experiences and on the impact of earlier on later experiences (Bower, 2005). Emotions are the way our bodies, brains, and minds react when aroused by external events that have meaning for us (Howe, 2005, p. 11). Attachment theory assumes that in close relationships, we "mentalize" other people's behavior—that is, we respond to how they behave according to our assumptions about their mental state. We base our assessment of their mental state on our previous experience, particularly with our parents and other people emotionally important to us, of how close relationships (attachments) work (Howe, 2005; see Wakefield & Baer, this volume, chapter 3). Resilience may also derive from our social networks, families, and communities. Carol, her children, and her friend are all part of what makes her resilient in the situation she faces; Walsh (2006; this volume, chapter 6) shows how important family resilience is in interaction with the needs of individuals within the family.

Resilience arises in the face of adversities, and social workers are often asked to deal with clients in adverse situations—that is, any situation that might be difficult to adapt to raises the risk of significant difficulties in adaptation for an individual, family, group, or organization. If the risk becomes reality and becomes an adversity, this may cause an emotional reaction that increases the level of difficulty. Adversities might come from any number of sources:

- *An individual's psychological makeup, home life, and interpersonal relationships within the family or social network.* Emotional reactions to adversities might interact with each other and affect parts of life that are distant from the source of adversity.

- *The organizations where social work takes place.* A small agency, with few resources, may feel less secure or caring to worker, client, or family than a large agency. Conversely, it may engage more personal commitment or be more flexible.
- *Wider society including the local community,* wider ideas about what is good health and social solidarity, and sociocultural and political ideas, such as concern about immigration or gender issues.

Finally, many patients have a great deal of adversity in their lives and so may transfer that adversity into the social work process or its setting. Sheppard and Crocker (2006) studied the locus of control of families with severe difficulties in parenting and child care. They compared families with an external locus of control—that is, those who looked outside their own resources for help in coping—and people with an internal locus of control, who were more pro-active in problem solving. People who experienced long-term adversities were more likely to have an external locus, and therefore likely to be less able to use their own resources when the family had problems.

Carol had experienced long-term adversity because of her husband's illness, but they had jointly managed parenting responsibilities in a way that enabled her to deal with her children appropriately, and respond to her husband's request to see the children, which initially she had not understood. As she gained additional information from the interview, she came to understand the changes in her husband's reactions, and was able to incorporate this understanding into a new response to the new situation. She did have the confidence and resilience to change direction. Practice theory might identify how the external information provided in this interview returns control over her situation by enhancing her understanding of how to respond to the way her husband has chosen to manage this new, and final, phase in his illness.

SUPPORT

Although *support* is a frequently used term in long-term social work, it is relatively untheorized, being taken for granted as an everyday concept. However, research is available to help us specify more clearly what support might be provided. Sheppard's (2004) study of social support needs and provision for depressed mothers, for example, identifies several potential professional actions:

- Emotional support, such as ventilation, giving esteem, encouragement, and feedback about successes
- Advice and information
- Working directly with the issue that is a problem, such as child care difficulties
- Emotional work around self-understanding and helping people make good decisions
- Financial support
- Social participation, such as facilitating contacts with friends and developing social skills

West (2004) outlines four kinds of support that psychological research has demonstrated to be helpful to people in organizational settings; these have a wider application and connect well with Sheppard's list derived directly from child care social work:

- Emotional support, by being a receptive, open, noncritical, but thoughtful listener, and being careful to look for people's needs to be listened to
- Informational support, by being prepared to offer information and consultation to deal with a problem
- Instrumental support, by routinely being prepared to do things that benefit the other person rather than oneself
- Appraisal support, by giving feedback on how things have gone and helping to plan how to learn and improve functioning

It is striking how emotional support emerges as important in these formulations, which are unconnected with identifiably emotionally stressful situations. Carol's needs for support were met by the awareness that there would be emotional reactions to the information provided, and preparation to respond to that, by listening to and accepting her emotional reaction, and by helping her to plan her next steps.

PROCESS

Process understanding has long been regarded as an important aspect of social work practice (Payne, 2005c), but again has only recently been researched in detail to provide practice theory that guides management of process. It is important to generalize about the overall process of social work in ways that can provide an empirical basis for action. It is also important to incorporate into a wise person's performance the markers of social factors in a situation. Process draws attention to the way in which a social work intervention is a relatively short-term action as part of an ongoing family and community situation and a trajectory of the issues that individuals, families, and communities face. For example, Carol had devised ways of managing her children's responses to her husband's long-term illness. However, the trajectory of change in the situation was altered by the information given in the interview, and my intervention was designed to support her in making the necessary change in response that was needed because of the new phase in her husband's illness and the family's relationships. This was achieved by a multiprofessional intervention, informed by agency policies and processes, reflecting research evidence about effective ways of practicing.

Berlin and Marsh's (1993) comprehensive study of the factors that might inform practice decisions, and instruments and techniques that might be used to take decisions rationally, is a decision-making approach to such process decisions, which identifies useful generic instruments that may be incorporated into social work decisions. Social workers increasingly require such instruments to help them make decisions so that they are fair, take into account the required range of information, and are accountable. Examples are comprehensive agreed-upon assessment processes for children and adults receiving social care services in the United Kingdom (CPA 2007; DfES, 2007), and instruments that may be used comprehensively in specialist settings.

In an important series of research studies, Sheppard and his colleagues (Sheppard et al., 2000; Sheppard & Ryan, 2002), using cognitive process interviews with social workers, have tried to capture the thinking processes associated with social workers' decisions. Such research is likely to inform practice theory in ways that offer the flexibility to deal with the complexities of "wise person" performances in social work. The processes outlined (Sheppard et al., 2000) are as follows:

- *Critical appraisal,* the initial judgments about the nature and quality of information required to work with a case; as with Carol, the doctor and I decided how to approach the initial information-giving
- *Focused attention,* selecting and concentrating on particular aspects of information given about the case; as with Carol, I focused on early statements in the interview about her children
- *Querying of information,* as I did when asking Carol about her children's awareness of her husband's condition

- *Evaluation of information,* in the way that I decided that Carol's response about her children did not require more assertive intervention to change how she was responding to their needs
- *Causal inferences,* as workers build hypotheses about the overall character of the case, as we did in deciding that the intervention was concerned with information-giving about a changed medical situation and the emotional consequences
- *Linking of critical appraisal with hypothesis generation,* as workers set up hypotheses to test their initial judgments; as in Carol's case, I decided that help was not required in working with the children, but set up opportunities to revise this if required
- *Partial case hypotheses,* which establish after some work, and in collaboration with colleagues and clients, more precise explanations of what is happening and decisions about appropriate actions
- *Whole case hypotheses,* which establish the nature of the case as a whole: whether it involves a child protection risk, for example. Such decisions might restructure the actions that a worker would take.
- *Speculative hypotheses,* of the kind that say: "If I did this, would that happen . . . "

Sheppard's project goes on to examine the ways social workers develop rules of analysis to test their hypotheses and guide action (Sheppard and Ryan, 2002).

CONCLUSION

I have argued that practice theory as it is currently formulated is inadequate, because it does not recognize the reality of social work practice as a performance by a professional incorporating professional knowledge in a persona of a "wise person." What I describe as a "wise person" is a professional recognized as wise in the ways of the agency and the social situations that it commonly tackles. Practice theory is unhelpful because of its assumption that it is possible to make universal prescriptions to achieve behavior and social change, while social workers need to be flexible to respond to the social and historical contexts in which they operate.

Four aspects of development create the professional "wise person." These are the pathways they follow into and through their profession; the balance achieved in various situations among different aspects of the territory of their practice; their developed experience in responding to value complexities; and the way they filter professional knowledge through their situational understanding of the agency and its role. The wisdom that constitutes social work needs to focus more on long-term care needs that form a major focus of social work practice, in addition to the current focus on behavioral and social change. This might appropriately lead to a research focus on understanding elements and aims in emotional labor and intelligence, caring, resilience, support, and process.

REFERENCES

Batson, C. D., Sympson, S. C., Hindman, J. K., Decruz, P., Todd, R. M., Weeks, J. L., Jennings, G., & Burris, C. T. (1996). "I've been there, too": Effect on personality of prior experience of need. *Personality and Social Psychology Bulletin*, 22, 474–82.

Berlin, S. B., & Marsh, J. C. (1993). *Informing practice decisions*. New York: Macmillan.

Bower, M. 2005. Psychoanalytic theories for social work practice. In M. Bower (Ed.), *Psychoanalytic theory for social work practice: Thinking under fire* (pp. 3–14). London: Routledge.

Brechin, A., & Sidell, M. (2000). Ways of knowing. In R. Gomm, and C. Davies (Eds.), *Using evidence in health and social care* (pp. 3–25). London: Sage.

CPA. (2007). *The single assessment process: Moving towards a common assessment framework*. London: Centre for Policy on Ageing. http://www.cpa.org.uk/sap/sap_home.html (accessed 27 April 2007).

Dalley, G. (1988). *Ideologies of caring: Rethinking community and collectivism*. Basingstoke: Macmillan.

DfES. (2007). *Common assessment framework*. London: Department for Education and Skills. http://www.everychildmatters.gov.uk/caf/ (accessed 27 April 2007).

Finch, J., & Mason, J. (1993). *Negotiating family responsibilities*. London: Routledge.

Foucault, M. (1986). *Care of the self*. Harmondsworth, Middlesex, U.K.: Penguin.

Gilligan, C. (1993). In a different voice: Psychological theory and women's development. Cambridge, Mass.: Harvard University Press.

Goleman, D. (1996). Emotional intelligence: Why it matters more than IQ. London: Bloomsbury.

Halmos, P. (1965). *The faith of the counsellors*. London: Constable.

Halmos, P. (1970). *The Personal Service Society*. London: Constable.

Hochschild, A. (1983). *The managed heart*. Berkeley: University of California Press.

Hochschild, A. (1995). The culture of politics: Traditional, postmodern, cold-modern and warm-modern ideals of care. *Social Politics*, 2(3), 331–346.

Houghton, P. (2001). *On death, dying and not dying*. London: Jessica Kingsley.

Howe, D. (2005). *Child abuse and neglect: Attachment, development and intervention*. Basingstoke, U.K.: Palgrave.

James, N. (1989). Emotional labour: Skill and work in the social regulation of feeling. *Sociological Review*, 37(1), 15–42.

James, N. (1993/2004). Divisons of emotional labour: Disclosure and cancer. In M. Robb, S. Barrett, C. Komaromy & A. Rogers (Eds.), *Communication, relationships and care: A reader* (pp. 259–269). London: Routledge.

Krill, D. F. (1990). Practice wisdom: A guide for helping professionals. Newbury Park, Calif.: Sage.

Marsh, P., & Triseliotis, J. (1996). Ready to practise? Social workers and probation officers: Their training and first year in work. Aldershot, U.K.: Gower.

Mayeroff, M. (1971). *On caring.* New York: Harper & Row.

McBeath, G. B., & Webb, S.A. (1997). Community care: A unity of state and care? In R. Hugman, M. Peelo & K. Soothill (Eds.), *Concepts of care: Developments in health and social welfare* (pp. XX–XX). London: Arnold.

Morrison, T. (2007). Emotional intelligence: Emotion and social work: Context, characteristics, complications and contribution. *British Journal of Social Work,* 37(2), 245–263.

Noddings, N. (1984). *Caring: A feminine approach to ethics and moral education.* Berkeley: University of California Press.

O'Sullivan, T. (2005). Some theoretical propositions on the nature of practice wisdom. *Journal of Social Work,* 5(2), 221–242.

Pawson, R., Boaz, A., Grayson, L., Long, A., & Barnes, C. (2003). *Types and quality of knowledge in social care.* London: SCIE.

Payne, M. (2004). Social work practice identities: An agency study of a hospice. *Practice,* 16(1), 5–15.

Payne, M. (2005a). *Modern social work theory,* 3d ed. Chicago: Lyceum.

Payne, M. (2005b). Continuing and lifelong education for social work. *Campus Social: Revista Lusófona Ciências Sociais,* 2, 51–60.

Payne, M. (2005c). Social work process. In R. Adams, L. Dominelli & M. Payne (Eds.), *Social work futures: Crossing boundaries, transforming practice* (pp. 21–35). Basingstoke, U.K.: Palgrave Macmillan.

Payne, M. (2006a). *What is professional social work?* 2d ed. Chicago: Lyceum.

Payne, M. (2006b). Identity politics in multiprofessional teams: Palliative care social work. *Journal of Social Work,* 6(2), 137–150.

Payne, M. (2007). Performing as a "wise person" in social work practice. *Practice,* 19(2), 85–96.

Sheppard, M. (1995). Social work, social science and practice wisdom. *British Journal of Social Work,* 25(3), 265–293.

Sheppard, M. (2004). An evaluation of social support intervention with depressed mothers in child and family care. *British Journal of Social Work,* 34, 939–960.

Sheppard, M., & Crocker, G. (2006). Locus of control, coping and proto prevention in children and family care. *British Journal of Social Work.*

Sheppard, M., Newstead, S., di Caccavo, A., & Ryan, K. (2000). Reflexivity and the development of process knowledge in social work: A classification and empirical study. *British Journal of Social Work,* 30(4), 465–488.

Sheppard, M., & Ryan, K. (2002). Practitioners as rule using analysts: A further development of process knowledge in social work. *British Journal of Social Work,* 33(2), 157–176.

Sibeon, R. (1990). Comment on the structure and forms of social work knowledge. *Social Work and Social Sciences Review,* 1(1), 29–44.

Specht, H., & Courtney, M. (1994). *Unfaithful angels: How social work abandoned its mission.* New York: Free Press.

Thorndike, E. (1921). Intelligence and its uses. *Harper's Magazine,* 140, 227–235.

Tronto, J.C. (1993). *Moral boundaries: A political argument for an ethics of care.* New York: Routledge.

Walsh, F. (2006). Strengthening family resilience. 2d ed. New York: Guilford.

West, M.A. (2004). *Effective teamwork.* Oxford: BPS Blackwell.

CONTRIBUTORS

JUDITH C. BAER, PH.D., is associate professor in the School of Social Work at Rutgers, The State University of New Jersey. She received her doctoral degree from the University of Houston. Her scholarly interests focus on infant mental health, attachment relationships, mentalization in adolescent development, and the nosology of mental illness. Prior to her current appointment, she worked as a practitioner and conducted research in the Department of Psychiatry at the Baylor College of Medicine in Houston.

SHARON BERLIN, PH.D., is the Helen Ross Professor Emerita in the School of Social Service Administration at the University of Chicago, where she taught for more than two decades. She received her doctoral degree from the University of Washington. Her empirical studies of cognitive therapy shaped her efforts to expand traditional models of intervention for social work practice. She is the author of *Clinical Social Work Practice: A Cognitive-Integrative Perspective* (2002) and coauthor, with Jeanne Marsh, of *Informing Practice Decisions* (1993). Her current interests focus on human rights work and the role of acceptance in social work practice.

WILLIAM BORDEN, PH.D., is senior lecturer in the School of Social Service Administration and lecturer in psychiatry at the University of Chicago, where he teaches courses on contemporary psychodynamic theory, human development, and comparative psychotherapy. He received his doctoral degree from the University of

Chicago. He is author of *Contemporary Psychodynamic Theory and Practice* (2009) and editor of *Comparative Perspectives in Brief Psychodynamic Psychotherapy* (1999). He has written on relational perspectives in contemporary psychoanalysis, integrative psychotherapy, and narrative psychology, and has conducted empirical research on stress, coping, and development across the life course. He has been a clinician for twenty-five years, working as psychotherapist and consultant in community mental health settings.

JAMES CLARK, PH.D., is associate professor and associate dean for research in the University of Kentucky College of Social Work and an associate professor in the College of Medicine, Department of Psychiatry. He is associate director of the University of Kentucky Center for the Study of Violence against Children. He received his doctoral degree from the University of Chicago. He has written on child maltreatment, substance misuse treatment, professional and research ethics, forensic mental health, consumer satisfaction search, and development of translational approaches in social work research. He has written recent essays on complex thinking, psychobiography, and the work of Erik H. Erikson.

JANET L. FINN, PH.D., is professor and director of the master's program in social work at the University of Montana. She received her doctoral degree from the University of Michigan. Her scholarship has focused on gender, welfare, youth, and community. She is author of *Tracing the Veins: Of Copper, Culture, and Community from Butte to Chuquicamata* (1998); coauthor, with Maxine Jacobson, of *Just Practice: A Social Justice Approach to Social Work* (2008); and co-editor, with Lynn Nybell and Jeffrey Shook, of the forthcoming work, *Childhood, Youth, and Social Work in Transformation*. Her current projects include studies of women's grassroots organizations in Santiago, Chile, and of experiences of childhood in twentieth-century Butte, Montana.

SUSAN KEMP, PH.D., is Charles O. Cressey Associate Professor in the University of Washington School of Social Work. She received her doctoral degree from Columbia University. Her research and scholarly interests focus on environmental and community-based interventions, low-income children and families, public child welfare, and social work history and theory. She is coauthor of *Person-Environment Practice: The Social Ecology of Interpersonal Helping* (1997) and other publications that focus on the history and contemporary form of approaches to person-place relationships in direct social work practice.

STANLEY MCCRACKEN, PH.D., is senior lecturer in the School of Social Service Administration at the University of Chicago and clinical director of the Heartland Training Center for Human Service Excellence at the Heartland Alliance. He received his doctoral degree from the University of Chicago. He has written on implementation of evidence-based practice, psychiatric rehabilitation, behavioral and cognitive-behavioral therapy, behavioral medicine, chemical dependence, and behavioral pharmacology. He is author of *Interactive Staff Training: Rehabilitation Teams That Work* (1997) and *Practice Guidelines for Extended Psychiatry Care: From Chaos to Collaboration* (1995). He has been a clinician for more than twenty-five years in the fields of mental health and substance abuse.

MALCOLM PAYNE is director of psychosocial and spiritual care at St. Christopher's Hospice in London; honorary professor, Kingston University, St. George's University of London (Medical School), and emeritus professor of social work at Manchester Metropolitan University, U.K. His scholarly interests focus on social work practice theory. He has written extensively on a range of topics in clinical practice and is author of ten books, including *Modern Social Work Theory* (1995), *The Origins of Social Work* (2005), and *What Is Professional Social Work?* (2006). Over the years he has been involved in efforts to establish the field of international social work, leading projects to develop programs and policy in Eastern Europe, Russia, and China. His current interests center on social work practice and end-of-life care.

TINA RZEPNICKI, PH.D., is the David and Mary Winton Green Professor in the School of Social Service Administration, University of Chicago. She received her doctoral degree from the University of Chicago. Her scholarly interests include case decision making, task-centered and behavioral practice, and practice research in the field of child welfare. She has written on issues of child welfare, family reunification, parenting, permanency planning, and evidence-based perspectives in direct practice. She is coauthor of four books on decision making and clinical practice in the field of child welfare and co-editor of *Using Evidence for Social Work Practice: Behavioral Perspectives* (2004).

JEROME WAKEFIELD, PH.D., D.S.W., is University Professor, professor of social work, and professor of psychiatry at New York University. He holds doctorates in social work and in philosophy from the University of California at Berkeley. His scholarship has focused largely on the conceptual foundations of clinical theory, and he has written about a range of concerns in philosophy, psychoanalysis, cognitive science, and the mental health professions. His recent work has centered on conceptions of mental disorder, and he is coauthor, with Allan Horwitz, of *The Loss of Sadness: How Psychiatry Transformed Normal Sorrow into Depressive Disorder* (2007). He has emphasized integrative approaches in his clinical training and practice in the field of mental health.

FROMA WALSH, PH.D., is the Mose and Sylvia Firestone Professor Emerita in the School of Social Service Administration and professor emeritus in the Department of Psychiatry, Pritzker School of Medicine, at the University of Chicago. She serves as codirector of the Chicago Center for Family Health. She received her doctoral degree from the University of Chicago. Her scholarly interests focus on family systems and developmental theory; contemporary family diversity; conceptions of loss, trauma, and resilience; and family and couples therapy. She has published widely in the field of family studies and therapy; her books include *Strengthening Family Resilience* (2d ed., 2006), *Living beyond Loss* (2004), and *Normal Family Processes: Growing Diversity and Complexity* (2003). She has been a clinician for more than thirty years and has provided training and consultation for mental health services internationally.

INDEX

Aboriginal Australians, relationship to place, 119

absolute objectivity, 94–95

acceptance: history of, 179–81; limits of, 183; love and justice, 186; in social work, 179–81

accepting the uncontrollable, 167

accompaniment, Just Practice framework, 193

action: to be taken, designing questions for, 217; causes of, 61; Just Practice framework, 193; love as basis for, 200; social work values as prescription for, 241

action stage, evidence-based practice, 216

activist mothering, 188–89

activist mothers, 189

adaptation: cognitive therapy, barriers to, 34–36; cognitive therapy, unre-

sponsive environment, 44; family resilience, 152–53

adaptational pathways, family resilience, 155–56

Addams, Jane: Berlin on, 183
—Hull House (*see also* settlement house movement): garbage inspectors, 126–27; relational acceptance, 180–81; role of Christian values, 182; sharing and inclusion, 182

adult literacy, 183–85

adult survivor of child abuse (case study), 96–99

African Americans: adult literacy, 183; Citizenship Education Program, 184; Clark, Septima, 184; relationship to place, 120, 128; rights of women of color, 188; Ross, Rosetta, 184; women, as activist mothers, 189; women activists, 183–84, 189

aries, reframing, 205; "Valuing Vulnerability," 205
—looking for: confirming otherness, 194; dialogue, requirements for, 194; empathy, in dialogue, 194; human interaction, in creating the self, 194; identification with others, in dialogue, 194; *Just Practice: A Social Justice Approach to Social Work*, 194; Just Practice framework, 194; liberation theology, 195
love and justice: *The Art of Loving*, 203–204; connecting the personal and the political, 203–204; conspiracy of hope, 203; dealing with mental illness, 202–203; Love Paradigm, 203; politics as acts of love, 196; relational spirituality, 201; respect, 203; responsibility, 203; sharing power, 201–202; social caregiving, 201; social justice, 188
—ethnographic examples: Caravan of Death, 197–200; the disappeared, Argentina, 199–200; *Maternal Thinking*, 200; Michael, a black teenager, 201–202; political activism in Colombia, 196; *Revolutionizing Motherhood*, 199; women's rights in Chile, 197–200
love and justice, early twentieth century: adult literacy, 184–85; African American women activists, 183–84; class-based judgments, 182; engaging the privileged, 185; limits of acceptance, 183
—settlement house movement (*see also* Addams, Jane; Hull House): Addams on, 182; common denominator, 182; new definition of religion, 182; role of, 182; spiritual basis for, 182; tough love, 181–82
love and justice, late twentieth century: antiwar movement, 187; civil rights

movement, 187; correctional systems, 188; decoupling from social work, 188; education systems, 188; health systems, 188; individual pathology approaches, a critique of, 188; legitimacy of interventions, 187; racism and inequality, 188; rights of women of color, 188; social justice, 188; *Social Work Practice and Social Justice*, 188; war on poverty, 187; welfare systems, 188; women's movement, 187
—women's activism: activist mothering, 188–89; activist mothers, 189; African American women, 189; history of, 188; militant practice of radical love, 189–90; othermothering, 189; political activism, 189–90; women of color, 188–89
love and justice, mid-century: acceptance, 186; *The Casework Relationship*, 186; confidentiality, 186; controlled emotional environment, 186; empathy, 185–86; genuineness, 185–86; humanistic psychology, 185–86; individualization, 186; nonjudgmental attitude, 186; purposeful expression of feeling, 186; Rogers, influence on, 185–86; self-determination, 186; social work relationships, characteristics of, 186; unconditional positive regard, 185–86
love and justice, (post)modern era: absence of a discourse of love, 193–94; accompaniment, 193; action, 193; authority of the worker and the client, 190; celebration, 193; context, 193; core processes, 193; critical reflection, 193; criticisms of social work, 190–91; dialogue, requirements for, 192; engagement, 193; evaluation, 193; feminist perspectives, 191–92;

love and justice (*continued*)
history, 193; integrating politics
and practice, 192–93; Just Practice
framework, 193–94; key themes, 193;
liberatory change, 192; meaning,
193; possibility, 193; post-structural
criticisms, 191; power, 193; power
and inequality in social work, 190;
social justice work (*see* Just Practice
framework); teaching/learning, 193
Love Paradigm, 203
Low, Setha, 123
Luborsky, Lester, 69–70, 72–73
Lukacs, John, 92

Mahoney, Michael, 17
maintenance stage, evidence-based
practice, 216
Mandler, George, 59–60
Maori of New Zealand, relationship to
place, 119
maps and drawings of place, 131–34
marginalized persons, place making,
137–38
Marx, Karl, 82
Massey, Doreen, 122
Maternal Thinking, 200
Maturana, Humberto, 204
McAdams, Dan, 86
meaning: biological roots of, 53;
derived from adversity, family
resilience, 164–65; factors shaping,
53–54; instrumental conditioning,
53; Just Practice framework, 193;
motivation for actions, 53; personal
(*see* personal meaning); processing,
levels of, 53–54; unconscious activation of, 53
meaningful locations, 118
Megill, Alan, 93
Meichenbaum, Donald, 17
memory: biological substrates of, 84;
human, modeling, 84–85; patterns

(*see* schemas); sea snails (Aplysia),
studying, 84–85; testing neural
structures, 84–85
Menand, Louis, 8
mental health agencies, preference for
cognitive therapy, 32
mental illness, love and justice, 202–203
mental linkage of ideas, 62–63
mental networks. *See* schemas
mental representation, 58–59
mental states, 59–60. *See also* ideas;
mind
mental structures. *See* schemas
the mentally ill, relationship to place, 123
Messer, Stanley, 6, 20–21, 57–58
meta-psychological theory, 92–93
The Metaphysical Club, 8
Meyer, Carol, 115, 117
militant practice of radical love, 189–90
mind: elements of, 58–59; habits
of, breaking out of, 36; life as a
precondition to, 85; modularity of,
74; narrow memory frameworks
(*see* habits of mind). *See also* ideas;
mental states
mindful practice, testing theories, 212
Mitchell, Stephen, 17
mode of intentional state, 59
modeling human memory, 84–85
modularity of mind, 74
Monahan, John, 105
moral case for integration of theories,
54
motivation: in cognitive theory, 61–62;
Freud on, 61–62; meaning as, 53; in
narratives, 94
motives, of the biographer, 91–92
multi-modal therapy, 18–19
multigenerational perspective, family
resilience, 157
multiscalar nature of place, 121
multisystemic perspective, individual
resilience, 150–51

the mentally ill, 123; Native Americans, 119; persons with disabilities, 123; phenomenological perspective, 119–20; repositories of meaning, 120; root shock, 121; separating place from self, 119–20; Western Apache, 119; Western paradigms, 119–20; *Wisdom Sits in Places,* 119
place-based stereotypes, 124
place making: assumptions about, 136–38; definition, 136; for the displaced or marginalized, 137–38; people care about place, 136–37; relevant unit of analysis, 137; work involved, 137; youth, as placemakers, 135–36
place narratives, 131
place-sensitive practice: child welfare services, spatial patterns, 129–30; environmental factors in childrens' development, 127–28; ethnographic imagination, 126–27; firsthand investigation, 127; foster placements, spatial distribution, 128; GIS (geographic information system), 128–30; mapping the environment, 128–30; spatial data, 127–28; urban planning and architecture, 128–29
pluralism, 7–9. *See also* critical pluralism
pluralistic perspectives, integration of theories, 57
policy community knowledge, 242
political, connecting to the personal, 203–204
political activism, 189–90, 196
politics: as acts of love, 196; integrating with practice, 192–93
Popper, Karl, 83–84
positive discrepancies: cognitive therapy, 34, 35; creating, 45; lack of, 35
positive illusions, family resilience, 166
positive outlook, family resilience, 165–67

positive self-memories, cognitive therapy, 35
positivist research, in practice theory, 238
possessive familism, 246
possibility, Just Practice framework, 193
postmodern knowledge, evidence-based practice, 215–16
post-structural criticisms, 191
posttraumatic reactions, individual resilience, 152
power: clinical setting, sharing, 201–202; of ideas, 61–62; and inequality, in social work, 190; Just Practice framework, 193; racialization, 124–25; sharing, 201–202
—of place: landscapes of power, 123; racialization, 124–25; sites of power, 122–23; socially constructed, 121; urban planning and architecture, 123–24, 128–29
practice: applications for family resilience framework, 157–62; integrating politics with, 192–93
practice context, designing questions for, 219
practice theory: definition, 237; formal, 237; influence on designing questions, 218–19; informal, 237; interpretative research, 238; positivist research, 238; practitioner, as wise person, 239–42; scope of, 237–38; untheorized treatment, 238; weaknesses, 238–42
practice wisdom, areas of practice: appraisal support, 250; attachment theory, 248–49; emotional intelligence, 244; emotional labor, 242, 243–44; emotional support, 250; informational support, 250; instrumental support, 250; overview, 242; resilience, 242, 248–49; social intelligence, 244; support, 242, 249–50

psychoanalysis linked with behavioral theory, 20. *See also* psychotherapy

psychobiography: definition, 83; Freud as father of, 92. *See also* biographical approaches; narratives

psychobiography, biographical approaches: *Criteria for the Life History,* 91; critiques of, 90–93; definition, 83; *Gandhi's Truth,* 91; history of, 90–93; *The Hitler of History,* 92; *Leonardo da Vinci and a Memory of His Childhood,* 92–93; limits of human nature, 90; *Lincoln's Melancholy,* 92; meta-psychological theory, 92–93; motives of the biographer, 91–92; overgeneralization of findings, 93; personhood, 89; sin of originology, 93; sociological imagination, 89; *Young Man Luther,* 91. *See also* narratives; personality psychology; studying the person

—case studies: adult survivor of child abuse, 96–99; caregiver assessments, 103–106; emotional trauma resulting from a fire, 99–103; longitudinal study on child placement, 103–106; Munchausen's-by-proxy, 104–106

psychocentric bias: alternative to, 40; correcting for, 47; tendency to revert to, 41–42

psychodynamic theory, 11–12. *See also* cognitive theory, integrating with psychodynamic

psychological constructivism, in psychotherapy, 13

psychological demands of environmental influences, 41

psychology in history, 102

psychotherapists. *See* practitioners

psychotherapy. *See also* psychoanalysis

—schools of thought: authenticity, 14; behavioral perspectives, 12; classical conditioning, 12; cognitive perspectives, 13; empathy, 14; environment, effects on behavior, 12; existential living, 13–14; experiential tradition, 13–14; humanistic perspectives, 13–14; mental structures (*see* schemas); openness to experience, 13–14; operant conditioning, 12; organismic trusting, 14; patterns of learning, effects on behavior, 12; person-centered tradition, 13–14; psychodynamic perspectives, 11–12; psychological constructivism, 13; relational, 11; situational factors, effects on behavior, 12; social learning, 12; unconditional positive regard, 14; warmth, 14

psychotherapy, integrating theories: assimilative integration, 57–58; barriers to integration, 56; cognitive theory with psychodynamic (*see* cognitive theory, integrating with psychodynamic); common factors perspective, 19–20, 56; folk psychology, 53; inter-theory competition, 54–55; moral case for, 54; pluralistic perspectives, 57; psychotherapy wars, 54; reasons for, 52–55; technical eclecticism, 18–19, 55; theoretical integration, 20–21, 56–57. *See also* integrative perspectives

—meaning: biological roots of, 53; factors shaping, 53–54; instrumental conditioning, 53; motivation for actions, 53; processing, levels of, 53–54; unconscious activation of, 53

psychotherapy wars, 54

PTSD (posttraumatic stress disorder): among refugee families, 160–62; CAFES (Coffee And Family Education & Support), 161; case studies, combat-related, 9–10; KFPEC (Kosovar Family Professional Educational Collaborative), 161; resulting

studying the person: biological substrates of memory, 84; BIV (brain in a vat) experiment, 85; dividing people into components, 84; formulation of self, 86; modeling human memory, 84–85; personality and social psychology research, 83–84; reductionism, 84–85; by studying sea snails (Aplysia), 84–85; testing neural structures, 84–85. *See also* biographical approaches; narratives; psychobiography

substantive distraction, in narratives, 94

support, practice wisdom, 242, 249–50

symptoms of distress, timing of, 156

TAFES (Tea And Family Education & Support), 161

Taylor, Charles: formulation of self, 86; recovery from childhood trauma, 98–99; value of narratives, 106–107

teaching/learning, Just Practice framework, 193

technical eclecticism: critique of, 23; description, 55; interventions, 18–19; overview, 18–19; psychotherapy, 18–19

testing neural structures, 84–85

testing theories, 212

the experiencing, acting, living "I," 6

theoretical integration: critique of, 24; description, 56–57; interventions, 20–21; overview, 20–21; psychotherapy, 20–21

theoretical systems, 4–6

theories: basis for interventions, 222–24; change, 213; clinicians' view of, 6; definition, 211–12; disconnect from practice, 6; as disembodied abstractions, 6; in evidence-based practice (*see* EBP [evidence-based practice]; empirical studies);

explanatory, 213; implicit, making explicit, 212; James, on the role of, 7; logic modeling, 212–13; mindful practice, 212; schemas of experts, 212; testing, 212

theory of defenses, 74–75

therapeutic techniques: CCRT (Core Conflictual Relationship Theme), 69–70; cognitive therapy, 36–37; disconfirming idiosyncratic beliefs, 70–72; patient symptoms, locating, 69–70; REs (relationship episodes), 69–70; symptom-context method, 69–70. *See also specific therapies*

therapists. *See* practitioners

therapy. *See* interventions; psychotherapy; social work

thinking processes of practitioners, 251

tough love, 181–82

transcendence, family resilience, 167–68

transtheoretical model, 20, 21, 216–17

trauma-related stimuli, desensitizing, 19

traumatic memories, processing in interventions, 19

traumatology, individual resilience, 151–52

truth: cash value of, 8–9; James, on the value of, 8–9; limits on knowing, 16; value of, 8–9

Tuan, Yi-Fu, 119

Type III error, 223–24

unconditional positive regard: love and justice, 185–86; in psychotherapy, 14

unconscious, activation of meaning, 53

unconscious mental states, 59–60

uniqueness, personal and biographical, 87–89, 108

untheorized treatment, 238